How to Sell
Every Magazine
Article
You Write

LISA COLLIER COOL

How to Sell Every Magazine Article You Write

Writer's Digest Books

Cincinnati, Ohio

"Genetic Counseling," by Lisa Collier Cool and Susan Smahl Plummer, which appeared in the June 1986 issue of *Cosmopolitan*, is reprinted with permission of Susan Smahl Plummer.

"Tumbling Away Tension," by Maria Neuda, is reprinted with permission of Maria Neuda.

First paperback printing 1989

93 92 91 90 89   5 4 3 2

Library of Congress Cataloging-in-Publication Data

Cool, Lisa Collier,
  How to sell every magazine article you write.

  Bibliography: p.
  Includes index.
  1. Authorship. I. Title.
PN147.C774 1986   808'.02   6-15864
ISBN 0-89879-355-6

Design by the Antler & Baldwin Design Group

To my twin daughters, Alison and Georgia

Acknowledgments

For their valuable contributions to this book, I'd like to thank:

Oscar Collier, my father and agent, who sold this book and shared his publishing wisdom with me as I wrote it.

John Cool, my husband, for his support and encouragement.

Paul Gupta, my brother-in-law and favorite lawyer, and Mark Norman, counsel to Writer's Digest Books, for their legal expertise.

Guy Flatley, Susan Benson, Tom Sedita and Susan Korones of *Cosmopolitan,* and Peter Bloch, Claudia Valentino and Laura Berland of *Penthouse,* for opening their "books" to me.

Patrice Adcroft, Elizabeth Crow, Ruth Drizen, Phyllis Evans, Julia Kagan, Connie Leisure, and Louise Tutellian, for providing insights into the magazine editor's craft.

Maria Neuda and Susan Smahl Plummer, for allowing me to reproduce their material.

Paula Dranov, for revealing her research secrets.

The librarians of the New Rochelle Library, for service above and beyond the call of duty.

Carol Cartaino, for seeing potential in this book; Nancy Dibble, for her meticulous editing; and Bill Brohaugh, for getting me started in the business of writing about writing.

And finally, my IBM PC for storing the 910,014 keystrokes used in writing this book.

Contents

Introduction

If you've always dreamed of selling your work; if your writing has been praised in school and on the job; if you enjoy reading magazines regularly; if you find yourself thinking, as you flip through an article, "I could have written this," or "If I were writing this, I'd include . . ."; then this book will start you on the road to turning those dreams and thoughts into cash and bylines, and quite possibly, a new career—as a professional magazine writer.

Magazine writing is one of the easiest—and most profitable—ways for the novice to break into print. I know because I've done it. My articles have been published in twenty-five major and minor magazines, and in newspapers. Not only have I sold over a hundred of my own articles, but as a magazine writing teacher, I've seen previously unpublished students take their ideas and sell them for prices between $75 and $750. More established writers frequently receive prices between $1,000 and $2,000; while top writers may make as much as $6,000 to $12,000 from a *single* article. One Pulitzer prize-winning writer I know sometimes realized as much as $20,000 to $30,000 per article through worldwide syndication of his material. No matter what the pay scale is, the message is the same: your ideas are potential income.

Beyond the financial rewards, magazine writing provides many intangible benefits: flexible hours, independence, lively topics, contact with glamorous and interesting people, opportunities to explore new places, experiences, and depths within yourself. And there's the never diminishing thrill of passing a newsstand and seeing your work being offered to thousands, even millions of readers, and feeling a sense of immortality when your words are preserved in archives and libraries.

To reap these benefits, you must combine your writing talents with sales techniques. Starting writers frequently have an inflated notion of the degree of talent necessary for success. As a literary agent and writing teacher, I've often seen writers of modest ability succeed and more skilled writers fail. In fact I've sold books by authors whose skills seemed marginal at best—and watched these works become giant sellers. Why? Because these writers, though weak in style, were masterful at *packaging* their ideas to sell.

In nonfiction writing, whether of books or articles, information is often what hooks the reader rather than literary brilliance. The ability to recognize a money-making idea, flesh it out with in-depth research, add sex appeal with lively packaging and, most important, put it in the hands of the right editor is the key to success. If your writing is clear and concise, and your material properly researched and organized, chances are it's good enough to sell. Great talent, while undeniably valuable, is not essential to nonfiction success. And while writing ability can be enhanced through hard work, sales skills can be acquired quickly, letting you earn money as you develop your writing skills to the fullest.

This book, like my writing course, is not an abstract discussion of creative writing but a practical guide to acquiring a professional approach to writing and selling your work. It is designed to help you realize every writer's ultimate goal—publication, and beyond that, continuing success in the magazine field.

But you can't sell unless you convince yourself of one thing—that your work *is* good enough to sell. One of the biggest problems I've met in my writing course is convincing students to actually submit their work. Many writers love to write, have trunks full of their material, but lack the courage to send it out. Or they let negative attitudes and insecurity color their writing with a weak and indecisive style and top it off with a fainthearted cover letter that all but invites rejection. Sometimes all that is standing between you and your first sale is *you*.

A stout heart is often essential to a writer's ultimate success, as the careers of well-known writers ranging from Edgar Allan Poe to Stephen King clearly demonstrate. Poe's great poem "The Raven" was so poorly received on its first submission that the pitying staff of the magazine, believing that the poem would never sell, gave the author some money out of their own pockets. Laurence Sterne, author of *Tristram Shandy*, had to subsidize publication of his novel, while D. H. Lawrence's *Women in Love* was rejected by every publisher in England. Science-fiction writer Ursula K. Le Guin submitted stories for six years without success; while best-selling horror writer Stephen King climbed to the top after writing sixty short stories and four novels that failed to sell. After being told that twenty or so publishers "[weren't] interested in a talking seagull," writer Richard Bach saw his novel *Jonathan Livingston Seagull* go on to sell more than million copies.

Rejection is a fact of literary life. While few writers relish it, almost all encounter it. Even the Nobel Prize doesn't guarantee surefire sales according to Isaac Bashevis Singer and Saul Bellow, both of whom have had turndowns since winning the prize. However, as Singer notes, rejection may be painful, but consider the alternative: "If I stopped working, I wouldn't get rejected anymore. But would that be good?"

However, that rejection you fear may not be a rejection at all. William Styron and Arthur C. Clarke maintain that their careers have never been blemished by rejection. While this, alas, has not been the case for me, I've seen several writers start their careers with sales on their very first submission. Recently one of my students landed a $500 assignment by mailing one letter to a very carefully targeted market. My students frequently seem shocked when I admit to being rejected regularly. At least 30 percent of my ideas fail to make it into print. But I get enough acceptances to keep me steadily employed. So could you—if you acquire a firm belief in your ultimate success.

One of my students came proudly into my class waving a letter. As we waited expectantly, she announced: "Guess what, I got my first rejection!" She was delighted that she had actually done it—sent one of her ideas out to an editor. And she was relieved to find that yes, there is life after rejection. While getting your first rejection letter may not seem like much of an accomplishment, it is a step forward. It shows you've crossed the boundary between the amateur who amasses material in private and the professional who puts it before the public. Trying brings you closer to the next milestone—succeeding.

Ideas Are Income

More than two million articles are published each year in the United States in 16,000 different magazines. Assuming that 20 percent to 40 percent are staff-written, that still leaves more than a million opportunities each year for the ambitious freelancer to sell his or her articles. One of them could well be your first sale—all you need to start is the right idea to work with.

Once you know how and where to look, ideas are everywhere. I've discovered article ideas while socializing with friends, scanning the headlines of my daily paper, watching movies or TV shows, even driving to everyday destinations. Your daily life can be equally fertile: much of what you think, see, hear, and do can be turned into good article topics. Develop a sense of the salable, and soon you won't be wondering *what* to write about but *how* to write fast enough to keep up with your flow of ideas.

Here are several sources of ideas:

Personal experiences. Research is minimal when you select the topic you are most expert on—yourself. Sharing your experiences with readers is emotionally and financially profitable, as you can help them overcome similar difficulties, spur them on to greater efforts, prevent possible tragedies, increase understanding of issues important to you, or simply provoke a good laugh. I'm always surprised in my class when students who've had truly remarkable experiences—such as a miraculous recovery from a rare disease or being a foster parent for a dozen handicapped children—never think of writing about them. Many magazines, especially women's magazines, are hungry for "real life dramas" and personal experience pieces.

A tragedy in my family led me to write "SIDS—The Sudden Killer of Infants Under a Year" for *Glamour*. By increasing public awareness of the problem and donating my fee to sudden infant death research, I felt that I had made a positive gesture toward coping with the death of my infant nephew. Though painful to write, articles about shattering personal experiences are often cathartic for their authors. One of my clients, a woman who suffered a severe spinal cord injury yet went on to marry and raise two children, told me that writing and speaking publicly about her handicaps helped answer her inner question of "Why me?".

Your experience need not be extraordinary to sell. Many writers have turned everyday topics into article sales—it's a matter of approach. Though I could scarcely know it at the time, when I set off to summer camp at age twelve I was gathering valuable research material for future articles. Twenty years later I used these experiences in two of my articles: "How I Spent My Summer Vacation," a humor piece, and "Selecting the Right Camp for Your Child." Some experiences translate well into helpful advice articles: my wedding inspired "Enjoying Your In-laws," published in *Modern Bride;* my work as a literary agent provoked "Telephone Techniques," published in *Family Circle*.

Imaginary experiences. Many intriguing articles originate with the simple question "What if. . . ." Whenever you find yourself daydreaming about something, ask yourself if there's an article in it. One day I was passing by a bridal store and found myself wondering "What if my twin daughters decided to have a double wedding?" Rushing home, I typed out a query on double weddings and sold it on one submission to *Modern Bride* magazine. During a vacation at an expensive resort, a friend began to wonder "What if someone with a really modest budget wanted to come here?" Calling her metropolitan newspaper, she sold "The Hamptons on a Budget," her first published piece. The "what if" could deal with national politics, fire safety, consumer complaints, family life—anything you can conjure up.

Tell other people's stories.   Look around your home, office, and neighborhood for colorful material. If you know someone who has had an unusual adventure—an act of heroism, a dramatic recovery from illness, a spectacular business success, a stroke of amazingly good fortune, an encounter with violent crime, or some other extraordinary experience—think in terms of either an "as told to" piece, written in the first person, or a third person human interest story. If the person's entire life is the stuff of fantasy, whether through glamour, riches, notoriety, or the bizarre, consider a profile piece or interview article. Particularly make note of any business success stories you encounter; many magazines are interested in entrepreneurs, especially people who've succeeded young or in an offbeat profession, as well as inventors, self-made millionaires, Horatio Alger types, female business owners, and those who've made their millions through shady deals or outright fraud. Or combine a few interesting stories into a collective profile: "The New Breed of (bankers, real estate tycoons, ballerinas. . . . you name it)", "Older Women, Younger Men," "From Housewife to Millionaire: Five Success Stories," "Yuppie Criminals."

It pays to listen.   You'd be surprised how many experts you already know, people who've amassed knowledge you could pass on to readers in your articles. Collect crime prevention tips from the retired cop down the block, investment strategies from the broker next door, ways to save on home mortgages from your banker. A single expert may be enough for an easy, research-free article. And the doctors, psychiatrists, and psychologists you know can provide material for hundreds of good articles, as well as giving you leads on the latest breakthroughs in their fields, which can translate into still more articles. Almost anyone you meet could be a potential source; cultivate the ability to listen—and learn.

Seasonal subjects.   Many magazines need articles to tie into Christmas, Thanksgiving, Easter, Passover, Independence Day, and other major holidays. Mother's Day and Father's Day are also frequently observed through appropriate articles, as are the anniversaries of major historical events like the one hundredth anniversary of Mark Twain's death. There are two tricks to selling seasonal and anniversary articles: submit early—at least six to eight months before the occasion—and think of something relatively fresh to say about it.

Articles can also be timed to coincide with a variety of less well known occasions. Over the years manufacturers and institutions have arranged for such annual occurrences as National Pickle Week and Secretary's Day. Your article could be submitted to tie in with any of these events. Consult *Chase's Annual Events* for likely tie-ins to your ideas. Sometimes the connection between your idea and some occasion is not immediately apparent; by pointing out, for example, that your nostalgia piece on your grandfather's experiences as a street peddler could commemorate Grandparents' Day might make the difference between acceptance and rejection, by giving the editor an obvious reason to publish.

Self-help. Readers enjoy reading articles that show them how to improve their mental, physical, or emotional health; enhance the quality of life; and succeed socially, sexually, professionally, and financially. Cater to this craving for self-improvement with practical advice: "Marrying a Millionaire," "Negotiating a Raise." "When Your Sexual Styles Don't Mesh."

Fun and games. Psychologists believe that all of us crave excitement and stimulation. Cater to this need by writing about sports, hobbies, vacation, travel, and recreation. Offer the reader vicarious stimulation by reporting on the experiences of those who live out the reader's fantasies: race car drivers, astronauts, movie stars, heroes and heroines.

The seven deadly sins and other woes. Any of the seven—pride, covetousness, lust, anger, gluttony, envy, and sloth—is rife with possible article slants (although surprisingly little is done with sloth). Envy could be shaped into "When a Co-Worker Is Promoted—And You Aren't," or gluttony could lead to "Help for Your Overweight Child." Since misery loves company, common problems like depression, grief, anxiety, fear, loneliness, failure, rejection, and shyness are good topics. Ideas might include "New

Treatments for Phobias" and "Living Alone and Liking It."

When your subject is emotional, working from personal experience can add power to your writing. One writer I know used her typewriter to vent her fury at the mandatory retirement policies that were forcing her out of a job she loved. Her piece, "I Refuse to Go Gentle," became her first published work, appearing on the editorial page of the *New York Times*. Or you may wish to draw on your experiences though a third person piece: transforming your annoyance at your demanding employer, say, into, "Coping with an Impossible Boss," in which the tyrant you work for, suitably disguised, serves as an illustration of one of the many problems you discuss.

Oldies, but goodies.   An article idea need not be particularly new, original, or earth-shattering to sell. In fact selling a familiar old idea can often be easier than breaking ground with a new one. Consider these article ideas: "Coping with Rejection," "Popularity—How Important Is It Really?", "Crash Diets Can Be Hazardous to Your Health," "You Can Make Money from Your Own Business," "The Helpful Home Computer," and "How to Hire a Secretary." None are particularly brilliant, but all are ideas that I or my clients sold to major magazines. The crash diet idea sold twice, once to a magazine and once to a newspaper. The home computer idea produced *four* separate sales—to a woman's magazine, two men's magazines, and a newspaper syndicate. So far the gross from these six ideas is $5,150.

"Coping With Rejection" is covered frequently in women's magazines; "The Ups and Downs of Popularity" is a staple of teen publications; and home computers have generated millions of words in magazines of every type. Basically these ideas are no more than old wine decanted into new bottles. Why then are these vintage ideas so easy to sell?

Ideas like "How to Put the Spark Back into Your Sex Life" can sell time and time again because magazines tend to run articles in a cyclical pattern. At *Family Circle,* says former articles editor Constance Leisure, "Approximately every two years we'd run an article on 'The Education of a Widow,' covering new wrinkles in estate laws, taxes, insurance policies and other practical aspects of widowhood. About once a year we'd do a piece on 'How to Improve Your Marriage.' " Though some topics have a longer turnaround time, most ideas run in a two- or three-year cycle.

The reason certain topics are repeated is twofold: limited subject matter and reader turnover. A magazine targeted at young, single women is likely to carry many articles on male/female relationships and none on building cars from spare parts. And since these young, single women age and marry, eventually new readers replace them. To serve this changing audience, certain perennially interesting topics are redone periodically.

A timeless topic is usually one that touches on a fundamental human concern such as food, shelter, clothing, finding and keeping a mate, sexual desire and gratification, pregnancy and childrearing, family relationships, companionship, avoiding danger, and preserving health. Any of these categories could inspire hundreds of different articles. Pregnancy, for example, is literally fertile: "Preventing Premature Deliveries," "Sex during the Last Trimester," " Are You Carrying Twins?", "Genetic Counseling— Is It for You?" are just a few possible articles.

However an idea can be *too* familiar. When several of my students come up with the same idea, the topic is nearly always some trend that has just about run its course, like the ubiquitous Cabbage Patch doll; a story extensively covered in the media, like the AIDS epidemic; or an extremely commonplace event like "How to Have a Yard Sale." While these tired ideas could be resuscitated by an expert writer, new writers are best off avoiding the topics that are on everyone's lips. Following a stampede isn't the best way for a new writer to attract an editor's notice. If you luck into something genuinely avant-garde, then pursue the story; otherwise, let it pass.

Reading like a writer.   For more ideas, read, read, read. Newspapers, magazines, and nonfiction books are crammed with interesting tidbits that could inspire fresh article ideas as well as fleshing out ideas you already have. Look beyond the obvious in your reading; when skimming your morning paper or favorite magazine, don't neglect classified ads that could turn you on to some novel business or suggest a potential profile. Letters to the editor can be another source of inspiration—here are actual readers telling you what they'd like to see in print and how they feel about the issues of the day.

Your reaction to your reading can suggest additional articles. Ever read an article and find yourself wondering about some related problem or question? Or do you find yourself disagreeing with what you read? Are you unsatisfied with the coverage of some tantalizing thought the author has tossed out in an offhand way, amid other topics? Such musings could be the beginning of lively new ideas for you to exploit.

The information you gather through omnivorous reading, accompanied by clipping and saving all items of potential interest, represents an investment that will yield dividends in creating and writing articles throughout your writing career. You'd be surprised how often some yellowed clipping that's been moldering in your drawer for a year or two suddenly connects with another thought you see elsewhere to create an article idea, or turns out to be the missing link to complete a project.

Once you start making a systematic search for ideas, you'll realize how many are lurking in your immediate surroundings just waiting to be captured. To keep track of all the ideas you're sure to discover, keep an idea list handy to jot down your latest thought whenever inspiration strikes. Write down as much of the idea as possible while your imagination is hot—the more you give yourself to work with now, the easier it will be to finish the article later. Since ideas are your stock-in-trade as an article writer, building up a good inventory is a sound business move. A good supply of ideas ensures a steady flow from your typewriter to editors. The more you can submit, the quicker you're likely to land some sales.

2
Shortcuts
to Sales

T hough the conventional wisdom has it that the starting writer should expect to paper his garret with rejection slips while waiting for that first sale, wouldn't you prefer to start selling right now? Collecting rejections may build character, but collecting checks builds a career. The secret is simple: think small, with shorter articles and smaller markets. While these won't pay top dollar, they will build up a portfolio of published work quickly. As many freelancers have discovered, those little checks do add up into a reasonable living if you work steadily and keep output high. However, you need not give up your dream of selling a cover story to *Esquire* or *Ladies' Home Journal*. Once you establish your credentials with the minor markets, you'll have more clout with the majors, putting those high-paying assignments within easier grasp.

If you'd rather start with the major markets, the "think small" approach suggests that you gain entry with short articles, a few paragraphs to a couple of pages. Such articles are often called features to distinguish them from longer pieces, usually referred to as articles. This approach can be surprisingly profitable, as I discovered while writing a little item for *Glamour's* "How to Do Anything Better Guide." I made $50 writing *four* sentences on "Free Plants from Your Fridge," a per-word rate rarely equaled by my longer articles. Many big magazines have sections composed of many small articles. These gazettes buy lots of freelance material for anywhere from $25 to $125, depending on length. Even if your piece in *Harper's* is a mere twenty-five words, you'll gain valuable credit for your bio. Large magazines periodically encourage readers to send short essays—be vigilant for these announcements, as well as submitting to regular departments carrying this sort of material. Once you've gotten your foot in the door, your chances of selling a longer article are much better.

Another way to approach big or small magazines is with editorials. While not all magazines carry editorials, those that do are often eager for material. Opinion pieces are anywhere from one to four pages, typed, and can either be humorous or serious, depending on the tone of the magazine you have in mind. Larger magazines pay up to $2,000, but $100 to $400 is more common.

A more modest approach is to write "fillers," those little items that fill out the columns of magazines and newspapers. While these pay only $5 to $30 or so, they're fun to write and a particularly easy way to begin. The best topics are off-beat facts, anecdotes, helpful hints, jokes, and other intriguing trivia.

The Big Versus Little Debate

There are pros and cons to both the major and minor markets. Large magazines offer good pay and wide exposure but expect professional polish and extensive research. Editors often demand major revisions, adding to the time spent on each piece. Articles are often heavily edited before publication and may not appear for a year or more due to larger inventories. And not all subjects will interest the mass audience. At smaller magazines you'll often encounter less editorial interference. When I wrote for smaller magazines, I seldom found a single editorial change in my published articles, while at major magazines, I've sometimes had to fight to save my original text. Publication is much quicker in smaller magazines, and this is helpful when you need clips to show editors. The other pluses constructive criticism from edi tors, more willingness to work with beginners, less competition with established writers, and the opportunity to write about more esoteric subjects; the minuses: lower and often slower pay.

If you'd rather think big and try to crack the majors immediately with full-length articles, you could find prompt success waiting. I've seen unpublished writers sell to *Glamour, Redbook,* and other major magazines their first time out. Though the big magazines may receive upward of 30,000 submissions a year, selling to one of them isn't like winning a sweepstakes. The odds are unimportant if you've got the right stuff. While some editors are reluctant to admit it, fearing an onslaught of submissions, just about every American magazine has bought from new writers on occasion. When I interviewed editors from a number of major magazines, almost all characterized their publications as either "somewhat receptive" or "quite receptive" to new authors. If you are convinced you've got what it takes to best the rather tough competition, by all means go for it.

The Invisible Marketplace

The top markets are easy to find—they're the magazines that fill newsstands and supermarket racks. Since they are so accessible, naturally they dominate your impression of the marketplace. But these hundred or so popular magazines, plus the three or four hundred others you might find at a medium-sized library, represent less than 1 percent of the possible outlets for your writing. While the majors can pick and choose from the top writers, literally thousands of other magazines are starving for good material. This invisible marketplace includes newspapers, Sunday supplements, features syndicates, and weekly tabloids but is often overlooked by the inexperienced author who sets his or her sights on the more obvious, but harder to hit targets like *Redbook* or *Playboy*—even though it offers the greatest opportunities for the beginner.

The first step to capitalizing on these opportunities is to locate them. Fortunately you need look no further than your bookstore or library to get up-to-date market information in the latest edition of the annual *Writer's Market.* (See the appendix for a list of other directories of magazine and newspaper publishing.) This directory, which lists over 4,000 paying markets for freelance articles, short stories, books, poetry, plays, and fillers, is the bible of many freelancers since the bulk of its one thousand plus pages are devoted to magazine markets. Published by Writer's Digest Books, it's well worth the $23.95 price tag.

Here's how it works. Let's say you have just written a piece about the martial art of *ninjutsu,* and wonder where to submit it. Scanning through the list of categories, you decide that either men's magazines or sports publications are your best bet. Under "Men's" you find twenty listings, five of which specify sports as an interest. Turning to the sports section, you find the subcategory "Martial Arts," listing seven other potential markets: *ATA Magazine, Black Belt, Fighting Stars, Fighting Women News, Inside Karate, Inside Kung-fu,* and *Karate Illustrated.* To get more detail, you scan the listing for *Black Belt* and read something like:

> **BLACK BELT,** Rainbow Publications, Inc. 1813 Victory Place, Burbank, CA 91504. (213) 843-4444. Publisher, Michael James. Emphasizes martial arts for both the practitioner and layman. Monthly magazine; 128 pages. Circ. 100,000. Pays on publication. Buys all rights. Submit seasonal/holiday material 6 months in advance. Photocopied submissions OK. Computer printout submissions acceptable SASE. Reports in 1 month. Free sample copy.
>
> **Nonfiction:** Exposé, how-to, informational, interview, new product, personal experience, profile, technical and travel. No biography, material on teachers or new or Americanized styles. Buys 6 mss/issue. Query or send complete ms. Length 1,200 words minimum, Pays $10-$15/page of manuscript.
>
> **Photos:** Very seldom buys photos without accompanying mss. Captions required. Pays $4 to $7 for 5x7 or 8x10 b&w or color transparency. Total purchase price for ms. includes payment for photos. Model release required.
>
> **Fiction:** Historical. Buys 1 ms/issue. Query. Pays $35-$100.
>
> **Fillers:** Pays $5 minimum.

Here's a quick translation of the abbreviations and new terms:

SASE, self-addressed stamped envelope. Most magazines expect you to send SASE with your submissions, at least until they start buying from you regularly.

Ms. or mss., standard publishing shorthand for "manuscript" and "manuscripts."

Query, a letter describing an article—Chapter Twelve will tell you how to write one.

All rights, this magazine buys every imaginable right to an article; see Chapter Fifteen for complete explanation of magazine contract terms.

Read Before You Leap

After compiling a list of potential markets, your next step should be reading at least one issue of each target publication. A surprising number of writers neglect this simple market check, frequently antagonizing editors with inappropriate submissions. In addition to being amateurish, such blind submissions waste your time and postage money. No directory can substitute for firsthand investigation.

If you can, read the last five or six issues. Not only will you avoid duplicating recently published ideas, another common cause of rejection, but you'll avoid being deceived by an atypical issue. Magazines often publish theme issues to commemorate various occasions or provide more detailed coverage of some particular topic; what you need to know is what they normally publish. Like *Black Belt* many magazines will provide you with a free sample copy to study; others charge a modest fee: two or three dollars is typical. To look at several issues, try the library or order through the magazine or a back date periodical store.

Starting Close to Home

Once you tune into the invisible marketplace, the choice can seem overwhelming. With so many magazines to sell to, how do you decide which ones to approach first? A lot of writers, including myself, have opted to start locally by writing about what's going on in their city or state and offering it to local or regional publications or to newspaper feature syndicates. The geographical approach can work for you whether you live in a publishing center like New York or California, a small town in Middle America, or somewhere in between. While New York City, my home town, doesn't suffer from any shortage of reporters and writers, I sold my first story by going *off* the beaten track, covering the activities of what may be the world's smallest political party, whose philosophy is summed up by their slogan "Vote for Nobody." When I learned of this group, I contacted several news services and found one that was willing to buy a two-page piece for $35. Encouraged by this, I located many other unusual groups, individuals, and events, and became a "stringer" for the feature syndicate—a non-employee who brings in material sporadically.

According to *Writer's Digest,* over 200 city and state magazines buy from freelancers, with pay scales ranging from a few dollars to $1,500 in the most populous regions. In addition most newspapers and their Sunday magazines will buy some freelance material. In daily newspapers freelance material is most likely to appear near the editorial page or in the special interest sections like gardening, home, fashion, arts. If you're lucky enough to find a local story with national interest, a newspaper syndicate might take it for distribution to its member papers all over the country. Check *Writer's Market* or *Literary Market Place* (published by R. R. Bowker, 205 East 42nd Street, New York, NY 10017, available at most libraries) for a list of syndicates. Two other markets for regional material are regional sections of national magazines— many women's magazines have these; check *Writer's Market* for specifics—and travel and airline magazines.

Regional magazines and newspapers are usually most interested in business stories, human interest pieces, descriptions of the sights and pleasures of the area, and profiles of prominent local residents. Depending on the tone of the magazine, local scandals, exposés, and crime coverage may also be marketable. Historical articles about the region are another possibility to consider. And while the local angle is usually very important, sometimes you can also sell more general interest articles by quoting local experts or referring to area residents in the text of the piece.

Other Good Starting Markets

Religious, ethnic, and minority magazines: In a recent interview, an editor of a small religious magazine confessed that he was starved for well-written inspirational material. While emphasis varies from magazine to magazine, a strong spiritual element combined with a popular, *not* preachy, style is preferred by most of the one hundred or so magazines of this type listed in *Writer's Market*. Since many of these magazines are directed to specific denominations rather than the general Christian reader, you can often multiply the pay scale (typically anywhere from two to twenty cents a word) by selling the same article several times to different denominational magazines. Chapter Seventeen gives detailed information on making such repeat sales.

Magazines targeted at Jewish readers, numbering about fifteen, tend to cover both secular and religious issues important to the Jewish community. Due to heavy competition, Israel travel pieces and Holocaust-related articles are more difficult to market than other aspects of the Jewish experience.

Another twenty-five magazines are directed at minority members and ethnic groups as diverse as the Danish-American and Pan-Asian literati. While it's not essential to be a member of the group you're writing for, it's important to key your article to the special concerns of the group. You can do this either directly, with profiles of ethnic or minority leaders and political issues, or indirectly, with general interest pieces using quotes and anecdotes from group members. Since not all groups have their own magazines, check listings before selecting your slant.

Business and trade magazines: About one-third of the magazines being published today fall into this category, making it fertile ground for the freelancer. Your own profession offers the most logical starting point, as you are probably already tuned into current trends and technology as well as having entrée to industry leaders for quotes.

Business articles are usually aimed at one of four likely readers: the entrepreneur, the executive, the retailer, or the manufacturer. The entrepreneur, who is usually a would-be entrepreneur, is the easiest to write for; since articles tend to focus on opportunities of which the reader may not currently be aware, you can give a general overview of a field. Such readers are also likely to be interested in articles on getting loans, finding partners, drawing up legal documents, and other practical business advice. Executives tend to expect a more sophisticated article like a profile, a technological update, financial strategies, or management advice. Retailers and manufacturers favor more "nuts and bolts" articles telling them exactly how to increase sales, reduce costs, or improve efficiency.

As with religious articles, the same material could be sold to several magazines since a topic like "Detecting Counterfeit Currency" could be of equal interest to grocers, restaurateurs, video store owners, and leather goods retailers, all of whom read different magazines.

Hobbyist and special interest magazines: Instead of costing you money, your leisure time activities could help you make money, through sales of articles on canoeing, flying, ceramics, doll collecting, photography, or dozens of other hobbies. In addition, once you start selling regularly, you could probably deduct many of your hobby expenses from your writing income—an added bonus from the IRS (check with an accountant). There is an abundance of magazines to sell to, ranging from *American Book Collector* to *World Coin News*. Often a how-to approach is emphasized, but historical, profile, travel, new product, or informational articles could also work. Some magazines like personal experience; others prefer objective pieces. Payment ranges from $25 to about $500.

Over 3,000 magazines cater to special interest groups from *Catholic Forester* to *4-H Club News*. While many are staff-written, there's room for freelance material at others. These publications include alumni and college magazines, in-house organs, and union and association publications. Some feature essentially promotional material that advances the interests of their sponsors; others carry a wide range of articles. Check the publications of any colleges, clubs, or associations you or your friends are connected with—good markets may already be waiting in your mailbox.

Juvenile and teen publications: *Writer's Market* lists over sixty magazines buying free-lance material aimed at readers in the two- to twelve-year-old age group; another fifty or so are targeted to teens.

You may have read some of these magazines in your own youth, but check current issues because today's child is a lot more sophisticated in his or her reading matter than yesterday's. Once-forbidden topics like sex, drugs, and drinking are discussed openly in many teen publications. For the under-thirteen market familiarize yourself with the age level of the magazine—two to five, six to nine, and nine to twelve years old are the usual divisions. To get a fix on appropriate levels of vocabulary and conceptual understanding for the age group you have in mind, either create a test market of neighborhood kids or study school texts used for the appropriate grades. Overly sophisticated or overly simple articles will not sell. Teen readership is sometimes broken down into teens and young adults, the latter being older teenagers. Quite a few youth magazines have some sort of religious message, but the majority are general interest. However, some magazines cater exclusively to one sex. Likely topics for juveniles are history, science, arts and crafts projects, health, safety and hygiene, children in other cultures, biography, and sports. For teens, profiles of teen leaders, community service, music and popular entertainment, summer jobs, self-help and self-improvement advice, and sports are all promising.

Miscellaneous: A number of other magazines deal with the off-beat, the occult, or the esoteric—as well as unusual life-styles. For example there are magazines directed at motor home owners, diabetics, vegetarians, astrology buffs, and parents of twins. Almost everyone is an expert in *something*, whether it's crocheting, constructing crossword puzzles, or raising children. Translating that knowledge into a salable article is merely a matter of finding like-minded readers.

Now that you have article ideas and some promising markets to fix your sights on, you have two-thirds of the sales equation. The next chapter will provide the financial component: strategies to tailor your work to the needs of the marketplace. Finding the right audience for your work is half the battle; selling to those publications is the other. With the right idea, the right market, and the right pitch, you'll have an unbeatable combination that could pay off big.

3

Slanted
for Success

T o pitch your ideas to prospective markets, you need a strong, recognizable *slant* or angle to attract the editor's attention and to distinguish your article from other submissions on the same topic. Slant is what makes a submission right for one magazine, wrong for another. While "Banks" could be a suitable topic for either *Penthouse* or *Cosmopolitan,* the idea would have to be approached quite differently for each of these magazines. For *Cosmopolitan,* realizing that the reader is a young, single woman starting in her career, you might concentrate on "Getting Your First Bank Credit Card." Since you've pegged the *Penthouse* reader as a politically aware male, your exposé article might claim "Big Brother Is Watching Your Bank Account," assuming of course that you have documentation of this assertion. The difference between these two articles on the same subject is the slant. After reviewing a few issues of each magazine, you would profile the average reader and find suitable slants. You'll find more information on doing reader profiles in Chapter Seven.

Angling for Sales

If little or nothing has been written on your topic, you don't need much of an angle to sell the piece. When I decided to write about pheromones, most editors had never heard of these natural chemicals that attract the sexes to each other. Though I had no particular slant, the novelty of the idea that love at first sight may merely be a chemical reaction was enough. I sold the piece on my first submission. With a really original or offbeat idea, seduce the editor with your facts not your slant.

With more common ideas slant can make or break the sale. At *Good Housekeeping* former editor Constance Leisure rejected two well-written ideas from professional writers: "Confessions of a Junk Food Junkie" and "Confessions of a Coupon Clipper." Why? In her words, "While both were perfectly good ideas that we've done before and might well do again, neither writer had taken the idea that one step further that makes it new again." If your idea is somewhat familiar—and most of the ideas you'll be working with are—a spark of originality in your slant will help kindle an editor's interest.

In addition to improving the salability of the finished product, a strong slant will also make it easier to write the article. Your research will be concentrated on material you can actually use, shortening library time. Interviews can be pared to the bone with pithy, productive questions. Chapter Eight will tell you more about research methods, and Chapter Nine will give interviewing tips. With your slant as a road map you'll stay on the right track as you work, reducing or eliminating unproductive detours and time-consuming rewrites.

To test your focus, imagine that you are describing the idea to a friend. Could you get the point across in just a few words? In *Adventures in the Screen Trade* screenwriter William Goldman describes his search for a handle on the 650-page best-seller *A Bridge Too Far*. His first step was to identify the main idea: to him it was "a cavalry-to-the-rescue story—one in which the cavalry fails to arrive, ending, sadly, one mile too short." Once he had this idea, his task was simple: "That was my spine, and anything that wouldn't cling to it I couldn't use."

Strengthening the Spine

If your spine seems soft or ill-defined, try narrowing your topic. Often the problem is that you've selected a very broad subject like sports—the sort of subject that must pass through several filters before a salable idea emerges. Narrowing it to table tennis helps, but it's still a topic in search of a slant. With further funneling, I found a slant that worked for me: "Confessions of a Table Tennis Hustler," an interview-based article I sold to *Gallery* magazine. Often reducing the story to a single dimension—focusing on a key person, place, or event—gives you an excellent angle on a complex topic.

Using the five W's (who, what, where, when, and why) will help you slant overly broad topics. Communication is a topic that would interest many people, but must be narrowed down quite a bit to become a salable article. Here's how to use the five W's to create salable slants:

Who? Ask yourself, "Who is communicating with whom?" To appeal to women readers, possible slants might be "Communicating with Your Husband" or "Communicating with Your Children." The second slant can be narrowed further by considering *who* the children are: "Communicating with Your Newborn" or "Communicating with Your Teenager." Salable ideas? Yes, says *Parents* magazine editor-in-chief Elizabeth Crow, who has bought both of them in the past. "We feel that 'Communicating with Your Children' is such an important topic that we do two or three articles on it a year from various angles."

What? The essence of a slant is what you plan to say about the topic. In fact the first question an editor usually asks when a writer presents an idea is "What are you going to say about it?" With "Communicating with Your Child," pose the question of *what* the reader might like to communicate: "Talking to Your Child about Money," "What to Tell and What *Not* to Tell Your Child about Sex," and "The Nonverbal Messages You Give Your Child"— three more slants *Parents* magazine has assigned in the past.

Where? Sometimes a good slant can be found by thinking about the environment your subject occurs in. For a national magazine slants on communication might include "How to Meet Men at Parties" or "Office Gossip—Can It Help or Hurt Your Career?" For a city magazine, how about "Behind Closed Doors—Why Neighbors Don't Talk to Each Other"?

When? Connecting your general topic to a certain season or occasion can create a timely and topical slant. Communication lends itself to such seasonal slants as "What His Birthday Gift Says about Your Relationship," "Should You Tell Your Children the Truth About Santa?" and "Avoiding Family Frictions at Holiday Time."

Why? The most intriguing slant of all, *why* allows you to write more imaginative articles. Applying it to communication yields dozens of promising new topics: "Why Employees Don't Listen," "Why Children Lie," and "Why You Can't Keep a Secret." When your topic is a bit out of the ordinary, the *why* of the matter is especially important to making the sale. For example *Savvy* magazine recently ran an article on the style of communication favored by Southern belles. Why should their audience of executive women be interested? Because the belle is out of the ballroom and in the boardroom, using her wiles to charm clients' money out of their wallets and into the company coffers.

Hooking the Reader

A good slant points the article toward a select group of readers, those of a magazine you're familiar with. While many writers dream up ideas and then look for an audience, reversing the process is far more efficient. Finding likely readers and writing for them shapes your articles into marketable commodities. Students often tell me that their ideas would appeal to "just about anybody." However "just about anybody" is the target audience of only one magazine in the United States, *Reader's Digest,* and it mainly reprints articles from other publications, with relatively few original articles—not the best market for the beginner. The other 16,000 or so American magazines are more similar to rifles than to shotguns, with articles aimed at segments of the population, whether it's people who watch TV or draft-horse enthusiasts. To sell to these magazines, your article should stalk the same sort of quarry through selective focus.

Identifying the slant favored by your target publication is a simple yet highly effective approach to slanting your article. When I first started writing, I wrote about confession magazines in a humorous article which editors told me they liked but couldn't see how to fit into their publication. Clearly a new slant was in order. Selecting a market, a magazine aimed at the entrepreneur, I studied the articles and realized that all of them had practical "how-to" slants. I revamped my piece into "How to Sell to Confession Magazines" and sold it to this magazine. Sounds obvious, right? Yet many writers have perfectly salable ideas rejected for the same reason; they send personal experience pieces to magazines that like objective reportage or humor to how-to oriented publications. Almost all article ideas lend themselves to a variety of slants. The more of them you can discover, the more markets will be open to your work.

Get Intimate with Your Reader

Though writing seems like a solitary occupation, the reader is a valuable collaborator in your work. What kind of reader should you write for? While some writers enjoy adopting a variety of voices, others do well casting their nets for readers somewhat like themselves. This approach has several advantages for the starting writer. As a young mother, for example, you're already attuned to the interests and concerns of other young mothers—making it easier to find the slants that will attract these readers. By writing the sort of articles you'd personally like to read, your work will gain the ring of conviction editors look for. As a fellow professional, church member, community resident, parent, or hobbyist, you'll have both authority and familiarity with the problems, expectations, and experiences of your readers.

To appeal to other kinds of readers, use a friend or relative as a role model. One male client of mine enjoyed great success writing for female readers by using his wife as a sounding board. He'd imagine how she'd approach the situation, what her priorities would be, anticipate her questions, and provide the answers. After writing it all up, he'd give it to her for a final quality check. Another client, a school dietitian, used her teenaged customers as prototypes in writing for the teen audience. Though childless herself and well into her fifties, she sounded completely in tune with today's teens.

Looking for Labels

If you're having trouble pinpointing your readership, return to your statement of purpose, or spine, looking for labels that suggest readers. Is the piece about a teenaged tycoon? This should interest both youngsters and entrepreneurs. Or you can add the labels—creating new markets for the work. An article about renovating brownstones clearly suggests urban dwellers, but it could suggest a lot more: you could focus on local brownstone owners for a regional publication, black owners for a black publication, older owners for senior citizens' magazines, young married couples for *Bride's* or *Modern Bride,* renovations combining home and office for business publications, even renovating with children in mind for parents' publications.

While imaginative slanting like this can multiply article sales—you could write and sell *all* of those brownstone articles, each to a different magazine—make sure the potential markets don't overlap in readership. Even the cleverest slanting would make it difficult to sell two articles on "Finding Men through Personal Ads" to such similar publications as *Mademoiselle* and *Glamour*. A very slight overlap is no problem—undoubtedly some readers of *Modern Bride* also read *New York* magazine—but the numbers are too small to concern editors. (For more on identifying noncompeting markets see Chapter Seventeen.)

Another cautionary note: Make sure you don't slant the article at *too* small a group of readers. You don't have to hit every reader of the magazine, but the percentage must be reasonably large. Only about 55 percent of *Family Circle's* readers have paying jobs, but an article on "How to Get a Raise" would still appeal to enough readers to be potentially salable; one on "How to Mount and Display Butterfly Collections" would not, even if a thousand or two of their six million readers would enjoy it. If your target audience is elderly black nuns living in the Boston area, your slant needs broadening; you could make this material a subcategory of a larger piece, showing how this group's problems could potentially affect all of us.

Other Common and Uncommon Slants

Sometimes narrowing the topic or finding the right reader aren't enough. Your subject still doesn't seem fresh and lively. Here are some other ways to add zip to your subject:

Give it a 180 degree twist: Taking some ordinary topic like in-laws, imagine the typical reader's first reaction: "Ugh!" Now figure out how to *reverse* this reaction. Using the title "Enjoying Your In-Laws," I sold the article to *Modern Bride*. Another twist is to juxtapose two apparently unrelated concepts to create a fresh approach; in a recent article, "Revamping Your Office Image," I showed the reader how to use Madison Avenue marketing strategies to promote her career.

Swimming against the tide has worked well for my best-selling client Harry Browne, who feels that the key to success is to appeal to the *minority*. The majority, he reasons, sees its views con-

firmed in print every day, while the minority is hungry for acceptance of its ideas. Taking a commonly held opinion and making a
case for the opposite viewpoint can be the key to an article sale.
One of the most popular pieces *Parents* magazine ever ran did just
this. Elizabeth Crow recalls: "For years, experts have been telling
us that children should never, ever be permitted to sleep in the
parental bed. When we ran an article called 'The Family Bed,'
showing that based on new studies it was OK to let your children
sleep with you, the readers were ecstatic to see their secretly held
belief given the *Parents* seal of approval."

   Point out how society is changing: An article written twenty years ago about women who work outside the home would have
taken an approach very different from one written this year. By
linking your general idea to a contemporary attitude, your article
will have an up-to-the-minute ring to it. At *Gallery* magazine, according to managing editor Marc Lichter, "We are now emphasiz
ing the concept of the 'new man,' who is neither traditionally ma-
cho or so liberated as to seem a wimp. The pendulum has swung
to both extremes and now hangs in the middle. A few years ago a
typical slant was how to please women—now the reader also wants
to please himself in a mutually satisfying relationship."

   Hitch your wagon to a star: Advertisers create favorable
impressions of unknown products by connecting them to brand
name products: "XYZ brand is the Rolls-Royce of typewriters." A
similar approach can enhance your slant by linking your idea to
the actions or statements of celebrities and authorities, popular
movies or best-sellers, major news events, and current fads. This
approach works best when the tie-in is subtle; a rehash of the news
of the moment will seem rather dated in the six to eight months it
takes a monthly magazine to print your article.
   Here's how it works. Let's say you've been thinking of writing
something about the toys that were popular when you were a
child. Since some readers will be older than you and others
younger, create a frame of reference by connecting yesterday's
fads with today's. If "Monkey Madness" is the current craze, you
might title the piece "From Moon Rocks to Monkey Madness—
Where Are the Fads of Yesteryear?" Presto! Your nostalgia piece
is a timely story that readers will want to see now.
   In a recent issue of *Good Housekeeping*, a writer increased

reader interest in her profile of an elderly female pilot by creating connections with the hit movie and book *The Right Stuff.* The slant was strengthened by a second factor: the profile subject was the first woman ever to receive a private pilot's license. First can be an excellent slant in itself—how many stories have you read about Louise Brown, the world's first test-tube baby? Try naming the second test-tube baby. Second doesn't count for much as a position, but *last* can sometimes work with end-of-an-era articles.

Extra excitement can also be created with "est" words: biggest, richest, oldest, latest, smallest, strangest, best. While it's important to be accurate, such qualities can be somewhat subjective; as an agent I sold two books about "the world's richest woman." Not only were they by different authors, but they were about different *women:* former Queen Juliana of the Netherlands and Doris Duke.

The Q and A slant: An extraordinary number of articles approach their topics by posing some question that might concern the reader and then answering it. If your topic is "Safe Deposit Boxes," an obvious slant is "How Safe Are Safe Deposit Boxes?" The question could be geared to a specific readership as well: "Should You Take Your Wife Trout Fishing?" Questions make excellent titles for your articles—open any magazine and you're sure to find a few questions in the table of contents.

Similarly, constructing your article around a problem/solution format makes for easy slanting. The main concern is to narrow the problem sufficiently: "Avoiding Credit Card Scams" is a better slant than "Protecting Yourself Against Rip-offs."

Playing the numbers game: A good slant for round-up or update articles is the numerical approach: "12 Businesses You Can Start For Less Than $100," "15 New Cures For Childhood Disease," "50 Ways to Lose Weight Fast." Chronology can also offer a slant: "A Day In the Life Of . . ." "The Night That . . ." "The One Minute. . . ." Selecting a limited time period automatically sharpens focus—in an article you can give an in-depth look at twenty-four hours but only an overview of a complete lifetime.

New and improved: Your slant need not be exotic to sell. A very common but highly salable approach is the "new and improved" slant. This approach spices up an average idea with new ingredients—the latest research, hot trends, and juicy gossip—

then tosses in a dash of originality with unusual viewpoints, intriguing questions, and surprising solutions. Managing editor Phyllis Evans of *American Baby* recently bought two articles of this type: "Infant Psychiatry" and a piece on the controversy about plastic surgery for victims of Down's syndrome.

Put Slant in Your Titles

Since first impressions can color an editor's or reader's perception of your article, conveying your slant in the title will create expectations the article actually fulfills. Enhance this first impression by making your title tempting as well as truthful. While you shouldn't make your search for a winning title into your life's work—half the time even your best title will be changed by the editor before publication—a modest investment of time can generate more editorial interest in your piece. Consider the editor presented with two articles: "Double Your Refund: 99 Money-Saving Tax-Cutting Tips from CPAs" and "How to Save on Taxes." Which do you think will be read first?

How do you create a winning title? Good titles are usually brief; five or six words is good. Longer titles can work, particular ly for humorous articles and editorials, but if you can't boil the idea down to a few words, why not try a title/subtitle combination like "Unnecessary Surgery—Learning Your Options before Your Doctor Operates." Many magazine titles follow the format (action verb) you/your (noun): "Revamping Your Office Image," "Revitalizing Your Love Life," "Earn $$$ From Your Handicrafts." Another straightforward approach is "How to (hire a secretary, buy a used car, select a pediatrician)."

Want something fancier? Look for titles in quotations, making sure you haven't picked something too common like "All the World's a Stage." Or reword familiar expressions for a zippy title: "Old Wine in New Bottles" was a title I used for an article on recycling old article ideas. Use the expression in an unexpected context: "I Do! I Do! Your Guide to Double Weddings."

Now that your idea's been fleshed out with a slant and a title, it might be right for one of the major, big-money markets. To learn how to break into the big time—right now, without a low-paying apprenticeship period— read the next two chapters, which offer an in-depth look at the market needs and pay scales of today's top markets: women's and men's magazines. With the right idea, your next sale might be to Glamour *or* Penthouse.

4

What Women's Magazines Want

Women's magazines are a major market for both male and female writers, offering both good pay and large readership. Since women tend to read more books and magazines than men do, according to many publishing surveys, addressing your articles to the female audience offers good exposure for your writing. However, to get started in this market, it's essential to realize that not all women's magazines are alike. There are several subcategories in this marketplace: magazines targeted at married women, single women, working women, fashion conscious women and sophisticated women, and more specialized audiences such as farm women and brides-to-be. Even within the same subcategory, emphasis varies as does ease of breaking in.

This chapter will take an in-depth look at some of the major women's magazines from several perspectives: the kind of articles most in demand, the easiest sections to sell to, overall attitude toward unpublished authors, pay scales, and suggestions for the beginner. Because of space limitations, not all women's magazines are covered here. In addition to checking *Writer's Market* or other directories for further listings, be on the lookout for new magazines just starting up. While their rates may not be the highest, they are likely to be quite open to new writers. Once you get in on the ground floor, expect pay to rise with circulation.

Since magazines have a high turnover of editors as well as occasional shifts in content, payment, and editorial policies, before submitting, call or write for the latest information on these markets as well as reviewing a few current issues of the magazine.

What Kind of Articles Are Easiest to Sell?

Self-help: A staple of most women's magazines, this type of article tells the reader how to overcome common emotional and psychological problems. There are two keys to selling the self-help piece: a strong slant and depth of ideas. The second aspect is easy to overlook, since the typical self-help article's ideas seem like sensible but fairly obvious solutions to the problem, with a few more thought-provoking suggestions thrown in here and there. But this apparent simplicity is deceptive—it takes research and a lot of thought to create a good, meaty self-help article. Quotes from psychologists, psychiatrists, social workers, and other experts are also important; mention potential sources in your query.

Here are some recent examples that may prove inspiring: "How to Deal with People Who Make You Angry," *Woman* magazine; "Is Fear of Rejection Cramping Your Style?" (quiz) *Playgirl;* "Daydreaming," *Vogue;* "Couple Talk: How to Establish Communications Skills," *Bride's.*

Fitness and Self-improvement: With fitness articles avoid overlapping with staff-written features on exercise and beauty. Articles that contain more illustrations than words are usually staff-written, like "The 15 Best Ways to Firm Your Fanny," while freelance articles tend to have few or no illustrations, like "Diet Sabotage—What Your Lover Gains by Keeping You from Losing." Self-improvement articles concentrate on sharpening your mental or physical skills or teaching you new ones—improving memory, eliminating bad habits, developing speaking skills, learning to listen—in general, ways the reader can move one step closer to perfection in some area.

How-to: These practical pieces could cover anything from "How to Flirt" to "How to Pick an MBA Program." Using bullet formation in your step-by-step guide is attention getting. Use plenty of examples of the problems and pitfalls to avoid. And go beyond the obvious—instead of writing "How to Be a Better Driver," what about "How to Double Your Gas Mileage"? Motivate the readers to learn by offering some obvious benefit: "How to Make His Kids Love You," "How to Triple Your Reading Speed," or "How to Be the Life of the Party."

Career advice: An increasingly popular topic as more and more women go to work, these articles are usually geared to either the young woman starting out on her first or second job, the homemaker interested in part-time work or home businesses, or the managerial woman, depending on the magazine you have in mind. It's important to focus on a very limited topic: "Should You Consult a Career Counselor?" "Making a Good First Impression," "The Office Family," "Revamping Your Office Image," "Quitting Your Job with Style."

Personal experiences: While the majority of personal experience pieces are written by female authors, I've seen many effective articles from the male viewpoint—for example, accounts of first-time fatherhood or becoming a father late in life: relationship or marriage stories; seasonal experiences like remembrances of one's parents or holidays past; tributes to courageous wives, sisters, or daughters. Female personal experience articles often center on unusual medical problems, losing vast amounts of weight, family or relationship problems successfully overcome, pregnancy or motherhood experiences, getting off drugs or alcohol, and erotic or romantic adventures and offbeat experiences of all sorts.

Human interest: Several types are popular: heartwarming actions of individuals or communities; dramatic escapes and acts of courage; tragedies or near tragedies, especially ones relating to women and children; true crimes; unusual families like one with many natural or adopted children or one that successfully helps handicapped kids or children from other countries; medical stories, particularly about women or children who've overcome serious diseases or suffered a baffling medical problem; and women who've done something extraordinary.

Personal finance: How to save money, make more, increase what you have, avoid rip-offs, get out of debt, and other helpful strategies.

Relationships: Slant your article either to married women or single ones, not both. Men are a surefire topic—angles include:

how to understand them, meet them, size them up quickly, attract them, live with them, reform them, get rid of them, marry them, get over them, and find new ones. Or your relationship article could deal with parents, children, siblings, in-laws, or other family members.

Sex advice: Sex definitely sells, but women's magazines vary widely as to how explicit the advice should be and what sort of terminology is preferred, ranging from the ultimate four-letter word to the clinical or even the coy. Study previous articles very carefully for tone and be sure to slant advice to either married or single women. Include plenty of case histories and quotes from doctors, psychologists, and sex therapists. Another common approach is to discuss "Communicating Your Sexual Needs."

Humor: Though humor is a bit more difficult to sell than most topics, you can improve the odds by familiarizing yourself with the two most common genres. The first, housewifely humor, is exemplified by the work of Erma Bombeck, Jean Kerr, and Peg Bracken, and usually deals with life with hubby and the kids, the eccentricities of repairmen, maids, supermarket clerks, and other facets of domestic life. For single readers humor falls into the dating-and-mating genre; typical examples are humorous classifications of men, "worst date" pieces, rueful romantic resumes, job jokes, satiric pieces about diet, beauty, and fashion.

Exposé: These in-depth pieces require extensive research but command good fees. While not as frequently used as some categories, the right subject can provoke newspaper coverage of your article, launching your reputation. Good topics include women's health care and what's wrong with it: the rise in cesareans, the controversy over breast cancer treatments, unnecessary hysterectomies; hazardous prescription drugs or birth control devices; weakness in laws protecting battered wives, rape victims, and women who suffer sexual harassment on the job; divorce issues including collecting child support from unwilling fathers, paternal "child snatching," and other custody problems; child pornography and other crimes against children.

Celebrity and other profiles: While celebrity assignments are considered plums to be given to top writers, keep them in mind for the future, as well as exploiting any contacts you currently have. Profiles of successful businesswomen and other female achievers are also good, either of one woman or several.

Tragedy: Sharing your own or someone else's sadness can

make an effective piece. The article should be very descriptive, emotional, tugging mercilessly on the heartstrings to make the reader feel the tragedy. However, the piece should not be relentlessly downbeat: it should end with a message of hope, a lesson learned, an acceptance of grief, or some other uplifting idea. These articles can either be drawn from your own experience or other people's.

Travel: Often staff-written, but there's room for some freelance material. Attention to readers' socioeconomic groups is vital—some magazines want USA travel only, while others favor the most exotic locations. Generally slants are either budget vacations, historical sites, or the latest playground of the rich and famous. Articles could also cover travel related topics like "What to Do If Your Passport is Stolen," "Making Your First Solo Business Trip," and "How to Select Luggage."

Popular culture/current trends: Since the major women's magazines cater to a mass audience, well-established trends are better than crazes of small subcultures, except at the most sophisticated magazines. Look to television, movies, and children's playthings for ideas.

Opinions: Many women's magazines have special opinion sections featuring short essays on either light or serious topics, passionately presented. For a good way to break in, see listings later in this chapter for submission ideas.

Other: Less popular, but occasionally bought categories include: historical pieces like "History of Makeup"; round-ups like "What Makes Me Anxious" with quotes from twenty or thirty celebrities or ordinary women, or "Childbirth Practices in Other Countries"; updates, "Ten New Operations that Could Save Your Life"; inspirational stories or essays, "The Long Road Back"; alternate life-styles, "Loving a Gay Man"; industrial stories, "How Chocolate Is Made"; informative, "All About Ballet Shoes"; and helpful hints, "97 Things to Do with Old Pantyhose."

A Word about Length:

Generally, a thousand words (four double-spaced pages) is the best length for opinion articles. For the other article categories, 2,000 to 3,000 words is the usual range, although a few magazines use longer articles—up to 5,000 words. Check listings in *Writer's Market* to be sure what length each individual magazine prefers.

The Best Markets

Here is a selected list of women's magazines with circulations of 500,000 or more, plus a few smaller ones. Since policies, prices, and personnel may change, check current issues before submitting, or send for writer's guidelines. For further listings of women's magazines consult *Writer's Market* or other directories. I've rated these magazines by placing a star next to the sections of the magazine most receptive to submissions from new writers. If the entire magazine is particularly open to beginners, an asterisk precedes the listing for the magazine. Rates are given to indicate possible payment; most magazines tend to start beginners at relatively low rates but offer steady raises as they get to know a writer's work.

For Married Women:

FAMILY CIRCLE: 488 Madison Avenue, New York, NY 10022; articles editor, Susan Ungaro.

Similar in distribution and readership to *Woman's Day, Family Circle* runs the same article types but places a bit more emphasis on humor, self-help, and inspirational pieces. A slight change in direction is expected shortly, with fewer how-to and more journalistic articles. Best bets for the beginner: same as *Woman's Day,* or self-help. Pays an average of $1 per word, less for beginners, more for top writers.

*"Readers' Idea Exchange" pays $50 for short fillers of a paragraph or two with helpful home, child care, or vacation tips.

GOOD HOUSEKEEPING: 959 Eighth Avenue, New York, NY 10019; articles editor, Joan Thursh.

The main ingredients of the editorial mix are celebrity and other profile articles, dramatic true stories and human interest material, and health articles; with small quantities of self-help, inspiration, and nostalgia articles. Career advice is more oriented to wife who works for a second income than the managerial woman—possible slants include reentry into the job market, combining work and motherhood, home businesses. Relationship and sex articles assume a married reader as a rule. Payment for articles is about $1,500 to start.

*"My Problem and How I Solved It" is a section devoted to personal experience pieces by women who've overcome domestic, emotional, practical, financial, and business problems. Published examples include: "My Successful Business Was Ruining My Marriage" and "My Daughter Didn't Want Me to Be Her Best Friend."

Payment starts at $500 and goes up to $1,000 for new writers, but can go up to $1,500 for more experienced writers. The optimum length is 1,500 words.

LADIES' HOME JOURNAL: 3 Park Avenue, New York, NY 10016; articles editor, Sondra Enos.

Like *McCall's, LHJ* is quite interested in contemporary issues affecting American and foreign women, as well as celebrity and other profiles, health, personal experience and self-help; career, marriage, child-rearing, and sex advice; and exposés. Payment for articles is about $1,500 and up.

*"A Woman Today" is a 1,500-word essay reflecting contemporary attitudes, experiences, and problems of women. Typical titles: "My Daughter, The Cheerleader," about a woman whose non-sexist childrearing somehow failed to take; "My Son, The Star" by the mother of a six-year-old Broadway actor. Payment is in the $200-$400 range.

MCCALL'S: 230 Park Avenue, New York, NY 10169; articles editor, Judith Stone.

Not afraid to tackle current social problems and issues, in the United States and abroad, this magazine also features medical and health articles; human interest and personal experience; self-help; marriage, child-rearing, and sex advice; and profiles of successful women and celebrities. Also interested in short humor pieces. Best bets for the beginner, according to assistant managing editor Lisel Eisenheimer, are short, timeless articles of 1,000 words "that we can keep in our larder until needed," lively humor or personal experience pieces, and regional material. For regional articles payment is about $200; for regular articles *McCall's* pays $1,500 to $2,500 for 3,000 to 4,000 words, up to $3,500 for very experienced writers.

*"The Mother's Page"runs short items that are useful, entertaining, or inspiring, paying $200; or 750- to 1,000-word essays paying $750.

*"Vital Signs" runs short medical items paying $100 apiece.

*"Back Talk" is a 1,000-word editorial, either light or serious, and could be controversial. Typical examples: "Babies Don't Come with Guarantees" and "Why Can't Teachers Speak English?" Pays $1,000 for 1,000 words.

*"The Single Life" also features 1,000-word essays, humorous or serious. A recent one, "A Guide to Married People," offered a lighthearted look at the wedded life-style through the eyes of an unmarried woman. Payment is about $1,000.

PARENTS MAGAZINE: 685 Third Avenue, New York, NY 10017; articles editor, Eileen Maguire.

Slanted mainly to mothers, articles cover parenting from pregnancy to the teen years. Focus is very important—concentrate on a single aspect of the topic: "Getting Babies to Sleep Through the Night,"rather than broad-spectrum advice on childrearing. Emphasizes the latest medical and scientific research, but with an informal tone. Also runs articles on fitness, education, current issues, career advice, marital relationships and seasonal subjects. For 2,500 words, payment is $500 and up.

REDBOOK: 959 Eighth Avenue, New York, NY 10019; articles editor, Karen Larson.

Though oriented toward married women, this magazine differs from the others in its category in that articles are slanted to a younger and more sophisticated reader. Typical articles cover the changing issues and problems of marriage and family life in today's world: exposé, health and nutrition, sex advice, and self-help topics. It seldom runs dramatic true stories, human interest, or celebrity material; instead has heavy emphasis on psychological subjects. Pays $750 and up to start.

*"Check Out" pays $50 for short anecdotes, craft ideas, recipes, and wonderful or witty sayings from your child (include photo of the child).

*"A Young Mother's Story" is a first-person true story relating to issues of marriage or family life; payment is $750 for 1,000- to 2,000-word articles. A recent example is "I'd Do Anything to Have This Baby," describing how one woman coped with a difficult pregnancy; another story described the experience of raising quintuplets.

WOMAN'S DAY: 1515 Broadway, New York, NY 10036; articles editor, Rebecca Greer.

Sold in supermarkets and newsstands, with a low cover price, this practical magazine emphasizes how-to articles slanted to a married reader with a modest income, such as "10 Ways to Save $1,000 in the Next Year" and "How I Dress Well on $100 a Year"—both actual, recent articles. True life dramas and human interest stories are frequently run. "Night of Uncommon Courage" is an example; also advice on marriage, children, health, jobs, and self-improvement appear. Travel articles cover USA only. Best type of article for the beginner—innovative money-saving ideas or true life drama. No set rate of payment, say the editors; what you are offered depends on the topic, length, and your writing background.

*"Neighbors" pays $50 for one- or two-paragraph suggestions on dealing with common domestic situations—examples include ways to improve children's table manners, birthday party ideas, vacation tips.

*"Reflections" is a 1,000-word editorial with a strong view-

point, usually serious, but occasionally more lighthearted—examples: "Experts Are Usually Right, Right? Wrong." and "Gourmet Food—Please, Not While I'm Eating." Payment is currently $2,000.

For Single Women:

COSMOPOLITAN: 224 West 57th Street, New York, NY 10019; executive editor, Roberta Ashley.

Editors classify the articles into two categories, emotional and nonemotional. Emotional subjects include self-help, sex advice, first-person erotic or romantic experiences, and relationship articles; nonemotional topics are careers, health (including infrequent pregnancy articles), diet, beauty and fitness, profiles of successful women or celebrities, and some current issues, rarely humor. Currently overstocked with emotional articles, check before submitting. A difficult market for the beginner, because most ideas are staff-generated and assigned to experienced writers, but does buy some material from new writers. Pays $750 to start.

*"Outrageous Opinions" is a lighthearted editorial section with essays from 250 to 1,000 words. Recent titles: "Busting the Bigger-Is-Better Myth" and "Some Opposites Attract, Others Grind You Down." Pays $300.

*GLAMOUR: 350 Madison Avenue, New York, NY 10017; articles editor, Janet Chan.

Aimed at a youthful, college-educated woman, this magazine seems quite receptive to new writers, judging by the experiences of clients and friends. It features psychological articles, relationships (mainly for singles), health, beauty, fitness, current issues, medical, personal experience, some pregnancy and baby pieces, some career, mixed with a smattering of offbeat topics and humorous (dating-and-mating genre) articles. Pays about $1,000 for articles to start.

*"Viewpoint" runs 1,000-word editorials on "a cause or grievance." Typical titles: "The Truth about Epilepsy" and "Making It without a College Degree." Pays $500.

*MADEMOISELLE: 350 Madison Avenue, New York, NY 10017; associate articles editor, Brie Quinby.

Heavily slanted to the single woman—no pregnancy articles—lots on relationships, dating, psychological topics, fitness, beauty, health, sex, some career advice. Likes a humorous tone where appropriate. Quite receptive to new writers. Pays $850 and up for full-length articles in the 2,500 to 3,000 word range, less for shorter articles of 1,500 to 2,000 words.

*Periodically has fiction and nonfiction writing contests with cash prizes and publication of winning entries; look for announcements in the magazine.

MS. MAGAZINE: 119 West 40th Street, New York, NY 10018; managing editor, Suzanne Levine.

Directed at a socially conscious, well-educated woman interested in the women's movement, articles cover social and political issues, intellectual concerns, health care, alternate life-styles, some motherhood and pregnancy pieces, Third World women, nonsexist child-rearing and relationships, career topics, and profiles of outstanding women. Quite different from other women's magazines, study carefully. Don't submit general pro-liberation pieces; concentrate on specific issues. Pays up to $1,000 for full-length articles.

*"The Gazette" features short news items; payment starts at $25.

PLAYGIRL: 3420 Ocean Park Blvd., Santa Monica, CA 90405; articles editor, Ruth Drizen.

The magazine that "goes all the way," featuring nude male centerfolds, *Playgirl* is aimed at a sophisticated reader. Article types include profiles and interviews, especially of celebrities; health, relationships, financial advice, business and career material, sexuality and exposés. Payment is about $500 to $800.

SELF: 350 Madison Avenue, New York, NY 10017; managing editor, Valerie Weaver.

Originally heavily slanted to the fitness buff, the magazine now emphasizes self-help, according to one of its editors, but uses an expanded definition encompassing physical and mental well-being, with articles on psychological issues, relationships, money, health, fitness, beauty, careers, and sex. Though most articles are targeted at single readers, pregnancy and babies are given some coverage, but as one editor put it, "If the kids are walking and talking, their mothers aren't our readers." Pays $750 and up.

*"Health Watch" runs 800-1,000-word features on health, "Your Money" uses 800-1,000 words on financial topics. Payment starts at $700 but is "negotiable" according to editors.

For Working Women:

SAVVY, The Magazine for Executive Women, 111 Eighth Avenue, New York, NY 10011; editor-in-chief Wendy Reid Crisp.

For women on the professional fast track—or those that aspire to be, *Savvy* runs profiles of successful female executives or entrepreneurs; management techniques, success strategies, health and fitness articles; some fashion and entertainment pieces; personal finance and investment advice, and travel. Articles tend to have a witty tone but a serious message. For shorter articles of 1,000 words payment is about $500; for longer articles of 2,500-3,500 words payment is usually between $750 and $1,000.

*"Facts of Life" uses anecdotes of 75 to 200 words that are "revelations, moments of truth, and other professional eye-openers," paying $50.

*"Frontlines" runs short news items relevant to working women and pays about $50.

*"Modern Dilemma" is an essay of about 1,000 words and pays about $500.

WORKING MOTHER: 230 Park Avenue, New York, NY 10169, articles editor, Susan Seliger.

Directed to the working mother with children living at home, this magazine is written in a popular style with short articles, 2,000 words or less. Typical topics are flex-time, finding child care, job sharing, working while pregnant, profiles of women who "have it all," light humor, and practical advice. Pays $500 and up.

WORKING WOMAN: 342 Madison Avenue, New York, NY 10173; executive editor, Julia Kagan.

For the managerial or executive woman, or business owner, this magazine likes to report on the latest business trends, current issues, profiles of successful businesswomen, improving management skills, business travel, health, and investment. Avoid overly basic business articles—reader is knowledgeable and sophisticated about the business world. Rates are variable: "We prefer to start writers off low, and grant raises as we get to know them." Top rates are in the $1,000 to $1,200 range for full-length articles of 2,000 to 3,000 words. Also uses short features of 250 words or more, starting at $50 and increasing with length.

Fashion Oriented:

VOGUE: 350 Madison Avenue, New York, NY 10017; managing editor, Lorraine Davis; features editor Amy Gross.

Oriented toward a relatively high-income, fashion-conscious woman, this magazine runs the gamut with self-help, career advice, health and fitness, pregnancy and motherhood, travel and current trends. Fashion articles are staff-written. Tone is sophisticated and somewhat literary. Best length is short, 1,000 to 2,500 words. Payment is $1 a word on average.

HARPER'S BAZAAR: 939 Eighth Avenue, New York, NY 10019; managing editor Betty Klarnet; health editor Denise Fortino.

Unlike most women's magazines, *Harper's Bazaar* is directed at older women—many articles deal with over-forty topics like face-lifts, belated motherhood, menopause, and "prime time sex" as a recent issue called it. However this slant isn't apparent in every article; topics frequently covered include health and fitness, interviews and profiles of prominent women, the arts, current affairs, travel, business and career topics, and life-styles. Pays $600 to $1,000.

To double your market prospects, consider giving your article a "sex change operation." With the right slanting, the same basic idea can be marketed in one version for the female audience, another for a male readership. Chapter Five will help you decide if your idea is right for the booming, high-paying men's magazine marketplace, as well as clueing you into market needs and fees.

5

The Men's Magazine Marketplace

While the majority of popular men's magazines feature nude photos (some much more explicit than others), they're also read for the *articles*—usually *not* about sex, but dealing with a wide variety of issues of interest to today's man. Or if you're more interested in dress than undress, a second category of men's publications, the fashion magazines, is a market to consider. These publications feature witty writing and stylish men's wear— and are definitely suitable to send home to mother.

What's Easiest to Sell?

Exposés: By far the most frequently bought article type, the men's magazine exposé article is hard-hitting, thoroughly researched, and uncovers scandals in government, medicine, politics, science, religion, business, banks, the military, or any other sector of contemporary life. Typical slants include computers and the invasion of privacy, CIA operations in the Third World, toxic waste dumping, price-fixing schemes, illegal IRS tactics, stock market scams, police brutality, the Colombia cocaine connection, and Pentagon cost overruns. For excellent exposé articles, study *Penthouse* which emphasizes the genre.

Wine and connoisseurship: While most men's magazine readers aren't rich, they enjoy reading about ways to eat, drink, and be merry. Articles can work on a practical level, "The Best California Wines," or a fantasy one, "Tasting a $10,000 Wine." Gourmet foods like exotic cheeses could be a good topic—but no cooking tips or recipes. Other trappings of the good life are covered: selecting and storing fine cigars, liqueurs and recreational drugs (sometimes).

Women: While the old "How to Pick Up Girls" article has fallen out of favor, updated versions sometimes appear: "A Crash Course in Scoring With Coeds" or "Rich Girls—How to Meet Them, How to Treat Them." More typically, articles concentrate on how to improve and solidify existing relationships, or deal with relationship problems: "When Women Stray." A humorous approach can also work.

Song: Since men's magazine readers tend to be on the young side—*Playboy* is the most popular magazine on college campuses for example—rock and roll and interviews and profiles of musicians frequently appear. Avoid overlapping with staff features like regular reviews of new releases.

Consumerism: Emphasis is usually on luxury items: videocassette recorders, home computers, electronic games, stereos, cameras, cars, sporting goods—"toys for men" *Gallery* calls them. Good angles are "how to buy," "how to protect," and "how to get the most from."

Sports: With really popular sports like football, searching for an original angle is the biggest challenge. Less common sports like windsurfing can be given more basic "how to get started" coverage. Also appealing are interviews and profiles of colorful characters in the sports world: race car drivers, hustlers, gamblers, and celebrity sports figures. Humor is also good: "Clichés of the Superbowl," "The Worst Plays in Major League Baseball."

Politics: A variety of slants to select from: profiles and interviews, exposé, humor, opinion, exploration of current issues, election coverage, historical ("The Most Crooked Election Ever Held"), and practical ("What the New Tax Laws Are Doing to Your Paycheck").

Military: While this topic is dwindling in popularity, good approaches include new Vietnam coverage (especially to coincide with news events or anniversaries), American mercenaries, military spending boondoggles, army exposés ("GIs on Drugs").

Fashion and current trends: While some magazines run many more fashion articles than others, "What's In, What's Out" articles can work for many markets, depending on content. Other typical topics: "How to Get the Perfect Fit," custom-made clothes, evening wear, ultra-trendy dress. If you want to write about current trends and fads, whether in fashion or living, move very quickly—men's magazines like to be in the vanguard of style.

Popular science: Down-to-earth reportage of scientific breakthroughs for the layman is highly salable. Futuristic speculation about possible implications of current research is also a good approach. Subscribing to several popular science magazines will tip you off to new research and suggest dozens of potentially promising topics. Scientific articles are a good but time-consuming specialty for a writer.

Health: While men's magazines don't run much on diet or fitness, health topics like cancer, stress, preventing heart attacks, innovations in health care could work; or an exposé approach: "Medical Genocide."

Life-styles: Exotic, erotic, extravagant, innovative, or offbeat life-styles are your best bets. Recent examples include articles on dinner parties of the smart set, yuppies, Miss America contestants, young Mafia members, fraternity boys, playboy businessmen, and pro wrestlers. The subject can also be approached through interviews and profiles or humor.

Technology: Readers seem to have an insatiable desire to learn what's going on in the world of high tech, what it might mean to them, how it will be used in the future, its sinister implications or astonishing benefits, conspiracies to suppress it, how to profit from it: by investment strategies or through personal use.

True crime: While this category isn't used as frequently as some, it does appear periodically so is worth keeping in mind if the right story comes along. Several approaches can work: new assassination theories (must be truly sensational, in view of the extensive coverage given this topic) reviving unsolved cases of the past, "did they get the right man?" stories, lively scams involving megabucks, offbeat murders or robberies, terrorists, organized crime exposés. The usual true crime story takes some case from the past, like the D. B. Cooper case (the first air hijacker—neither the ransom nor the hijacker was ever found), uncovers new and reevaluates old evidence to offer a theory about the crime's solution.

Money: Always a good topic, but make sure your angle is appropriate to the probable level of income and financial savvy of your intended readership. In addition to investment and tax advice, consider discussing the dollar implications of current or projected legislation: "Child Support—How the Government Can Force You to Ante Up," or "$400 Toilet Seats and Other Tales of Military Spending." The concept of *saving* money doesn't appear to be of much interest to the would-be playboy—you'd have to have some truly astonishing plan to make this work like "How You Can Buy a House for $1."

Humor: A staple of most men's magazines, witty pieces on any of the preceding topics could work, especially sports, sex, fashion ("The Slob's Guide to Style"), women, and money. Humor can lean toward the raunchy; be elegantly satiric about current events or trends; drag the reader into the mires of sick humor; or simply offer an outrageous view of the world. Adding an element of wit to your article often enhances salability even if you're not writing humor per se.

The Best Markets

While the two most popular men's magazines, *Playboy* and *Penthouse*, rival the best-selling women's magazines in circulation, sales figures are much smaller for the rest, so I've tried to include all magazines with a circulation of 250,000 or more, plus a few smaller ones. I haven't included business or sports magazines though these also buy articles oriented toward male readers, but I've concentrated on those that focus on male life-styles exclusively. I've also omitted magazines that *only* run articles on sex (if these interest you, look at *Cheri, Penthouse Variations, Stag,* or check any large newsstand for potential markets of this type).

As with the women's magazines, check before submitting for any changes in prices, personnel, or editorial policies since this material was compiled. Also be sure to read a few sample issues before submitting. Asterisk indicates markets that are quite receptive to new authors.

Pictorial Magazines

CAVALIER: 2355 Salzedo Street, Suite 204, Coral Gables, FL 33134; editor, Douglas Allen; managing editor Nye Willden.

In conjunction with its pictorial emphasis on female fights, this magazine is quite interested in general sports articles: "Tote Board Blues" about horse race betting, and "Boulevard Bash" about the Miami Grand Prix, are recent examples. Also runs articles on sex, consumerism, interviews and profiles, exposé, and wine; paying about $500 or so for 3,000 to 3,500 words.

*"Reader's Hang-ups" runs sexually oriented personal experience pieces of 2,500 words or less, paying $150.

CHIC: 2029 Century Park East, Suite 3800, Los Angeles, CA 90067; managing editor, N Morgan Hagen.

From the publishers of *Hustler,* this rather explicit magazine runs exposés, profiles, music, relationships, sports, and current events articles. Representative articles include: "The Rough Stuff," on off-the-road racing; "The Nine Fatal Errors of 'WHOOPS,' " exposé of nuclear energy plants; "Interview with a Coyote: Smuggling Aliens into the U.S.," and "Cocaine: the Cut that Kills." Pays $750 and up for 5,000 words.

*"Dope" pays $300 for drug-related features; "Cocaine: The Cut that Kills" was a recent example.

*"Sex Life" pays $300 for sex and relationship articles; example: "How to Make Women Fall for You."

*"Odds and Ends" pays $50 for offbeat photos and news items.

*"Close-up" pays $200 for 1,000-word interviews; typical example: "Mike Cockrill and Judge Hughes: Art's Bad Boys."

GALLERY: 800 Second Avenue, New York, NY 10017; managing editor, Marc Lichter.

Quite interested in exposé articles and humor. Along with its "Girl Next Door" amateur erotic photography contest winners, *Gallery* also runs relationship and life-style articles, interviews and profiles, sports articles, popular science and technology pieces, political material, and a variety of other articles. Little coverage of fashion, except humorous or very basic how-to. Typical articles: "Wilderness Lost," an environmental piece; "The Wall," an essay by a Vietnam vet; "Outlaw Art," on graffiti. Also has a section "Private Lives" featuring presumably true erotic material. Articles are usually 3,500 to 5,000 words, but also uses shorter features of 1,000 words and up. Payment for shorter articles starts at $200, for longer articles the range is $750 to $1,500—"more if it's really extraordinary," says one editor.

GENESIS: 770 Lexington Avenue, New York, NY 10021; articles editor, David Ivins.

Emphasizes current events, profiles and interviews, exposé, sports and humor, technology, popular culture, and consumer-oriented articles; plus "Friends and Lovers" nude photo contest. Representative articles include "Chuck Norris," a profile; "Wrestling USA," a life-style piece; and "Score U," a humorous piece on meeting coeds. This magazine plans to place greater emphasis on sex-related articles in the future, so recheck market needs before submitting. Articles are 3,000 to 5,000 words; payment is $400 to $750.

HUSTLER: 2029 Century Park East, Suite 3800, Los Angeles, CA 90067; managing editor, Jim Goode.

Definitely the bad boy of men's magazines, this highly explicit publication isn't for the faint-hearted. Exposés and sensational journalism are the mainstay here; typical examples include "The Death of Los Angeles," futuristic speculation about earthquake damage; "Onward Christian Soldiers—A Brief History of the Warrior Caste in America." Also uses interviews and profiles, celebrity material and some sick humor pieces, and has amateur photo contests. Articles run about 5,000 words and pay $1,200 to $2,500.

"Kinky Korner" buys "honest sexual experiences" of seven double-spaced pages for $250. Off-color jokes bring $50 from "Hustler Humor," if selected.

OUI: 300 West 43rd Street, New York, NY 10036, executive editor, Barry Janoff.

Humor and exposés are also good bets here; typical examples include "Are You an Alien?", a quiz, and "Deadly Fire," an exposé of arson causes and costs. Also covers sports, the arts (movies, mainly), sexuality, how-to, life-styles, current trends and "happenings," and profiles and interviews. Articles are 1,500 to 3,500 words long; payment starts at $300 and can go as high as $2,000, depending on length, research required, exclusivity, and news value.

*"Openers" runs short news items and new product announcements, pays $10.

PENTHOUSE: 1965 Broadway, New York, NY 10023; executive editor, Peter Bloch; senior editor, Peter McCabe.

Chock-full of lively exposés and humor, *Penthouse* runs more articles each month than most men's magazines, but due to its high rates and circulation is a very competitive market. Subjects include politics and political humor, sports, interviews and profiles, sex, music, relationships, and health. Typical articles: "20 Worst College Football Teams," "Back to School" (humor), "No Sweat," on the hazards of some forms of exercise, "The War on the Chiropractic" (medical exposé), "The New Mafia," and "Are You in the Right Job" (quiz). Articles tend to be on the long side, about 5,000 words, pay is $2,000 to start and can go up substantially for a major piece or cover story, say editors.

PLAYBOY: 919 North Michigan, Chicago, IL 60611; articles editor, James Morgan.

The founding father of the men's pictorial magazine, this is probably the most difficult but most prestigious market of its type. Pictorials are tamer than most. Famed for its interviews with such luminaries as ex-President Carter, *Playboy* also covers the arts, current events and politics, humor, sports, finances and business, science, women, trends, business, and a variety of other male-oriented topics, written with wit and research. Typical articles: "Child Support: Pay Me Now or Pay Me Later" (exposé); "Modern Girls," "Women of Mensa," "John DeLorean—Candid Conversation," "Farewell to the Staple" and "Yupward Mobility" (both humor); "Playboy's Pigskin Review." Runs an exceptional number of articles each month, paying $3,000 and up for 3,000 to 5,000 words; $500 and up for short features of 1,000 words; for interviews of 10,000 to 15,000 words payment starts at $4,000.

*"Playboy After Hours" buys offbeat and humorous news items for $50, also some original pieces, paying $500.

*"Playboy's Party Jokes" buys sexy and sick jokes for $50.

Fashion Oriented

ESQUIRE: 2 Park Avenue, New York, NY 10016; senior editors, David Hirshey (features and longer articles) and Adam Moss (features and entertainment pieces).

Calling *Esquire* a fashion magazine demands a very broad definition of the term, since clothes are only a small part of the eclectic topics covered in this sophisticated and intellectual publication. The cover proclaims that the magazine emphasizes "man at his best," while representative articles include: "How to Buy a Hunting Dog," "How to Profit from Patriotism," "Hemingway at Large," "Second Thoughts" on fatherhood, and "My Venice, Myself." Topics covered include world affairs, the arts, today's political scene, travel, relationships, connoisseurship, music and popular culture, life-styles, finances and business, profiles, and sports. A very competitive market, with rates starting at $2,500.

GENTLEMAN'S QUARTERLY (GQ): 9100 Wilshire Blvd., Beverly Hills, CA 90212; managing editor, Eliot Kaplan.

Oriented toward an upscale, fashion-conscious male reader, GQ expands the concept of fashion into life-styles, connoisseurship, health and fitness, the arts, investment, business, psychology, profiles, and business articles, usually written with a tongue-in-cheek tone. Recent examples are: "Building the Vintage Cellar," "The Case of the Missing Raphaels," "A Day in the Life of the Vertical Club," reportage on a tony health club; profiles of actors, writers, directors, and sports figures; "Guess Who's Coming to Dinner," gossipy material about chic dinner parties; and "Sweethearts of Gamma Nu," about the life-style of one college's "Animal House" sorority. Articles are 2,500 to 4,000 words, paying $500 and up for shorter articles; $1,000 and up for longer ones.

*Also buys for some of its columns and departments; check writer's guidelines for current needs and rates.

MEN'S GUIDE TO FASHION (MGF): 419 Park Avenue South, New York, NY 10016; managing editor, Steven Slon.

A bit sexier than other fashion magazines, this relative newcomer on the scene (started 1984) features psychology, fitness, relationships, sexuality, grooming, money, and life-styles. Typical articles: "Why You Need Aerobics Now," "Sex With an Ex-Lover," "Five Easy Ways to Boost Self-Confidence," "Why More Men Are Staying Single," and "The Startling Good News About Stress." Articles are short, about 2,000 to 3,000 words; payment is $500.

Naturally not all your ideas will dovetail with the major markets' needs. This lucrative but limited segment of the marketplace represents only a small fraction of the potential customers for your work. As a freelancer, make your first objective locating magazines that will buy your work regularly. Finding these can be a process of trial and error. As you investigate potential outlets for your writing, you'll often be faced with the task of quickly sizing up an unfamiliar magazine as a prospective market. In the next chapter I'll show you exactly how to psych out the market needs of any magazine—and locate dozens of new markets in the process.

6

Finding Your Niche

O nce you have a general impression of the size and scope of today's magazine marketplace, your next concern is selecting the right markets as targets for your initial efforts. For many writers the answer is to follow the path of least resistance—by starting with magazines which cater to their own interests, tastes, life-style, hobbies. While you may already be reading some of these, others are waiting for you to discover them. By systematically exploring as varied a collection of magazines as you can cram into your writing schedule, you're sure to discover many promising new outlets for your work. Even when you start selling regularly, this type of market research still pays off in increased sales and resales of published pieces.

Expanding Your Market Horizons

The publishing industry is a volatile one—editorial turnover is high, and a major shake-up can dramatically change a magazine's emphasis. New magazines spring up periodically; old ones sometimes die or merge with stronger ones. Writer's directories, valuable as they are, invariably contain some obsolete information by the time they go to press. Even the actual magazines currently on the stands now can be misleading, reflecting the editorial emphasis of several months ago, while major changes in staff or policy may be creating a new submission climate. Even minor changes can be significant: your query could be languishing on the desk of an editor who's moved on to the greener paychecks of another publication, or your editorial may be perfect for a column that was canned in last month's editorial meeting. While even the savviest freelancer can't keep abreast of every change, a modicum of regular market research will keep such snafus to a minimum.

While the best way to keep on top of the magazine scene is through a network of personal contacts, few freelancers have direct access to this pipeline. Instead they usually read the reports of those who do, in *Writer's Digest, The Writer* (for market needs, personnel changes, announcements of new publications) and *Publishers Weekly* (for personnel changes, relatively little magazine coverage otherwise). Writers' groups and conferences offer additional opportunities to garner market updates—some groups also publish newsletters with market information as well.

Other useful strategies are to become a regular reader of all the magazines that appeal to you, either at the library or through subscription. Sending away for writer's tips is also worthwhile, though some are overly general. Calling the magazine before submitting to double-check on current personnel is the easiest way to avoid submitting to departed editors, since very recent changes may not have found their way into print yet.

To learn of brand-new magazines *before* they are announced in writers' magazines—and inundated with submissions—make a habit of haunting the largest newsstand you can find in your area, looking for new faces on the racks. Watch also for cover announcements on familiar magazines—some magazines launch their first issue within another magazine, then go public with their second issue. Your favorite magazines may also carry ads to subscribe to as yet unpublished magazines—though some of them never get off the ground. Clubs and organizations sometimes get announcements of forthcoming magazines in the members' field of interest.

New magazines are particularly good markets for a beginner because they lack the stable of frequent contributors more established magazines draw upon for articles. While rates tend to be lower, getting in on the ground floor establishes a positive relationship with editors, putting you in line for the plum assignments if the magazine does take off. Getting in with new editors at established magazines is equally desirable—since they don't have a large workload yet, they are often fast and eager to buy.

Should You Specialize?

Naturally it's easier to keep abreast of the field if you limit yourself to certain market categories. While a few writers truly play the field, covering the gamut of subject matter, most writers concentrate on a few major categories, and a few specialize in a single article type such as medical pieces. There are appealing reasons to specialize: editors like to hire someone who's done similar articles in the past; a layman can often master a single field through concentrated study, reducing or even eliminating research on new pieces; editors may create special assignments for you once you're established; specialists often earn more; and finally, a collection of articles on the same topic can easily lead to a book project.

If specializing in a single field appeals to you, the most marketable specialties are: popular medical articles, business, travel, popular science, technology and computers, sophisticated self-help, outdoor and sports articles, and journalistic exposé pieces. However, any frequently bought category of article is suitable—review magazines in your area of interest for further inspiration about possible specialties.

A middle-of-the-road approach, less limiting than single-field specialization, but offering many of the virtues of specializing, is to select three or four areas of concentration. This approach retains credibility with editors; after you make a few sales you have a good portfolio to support new proposals with, while avoiding burnout in any particular specialty. Often writers fall into this pattern; as they start to sell, they discover that certain types of writing seem to come more easily and pursue those. Since you avoid being typecast in one specialty, it's easy to branch out into new areas if your interests change as your career develops.

Being a jack-of-all-trades has its virtues too. When editors learn to think of you as "this pen for hire," you're likely to be offered interesting and diverse assignments as you write celebrity gossip one week, career advice the next. By casting a wide net no opportunity is likely to be missed. While this approach is more work—you're starting new with each piece—it's also fun as you broaden your horizons through your work.

Under the Covers

To turn your market objectives into sales, you need a strategy to size up unfamiliar magazines quickly—a way to read as a prospective writer. A *reader* skims through a magazine reading the articles that strike his fancy and skipping the others. A *writer* analyzes everything in the magazine from the ads to the articles, looking for clues that will show him or her how to sell to that magazine. This attitude is what gives you that extra edge over the competition, making points with the editors and ultimately leading to sales.

Here's what to study:

The cover: While you can judge a magazine by its cover, you're likely to get a superficial impression. *New York* magazine is obviously a regional publication, but with eight million stories in the "naked city," which one should you pitch? Let's take a closer look at that cover; three stories are featured as I write this: "*AIDS* in the Emergency Room," "Jackie Gleason's Second Honeymoon," and "Interiors: Intimate Details." Since cover stories are the ones editors see as the most important in that particular issue, right off we know that these editors are interested in current events, medicine, television, and decorating—possible areas to consider for your submissions to this publication.

The table of contents: Since considerable creativity goes into the composition of the contents, often writers are confused by the differing terms and are unable to distinguish staff-written material from freelance pieces, or they waste time scrutinizing staff-written magazines that are not potential markets for their material. In the table of contents, staff-written pieces often appear without author bylines, while titles of freelance pieces are normally credited to their authors. If *no* bylines appear in the table of contents, the magazine is almost certainly staff-written; for further confirmation compare bylines of the actual articles with the list of "contributing editors" or "staff writers" in the masthead of the magazine. (If no bylines accompany the articles either, the magazine is definitely staff-written.) Checking for author biographies (usually called "bios" by editors) at the end of published articles will also help you to identify freelance articles: "Joan Smith owns Renovations Unlimited and is currently writing a book on home renovation" implies that the author does not work for the magazine regularly.

The table of contents is likely to be divided into at least two categories, one containing "articles" and "features" and another listing "columns" and "departments." While some magazines favor more fanciful terms, or group material by subject, your goal should be to learn which articles are regular, monthly features ("Cosmo Goes to the Movies") and which are one-shots ("Birth Control Update"). While the majority of freelance work will appear in the articles and features section, some regular columns and departments also buy freelance material. Others are completely staff-written. To determine which columns or departments are potential markets for you, compare each bylined name with the masthead—if the writer works for the magazine, the column isn't open to freelance work. Another test is to check two or more issues. If a different byline appears each month, the column is probably done by freelancers. Also look for small print at the end of the column—some magazines include writing tips and prices paid to encourage submissions.

The articles: Having several issues on hand is particularly helpful since some articles types may not appear in each issue. You'll want to note *length* (one printed magazine page with no ads is usually about 1,000 words; or count the number of words in one inch of a column and measure the article with a ruler to get a more exact count). Then look at what kind of *research* is favored: numerous quotes from experts, book references, newsbreaking reportage, popularization of scientific research, personal experience, author expertise, or intellectual analysis of ideas. Now consider *tone:* witty, practical, sophisticated, intellectual, sexy, step-by-step how-to, emotional, or chatty. Finally, look for *distribution* of subject matter: if the last three issues contain ten self-help articles and one humor piece, you'll have some idea of the relative demand for these two article types. Knowing the magazine's editorial standards will help you structure suitable queries.

The columns and departments: In addition to being possible markets for your writing, these can also indicate what *not* to write about. A column may completely satisfy the magazine's need for a certain kind of material, or it may limit submission possibilities for a particular topic. While some magazines buy freelance book or record reviews for example, freelance sales are unlikely if a regular column already covers new releases. Sometimes taking a specialized angle may overcome this problem: "The All-Time Best Love Songs," or "Finding Nonsexist Children's Books." If a column covers a very broad subject area like travel, check several recent issues before making submissions in the same area. Freelance articles on the subject, if any, are likely to be either longer or more specialized. Being aware of recent coverage also prevents you from making overlapping submissions.

The regular features can also help you construct a profile of the typical reader. Consider what these departments tell you about the *Cosmopolitan* reader: "COSMO Goes to the Movies," "COSMO Reads the New Books," "Horoscope," "Astroforecast for Your Man," "Irma Kurtz's Agony Column," "Outrageous Opinions," "Dieter's Notebook," "Travel Update," "Money Talk," "Your Body," "COSMO Tells All," "Red Hot Right Now," "What's New in Beauty." Right off you see that the Cosmo girl is quite interested in her looks, her body, and her mind. She is educated ("COSMO Reads the New Books"), but immersed in popular culture. ("Horoscope," "COSMO Goes to the Movies," "Red Hot Right Now"), probably single (the "astroforecast" is for her *man*," not her husband). Extrapolating from this, you can imagine the typical reader as an upwardly mobile administrative assistant searching for her male counterpart.

The ads: Since advertisers spend vast sums to pinpoint appropriate markets for their products, put this valuable research to use in learning all you can about the demographics of the readership: his/her age, sex, life-style, income level, social class, and interests. Let's take a look at *Parents Magazine*. Its name immediately identifies children as the reader's most salient interest, but who exactly is that reader? A quick glance at the ads: Solarian flooring, Sure & Natural Maxishields, L'Oreal makeup, and O-Cedar brooms suggests that your main audience is women—mothers—with modest to moderate income (we don't see ads for luxury cruises, high-tech consumer goods, or sports cars). With this in mind, finding suitable angles on articles slated for this publication is much simpler.

Scrutiny of the ads can also suggest *topics* to write about; since *Parents Magazine* has many ads for children's books, toys, vitamins, and baby foods, good articles might be "Teaching Your Child the Joys of Reading," "Education Through Play," and "Nutrition for Your Infant."

The editor's page: Though some magazines don't carry one, this page is your opportunity to meet the top editor "up close and personal" as sportcasters say. Often the editor either discusses what interests him/her about some of the major articles, or imparts philosophical reflections about the magazine's subject matter. Both give you insights into the editor's mental outlook and interests that can be reflected in your queries. In a recent issue of *PC: The Independent Guide to IBM Personal Computers,* "What's Inside," the editor's page, talked about one writer's feeling "excitement" about new communications software, another putting in late hours testing and retesting 2400-baud modems, and a third investigating public electronic mail systems by sending cryptic messages to colleagues. What this suggests to me as a writer is that this editor is looking for articles that reflect a passionate excitement and in-depth knowledge about IBM PC-related hardware and software, as well as a sense of fun about the subject.

The editor's page may also refer to personal information about the top editor that might suggest article topics. In a recent issue of *Parents Magazine* editor Elizabeth Crow talks about the infancies of her three children, theorizing why only the third slept reliably through the night. A writer might follow up on these leads with such article proposals as "Avoiding Sleepless Nights with the New Baby" or "Birth Order and Personality," both of which should strike a chord with this editor.

Letters to the editor: If the magazine runs reader mail, two helpful nuggets can be gleaned from it. First, you can infer subject matter of previous articles you might have missed, broadening your understanding of the magazine's emphasis. Second, the readers' reactions both tell you what does and doesn't work in this magazine. The reader's comments can sometimes suggest affiliated article topics to consider for future queries: if reader X complains that something wasn't covered, your query might focus on that subject.

"In the next issue" announcements: Like letters to the editor, this clues you in to additional topics that interest the magazine and shows the editor's priorities as major articles are emphasized in such announcements. For more guidance on profiling readers, a good book to consult is *Write on Target* by Connie Emerson.

As you sharpen your ability to size up market needs, you'll find the process becomes automatic—that even casual reading turns up ideas and approaches that could open up more markets for your writing—while regular market updating keeps you attuned to what editors want right now. But valuable as market study is—and it's vital to success—the knowledge you gain can only be put to practical use when you have a product *to offer: your writing. In the next chapter I'll show you how to turn out quality writing in volume, with proven tactics to raise efficiency and profits.*

7

Get Your Writing into High Gear

One of the most valuable lessons I've learned as a writer is that less work can equal more money. Eleven years ago I sold my first article, a two-page newspaper feature. I wrote all night and part of the next day, typing more than 5,000 words as I searched for the 500 that I needed. It was the hardest $35 I ever made. Recently I wrote a twelve-page article in less than half the time I'd spent on those two pages—and made about twenty-five times as much money. Faster writing can be equally profitable for you; an increase in output can easily translate into an increase in income as you submit more, reach more markets, make more sales, see more work published, enjoy more success as a writer.

While a few writers already work at whirlwind speed, like my client who finished a 600-page novel in just ten *days* and sold more than 150,000 copies of it, many writers are unwittingly hobbling themselves with time-wasting habits. As a literary agent I've seen many writers double and even triple their writing speed with improved writing methods. Fast writing should never be hasty or careless writing; with the right attitude and approach, faster writing becomes *efficient* writing. Frequently, raising quantity also raises quality; by letting the creative flow sweep past minor snags, your story acquires a momentum that carries it to a swift and graceful conclusion with a minimum of unproductive detours.

However, fast writing isn't just a numbers game; trying to meet some arbitrary quota of pages may actually *prevent* you from achieving your best pace. Consider the supposedly impossible goal of the four-minute mile—as long as runners believed that it couldn't be broken, it wasn't. If you feel that ten pages is the most you'll ever do at once, you're limiting yourself to fulfilling that goal—which may fall far short of your real capabilities.

To systematically unlock your true potential—it may be far greater than you imagine—you should examine each of the three crucial stages of writing: *preparation, composition,* and *polishing.* By reducing or eliminating unproductive habits and attitudes that now hold you back, you can look forward to peak performances at the typewriter—and enjoy the process more. To get the most out of your writing time, try these five steps to faster writing:

Getting in Gear

Recently a sports trainer told me that the most frequently neglected, but vital, element of a successful performance is a well-planned warm-up routine. Without it the athlete is neither physically nor mentally prepared. Many writers make a similar mistake by failing to flex and stretch the brain before starting work. How many times have you rushed over to the typewriter only to stare numbly at a blank sheet of paper, hoping inspiration will strike? Or do you find yourself compulsively cleaning your desk, telephoning a few friends to discuss the frustrations of writing, or inventing new ways to color code your research materials? Such procrastinating routines are a common symptom of inadequate warm-up.

To limber up your writing muscles, try these routines:

Focus: Nancy, one of my writing students, was puzzled by the class's unenthusiastic reaction to her writing. After all, the research was good, the style competent, the topic interesting. The flaw? The piece was an orphan: conceived in passion, but written after the heat had cooled. My class and I sensed that Nancy didn't really care about her subject—and neither did we. No wonder Nancy complained of the effort required to finish the piece—few tasks are more daunting than mechanically typing ideas that no longer interest you. Cold ideas make for slow, tedious work.

To rekindle the spark, concentrate on the aspects of your piece that most excite you. Imagine you are describing the idea to someone else. What's the most exciting aspect of the work? What's fun about it? Unusual? Challenging? Important? Creative? Why are you writing it? Getting yourself psyched up, eager to work, is the first step toward faster writing.

Facts: Now give the spark some fuel—information. I'm assuming you've already researched your subject thoroughly; if not, gather the necessary information before proceeding further. Rapidly skim all research material *once,* without making notes or underlining. Avoid consciously attempting to memorize, sort, or organize. Just absorb. You'll be amazed, once you start work, how much you'll remember from one quick reading. The right fact will surface when you need it, and any little mistakes can easily be corrected during the editing stage. Avoid shifting back and forth from research material to first draft—this makes for slow, disjointed writing. And just mark any holes in your research for later attention. Over-researching your first draft is just another way of procrastinating. Go with what you have—as far as it will take you.

Form: Now that you are tuned into your topic, warm up your style by rapidly skimming a model chapter or article. If you have previously written something similar, reviewing earlier work can be a great confidence booster as well as a good warm-up. If you haven't, reading a piece by someone you admire is helpful, as long as it isn't *too* close to what you are doing. To avoid unwitting plagiarism or derivative writing, get inspiration from writing of a slightly different genre, or on a slightly different topic. The easiest way to get in gear is to glance through a recent issue of the target publication. However, never spend more than fifteen minutes on this exercise. Spending your morning rereading the last six issues of *Cosmopolitan* may be entertaining, but it isn't writing.

Organizing Without an Outline

By now you should be eager to write, but don't neglect the final stage of your preparation—organizing. Careful planning eliminates many delays when you start to write. No time is lost pondering what to cover next: the right topic is already at your fingertips. Since you know how many subjects have to be covered in the given space, you'll find it easier to judge if an individual section is running long or short—and to make immediate adjustments. And you'll seldom waste time on rewrites to correct oversights or rearrange topics. A good plan is like a map—not only does it show you the best route (not necessarily the *shortest* one), but it keeps you from losing yourself in interesting digressions you encounter along the way.

Valuable as organizing is, you can have *too* much of a good thing. While some writers enjoy constructing elaborate formal outlines filled with roman numerals and capital letters, I've found that such detailed outlines just slow me down. Instead of thinking about the actual content of the projected work, I'd become bogged down with technical details. I'd think of a topic and start wondering if it was a subcategory of the preceding one or a new heading. Or I'd have an "A" without a "B" and find myself blocked temporarily. Then I'd notice that most nonfiction writing already contains a handy outline—the subheadings of the chapter or article.

Instead of a formal outline, I re-create this effect with a flow chart: jotting down a few spontaneous notes to remind myself of the movement of the piece. While this approach is equally helpful in fiction or nonfiction, a special benefit for the nonfiction writer is that these notes can sometimes be recycled into subheads for your article or chapters. A flow chart for an article I recently wrote on "Genetic Counseling" for *Cosmopolitan* looked like this:

Definition and benefits of counseling
Who should get it
Genetic detective work—case histories and diagnosis
Will my baby be normal?—tests and procedures
Genetic prophecy—future of the field

To create your flow chart, ask yourself questions—figuring out what the reader would like to know about this character, situation, problem, or adventure will help you set the right priorities. The answers help you construct paragraphs: as you think, "When should the reader consult a genetic counselor?" you write "One of the most common reasons for consulting a counselor is. . . ." Anticipating the reader's objections or preconceptions also gets your writing flowing briskly: "Incompetence is the *least* common reason for being fired. Actually, most firings result from. . . ."

Continue the organizing process with "pre-fab" constructions in your draft for a quick framework. Avoid letting these guidelines become rigid formulas to follow. Instead, use the following common organizing principles, or others you've invented, as flexible approaches to drafting. You may also wish to combine these approaches in your piece, using different ones in different sections.

Numbers: This chapter is organized into five steps to faster writing. Your article could contain twenty ways to save money on taxes, a guide to the five most common mental disorders, three entrepreneurs and their success strategies. Numbers can also be used as a mini-organizing principle; write: "Three of the most common mistakes new mothers make are. . . ." and three easy paragraphs will follow.

Time: From *Day of the Jackal* to *Thin Thighs in 30 Days,* countless books and articles are constructed chronologically. Be creative—although starting in the past ("I was born in the house that my father built") is logical, it can be dull. Often a better plan is starting with the present, the exciting things going on right now, moving to the background material, the past, then finishing up with intriguing suggestions about the future. Or begin with the future, using exciting speculation about the implications of today's technology, say, then go to the present.

General to specific: If your basic idea is somewhat surprising, start by stating the premise in general terms: *hypnosis can improve your sex life.* Elaborate on it with convincing examples, then explain in detail what the techniques are and how to use them. For more commonplace ideas it's more effective to start with the specific, through anecdotes or examples, and then move to the general.

Problem/Solution: The plots of many novels revolve around a series of problems confronting the characters: ranging from being transformed into an insect overnight to determining just who did kill Roger Ackroyd. Equally suitable for nonfiction, the essence of this approach is presenting the readers with a dilemma—coping with failure, say—and skillfully guiding them through the nuances of the problem, then gradually unfolding the answer.

Beginnings

A surprising number of writers find composing the first paragraph extraordinarily difficult. Naturally you want to hook the reader, impart some clever idea, set a standard to follow, and generally get launched with a bang. With these expectations the first sentence seems like an insurmountable stumbling block. You write and discard opening after opening. This stage alone used to take up as much as a quarter of my writing time. Since then I realized that I had set up a sort of catch-22 situation, where I was trying to find one of the borders of an unexplored wilderness before I had charted the terrain. I didn't know where to begin because I didn't know where I was going or where I'd end up.

Remembering that the first draft is clay, not marble, is the key to solving this problem. Since the opening can, and often will, be changed before you submit, it doesn't matter *how* you begin— as long as you *do* begin. Any starting point will do. "An image, a line, a phrase you saw on a cocktail napkin last month—any of these can be the first layer," says Martha LaBare, author of *Shooting Star and Other Poems.* "Some of the other layers will appear immediately, others only in revision. Writing is a process of discovery."

If you're stuck for a good opening, a formula beginning—for instance, starting with an anecdote—can get you moving. Often the reason that certain kinds of openings are used frequently is that they work; and you may be so delighted with the results that you keep your first opening. Or you may find, as many writers do, that the ideal beginning only occurs to you after you've completed the whole piece. Either way, a stock opening serves its purpose— getting some words on paper.

Sometimes your best move is to skip the beginning and move directly into the middle or even the end. Start with any section which seems particularly vivid in your imagination. Poets often start work with a group of lines already composed in the mind, then build around them. This nonlinear approach might be compared to tossing a stone into the water and sketching the ripples around it. As the sections that live in your mind take shape on the page, new words will flow from what you have. Working out of sequence may seem to be unnatural or to violate some supposed rule of writing, but the only right way to write is the one that works for you.

Keeping the Momentum:

Now that you've plunged into the piece, keep prodding yourself onward. As you work, watch out for four mental saboteurs that even the most experienced writers sometimes encounter:

It isn't good enough: If you were painting a portrait, would you start by delineating each eyelash? Yet many writers make this very mistake, anguishing over each word of their rough draft instead of blocking out the work in broad strokes. Perfectionism is a common pitfall—I've known writers to spend an hour revising and polishing a *single* sentence in a draft. Naturally after such a microscopic scrutiny of one sentence, all perspective on the work as a whole disappears. The next sentence seems even more difficult as the internal critic, once activated, casts its withering gaze on each fledgling thought, murdering it in its infancy.

It took one of my clients three books to find the solution to this problem—and once he did, he went on to write seventeen more books with less effort than the original three. Here's how he describes it: "I used to sit, finger posed over the keys, waiting for that perfect sentence to pop into mind. Once I realized that you can't build bricks without straw, I started typing any thought that struck me, no matter how poor it seemed at the time." By working hastily, he was able to capture most of his ideas as quickly as they occurred to him. The next morning he'd discover, buried in his raw outpouring, many gems to polish into a brilliant final draft. "My real writing is rewriting," he concludes. "The draft is just an extension of the thought process."

I don't know enough: Despite the most careful preparation, you may discover a missing link in your chain of ideas, a seemingly insoluble problem. To keep your draft moving quickly, let your subconscious fill the gaps in your work. Whenever you hit a snag, jot down "tk," the old printer's abbreviation for "to come," and move on. As you race forward, your subconscious will be busily mulling over the problem. The answer will surface when you least expect it. Often my best ideas occur to me during my breaks; as I sip a glass of iced tea, sentences and even paragraphs that had eluded me seem to write themselves in my mind. Your subconscious is a powerful writing tool—put it to work for you.

   I'm not getting anywhere: Frustration is a familiar feeling to most writers when for no particular reason some ideas resist being written. While your first impulse may be to give up temporarily, two more productive solutions can help overcome these difficulties. One is to switch to another section—or even an entirely different project—that seems more exciting. Fresh material may spur you on to new efforts. Or a bit of pressure, judiciously applied, may do the trick. Since work tends to expand to fit available time, tight deadlines reverse the process, contracting it. As a very productive publicist told me, "There's nothing like knowing it has to be ready by five o'clock to get the adrenaline—and creative juices—flowing." Create imaginary deadlines if you lack real ones, or try a combination of time quotas and rewards for meeting your self-imposed goals. For example, you might promise yourself that when you finish the article, you'll treat yourself to a fine French dinner.

   I'm having trouble getting back into it: While some writers favor marathon sessions, others work best in a series of sprints. If you cannot complete the project in one sitting, prevent cold starts by leaving yourself an entry point for the next day's work—the beginning of the section. A quick list of thoughts to develop can also serve as your landmarks for reorienting yourself.

Quick Fixes

   When you first try fast writing techniques, you may find that your work needs *more* editing than before. While this may seem to cancel the benefits of speedier composition, I've discovered that the reverse is true. My old, slow method of writing required little editing since I combined writing and editing. While this sounds more efficient, trying to simultaneously create and critique *inhibited* my writing. Why? Because I was urged in contradictory directions by the two processes—simultaneously creating and critiquing. Rejecting undeveloped ideas before they were fully explored, I often found myself staring at a blank sheet. My new method allows me to fill that sheet, *then* improve it. *Separating* the stages, with rougher drafts and heavier editing if need be, allows you to concentrate just on the present task, whether it's editing or writing, with a dramatic increase in efficiency.

Subdividing the editing into its components makes for even faster work since you can first focus on the big picture—the entire piece—then on individual elements. Finally you'll put it under a microscope to spot copyediting errors. Here's the best sequence:

Let your draft age a day or two before editing.   I've found that too much study of the same work numbs the brain, making it impossible for me to look at my work objectively. Instead, start researching the next project, send out a few queries, or begin another piece. Keeping a variety of work on hand will eliminate time lost to blocking, waiting for research materials, or encountering other delays. While this arrangement doesn't increase the speed of each project, it improves overall efficiency, increasing your total output. This short delay between writing and editing freshens perspective, allowing for faster editing of the completed piece.

Read the piece once, quickly.   Since you want to perfect the piece with as few revisions as possible, you'll want to address the most glaring problems before proceeding to another draft. If you've really sped through the first draft, your first problem is likely to be filling the holes with additional information and ideas. You may also want to add some new topics if the piece is too short. After deciding what to add, consider what to *subtract*. Almost all writing can be improved by selective pruning, painful as it may be to see your precious words eliminated. Fast writing often includes superfluous material in the rough draft since the technique aims at maximum inclusion initially, but you don't want your fast writing to be a slow read.

Rethink and rearrange.   Once you have a completed draft, with the fat trimmed and extra meat added, study the arrangement of ideas. Using the mental flow-chart technique should give you good organization, but in context you may see that some segments have more impact elsewhere in the piece. Instead of redrafting at this point, you may want to number the paragraphs in the new order for now.

Scrutinize style. While each writer has a unique style, most gravitate either toward the elaborate or the plain. Each has its virtues but necessitates different editorial approaches in order to emerge as lively reading. Overwriting is the hazard of the elaborate stylist; editing should be directed at controlling any excess that bogs the reader down, while retaining expressive flourishes that enhance meaning. Underwriting, the negative expression of the plainer style, can be jazzed up with more vivid language, increased use of comparisons, and intriguing facts, examples, and enriching details.

Fine-tune your copy. To detect more subtle flaws of diction and style, try reading the material aloud. Awkward sentences the eye might pass over become obvious when spoken. If you find yourself stumbling over some of your prose, imagine how it will strike the reader. Reword.

Letter perfect. Since editors associate copyediting errors with potentially larger problems, meticulously check and recheck your final draft. If possible, do the second check the following morning. You'll be surprised how new errors leap out at you after a short break.

As you use this checklist, alert yourself to problems that crop up frequently. Once you become aware of where you're going astray, you can program yourself to avoid the problem in future pieces. By making a list of words I frequently misspelled, I finally became an excellent speller. Other writers I know managed to overcome major stylistic flaws. With practice your fast writing will need less and less editing, as you catch potential editing problems when you write.

Fleeting thoughts: Fast writing offers more than just a high page count and improved efficiency in your work. Fast writing can also be fun writing. My old way of writing—anguishing over each sentence then laboriously plodding on to the next—was hard, hard work. I felt I was losing sight of what I like about writing—the joy of turning thoughts into well-crafted sentences. Faster writing brings me closer to my thought rhythms as I work at a pace I enjoy. Watch a young child write a story and you'll see words appear happily, uncritically, naturally. Bring to that simple process the adult perspective of honing, polishing, completing, and you have faster writing at its best.

Faster Times at the Typewriter

Use these techniques to enhance your mechanical efficiency:

Type drafts.   One of my clients was able to double his writing speed by eliminating longhand drafts. Your first draft may be good enough to be final; if so, eliminating that extra step of typing up completed material will speed your work considerably. Typing the material is also helpful in getting the right length.

Reduce retyping.   Many writers waste time retyping their rough drafts. Newspaper writers are notorious for sloppy drafts and fast writing. If you don't like it, X it out and move on. Stopping to retype breaks flow.

Use inserts.   Often a great idea for an earlier section will strike you in the middle of your rough draft. Just type it on a new sheet, labeling the page 2A, 3A, or whatever to indicate where the new material belongs. I've seen drafts with more insertions than original pages.

Cut and paste.   Often when you edit the piece, you'll find large sections that need no revision. To avoid retyping on intermediate drafts, simply type the new material on separate sheets and organize the material into the correct order with scissors and paste or tape. Less meticulous writers staple the new material in place. Then photocopy the assembled page, and presto—a perfect looking page with minimum typing time.

After your piece is finished, edited, and polished, then retype it to produce a perfect, error-free copy for submission.

Last Chance Checklist

Unsure if your material is really ready to go out? Here's a systematic approach to reviewing your article one last time:

Beginning: Does your lead hook the reader with an interesting anecdote, intriguing question, promises of valuable information to come, vivid descriptions, provocative quotes, witty definitions—does it arouse curiosity and get the reader's attention? Does it fit the tone and topic of the article? Does it seem similar to the leads favored by your target publications? Is your basic thesis clearly stated somewhere on the first page?

Middle: Does the middle develop your thesis with carefully researched facts, convincing arguments, authoritative quotes, surprising statistics, or revealing case histories? Are the arguments and points arranged in a logical manner? Are there any weak links in your chain of reasoning? Does the style conform to that of your target publications? Do you have enough subheads?

End: Are all loose ends tied neatly together? Do you end with a sharp summary, some memorable new point, a powerful additional argument, thoughtful quote, or some other refreshing last thought? Does your ending convey a sense of finality? Do you need to add a box with names and addresses to contact for further information? Is the length of the article as a whole right for the magazines you've selected on your submission list?

If you think some extra editing would help, Chapter Ten will illustrate the editing process as I applied it to one of my recent articles. Or if you're pleased with your article, check Chapter Thirteen for submission strategies to use. Still not quite sure about the piece? Don't be too much of a perfectionist—you can edit a perfectly good article into oblivion. Though I believe in careful writing, I've found that some writers seem to have a hard time letting go of their work. There comes a point when you have to declare a piece finished and move on. How do you tell when you've gotten there? If you feel the article is at least 90 percent as good as it will ever be, and are unable to improve it significantly with one additional editing session, send it out. It's ready.

8

Stalking
the Stray Fact

Knowledge has power—and potential profit for you. Readers like to learn from nonfiction writing; editors like to satisfy this hunger with informative articles. A solid foundation of facts is often what separates so-so material from salable work. And beyond the basic facts, what hooks readers and keeps them hooked is the depth of ideas in the material. By connecting your own insights with the accumulated wisdom of the past gleaned through your research, your analysis and interpretation of the facts will become more penetrating, more *satisfying*. Though some excellent articles can be written without bolstering of books or experts—especially humor, personal experience, or editorial opinions—research is the backbone of most nonfiction writing.

Making research pay off for you is a matter of technique. To some writers, fact finding seems frustrating and dull, usually because they have no clear idea how or where to find the information they need. With the right tools, literary detective work becomes a craft. As you learn to systematically track down elusive facts quickly, research soon becomes a profitable—and enjoyable—pursuit, paying off in increased sales opportunities and better writing. And there's the thrill of discovery as you successfully unearth facts others have overlooked and use them to improve your work. Useful guides to library methods are Lois Horowitz's *Knowing Where to Look* and *A Writer's Guide to Research.*

Armchair Research

For faster, easier research, start by using the world's best computer, your brain. Without any special effort, you've already accumulated a huge data base of facts through listening, observing, and reading. When you start to access these mental files, you're likely to be surprised how much helpful material you've already accumulated on your subject. You'll also pick up useful leads about where other facts could be found.

Here's how the process worked for me on a recent assignment from *Cosmopolitan* to write about "Computer Careers." After reviewing my somewhat scanty knowledge of the subject, I found:

1. Enough general information on computers to write an introduction to the piece. For more efficient and profitable time at the library, select topics you already have some background in; starting from scratch makes your task much more difficult and time consuming, lowering your hourly pay rate. Or for more enjoyable research, select an article subject that interests you powerfully—one that you might read up on even if you weren't hoping to sell the piece.

2. The names of three computer experts in my circle of acquaintances whom I could approach for more information. After consulting my experts, I was able to select ten job categories to focus on in my article, and get capsule information on some of them. A short chat with an expert can greatly accelerate your research: not only may the expert have facts on hand that might take hours to dig up on your own, but he or she can help you target your research efforts to the most fruitful lines of inquiry by offering reading lists and names of experts to contact. If you don't have a tame expert on hand, research can also help you find one and get a more productive interview once you do. (Chapter Nine will tell you how.)

3. The title of a book on computer jobs that I'd seen in a friend's office and could arrange to borrow. Though this particular book proved less helpful than I'd hoped, I've often found that I had some of the facts I needed right in my own home—on the bookshelf or in my collection of newspaper and magazine clippings.

4. Various formats for "Careers in XYZ" articles I'd read in the past. By analyzing these approaches, I was able to determine what sort of information the reader might expect from my article—exact salary, job description, how to break in, how to move up, overall job outlook, and working conditions for each position—and create a model layout. Knowing what you need to know *before* you start researching provides a convenient road map for your investigation, both keeping you on the right track and avoiding repeat trips to collect overlooked but essential information.

Research Shortcuts

Your library may have some new services that will make your research easier. If you need just one or two pieces of information to round out a query, you may be able to get the facts by phone. Many libraries have telephone reference services; the New York Public Library, where I do most of my research, has given me dozens of helpful facts for the price of a local call. This is particularly helpful when you're in the middle of writing the piece and realize that you need to know the population of Lubbock, Texas, or the date of Edmund Wilson's death.

Some larger libraries also offer computerized bibliography research. Taking advantage of the many research-oriented computer data bases now available, this service uses a computer to prepare a listing of research sources on your subject, showing title, author, and date and place of publication. Some data bases also provide brief abstracts, or summaries, of the material's contents. After the computer determines where the material is, you simply locate the correct periodicals and newspapers in your library, read them, and the research is finished.

Here's how it works. You spend a few minutes describing the project to a research librarian who helps you define the parameters of the search. Choosing from a long menu of data bases, the two of you select the indices to be used, such as *Newspaper Index* or *Business Periodical Index;* a time frame to examine, 1985 to present for example; and some key words to enable the computer to identify appropriate material like "Computer Employment/Data Processing Employment." You pay nothing for the expert services of the librarian but are charged a modest fee for "connect time," the time the computer spends searching the data bases. A recent computer search at the New York Public Library cost me $20 and provided an eight-page listing of sources on my subject.

If you have your own computer and a modem (a device that lets your computer communicate with other computers over telephone lines) you can subscribe to bibliographic computer data bases which allow you to rapidly search large data bases for research material on your subject. Some data bases provide summaries of the material; others give you just title, author, date and place of publication. For an additional fee, most will also provide photocopies of the full text as well. Currently the "big three" such services are Dialog (3460 Hillview Avenue, Palo Alto, CA 94304; (415)858-3785), BRS (1200 Route 7, Latham, NY 12110; (518) 783-1161), and Orbit (SDC Information Services, 2500 Colorado Avenue, Santa Monica, CA; (213) 453-6194). For further information on do-it-yourself computerized research, read *Answers Online* by Barbara Newlin (Osborne McGraw-Hill, 1985).

Even without a computer, a library can offer shortcuts. For instance, for a few cents a book, the impossible-to-find source can be yours (temporarily) through an interlibrary loan. Thousands of libraries, including the giant Library of Congress, cooperate in this program, allowing you to get just about any book, magazine, newspaper, government pamphlet, or even doctoral dissertation you could possibly need from another participating library.

Doing It by the Book:

Even after eleven years of researching and writing articles, I'm still discovering new research sources among the 4 million books, 312,000 reels of microfilm, and 12,000 bound periodicals at my library. (While the New York Public Library is one of the giants, even a medium-sized library will have well over 100,000 volumes on hand, as well as thousands of bound or microfilmed periodicals.) Sifting through these materials is less daunting than you might think; usually you can research a typical article in a few hours. Researching *several* articles or queries in a single visit to the library will increase efficiency.

Here's how to research a typical article:

Start with magazines. Magazine indices can be good tools for marketing your article, as well as for researching it. If *Woman's Day* and *Redbook* have covered the topic within the past eighteen months, but *McCall's* and *Ladies' Home Journal* haven't, you'll know that the subject is appropriate for the women's market, and which magazines are your best submission bets. With a new slant, *Woman's Day* and *Redbook* might run another piece; or you could market a similar approach, written in your own way of course, to *McCall's* or *LHJ*.

For general interest articles on the subject, check *Magazine Index,* available at most libraries. You view it through an easy-to-use microfilm reader. (Instructions are on the side of the reader, or ask the librarian for help.) *Magazine Index* covers articles which appeared during the past five years and includes most popular publications. Articles are listed by subject; heavily covered subjects are also subdivided: "Sex—Attitudes."

If you don't find many listings on your subject, be imaginative in searching for other possible headings; in researching "Failure," I found the best material under "Success." Sometimes you'll have to try a number of categories: for a recent article "Dating in the 80s," I looked under "Dating," "Dating Services," "Marriage," "Personals," "Videotapes—Social Use," "Computers—Social Use," "Baby Boom," "Yuppies," "Single Men," "Single Women," "Singles," and "Sex Roles."

Also be alert for listings of book reviews included under any of your subject headings. These will give you some leads on new books on the topic that the library might have; under "Baby Boom," I found a reference to a book review of *Great Expectations: America & the Baby Boom Generation.* Locating the book, I discovered that it had an excellent chapter on romance among baby boomers, providing some quotes and statistics for my article.

If your library doesn't have *Magazine Index* yet or you need material that is more than five years old, use *Reader's Guide to Periodical Literature* and *Access: The Supplemental Guide to Periodicals.* (Some ultra-conscientious writers use both *Magazine Index* and *Reader's Guide*—the two publications are not exactly the same but have considerable overlap.) *Reader's Guide* and *Access* are multivolume publications, organized by year. Start with the most recent supplements and work *backward* since older research may have been overtaken by later developments.

If you need really old material—it can provide interesting contrasts to contemporary attitudes, anecdotes for travel pieces, and background for historical articles—check *Poole's Guide to Periodical Literature,* which indexes material published before 1900.

To track down more specialized articles like psychological studies, scientific papers, and medical reports, ask the librarian about subject indices or abstracts (indices which include short summaries of articles) pertaining to the topic, or check *Subject Guide to Reference Books,* a reference book *about* reference books. Among the thousands of subject indices are: *Business Periodical Index, Index Medicus, Psychological Abstracts,* and *Biological Abstracts.*

After you've assembled a list of likely articles, your next step is to either locate the bound periodicals on the library shelves or request them from the call desk, depending on your library's system. Prepare yourself for a slight disappointment here. Not even the largest library is likely to have every issue of each indexed magazine; typically, I find that 20 percent of the magazine articles on my bibliography turn out to be unavailable. Usually this presents no particular problem, but if it does, you can have the librarian help you track down another library that does have the elusive material. If you're in a rush, you can often buy old magazines quickly through back date periodical stores, or if time isn't a problem, order them from the magazine itself.

Once you have the magazine in hand, rather than reading each article and making notes while at the library, I've found it more efficient to merely read the first paragraph or two to establish the value of the material, then photocopy it for future reference. It's surprising how much reading you can cram into otherwise wasted time, so keep your photocopies handy for review on your morning commute or other odd moments of free time. While photocopying everything that looks at all likely entails feeding handfuls of loose change into the library's photocopier, the time saved is well worth it.

Newspapers are next. Since the typical newspaper article is short but crammed with facts, statistics, and names, newspapers are an excellent source of material for articles on current events, personality pieces, and other factual stories. To find the stories you need, the microfilm reader containing *Newspaper Index,* newspapers' equivalent of *Magazine Index,* should be your first stop. However, bear in mind that most libraries will only have the local paper and possibly *The New York Times* and *Wall Street Journal.*

Your librarian can either arrange to borrow other papers through interlibrary loan or help you determine the nearest library that does have the paper which interests you.

Other helpful newspaper indices are the *New York Times Index, Wall Street Journal Index,* and the *Official Index of the London Times.* For older newspaper items, you can check the *New York Daily Tribune Index* (1875 to 1906), *American Newspapers 1921-1936,* which also tells you which libraries or organizations actually have copies of the indexed papers, and *History and Bibliography of American Newspapers 1690-1820.* Older newspapers are likely to be available on microfilm.

For newspaper research dealing with the local scene, find out if your town or area newspaper has a morgue (clippings library). Many papers let freelancers have access to these reference materials, which may range from clipping files of the newspaper's own coverage of local people and events, arranged by subject or name, to more elaborate systems that include clippings from a wide variety of newspapers and magazines as well as such items as high school and college yearbooks for local socials, old business and phone directories from the area, and rare photos. Local or area material can often be sold nationally, especially if your piece is an exposé, human interest story, true life drama, or true crime story. Copies of the local papers will probably also be available at the public library, organized by date not subject.

Hit the books. To complete your bibliography, check the library's subject guide for books on your topic. Naturally this won't include all published books on the topic, only those actually available at that particular library. There are a variety of books designed to help you find other books, including several guides to reference books; subject bibliographies like *Science and Engineering References Sources* (look in *Bibliography Index* to identify the correct one) and *Books in Print* (lists all current books by author, subject, and title) are particularly helpful. An even more detailed work is *Cumulative Book Index,* which lists everything published in English from 1928 to date.

When you're looking through the library's card files or book catalog, a time-saving trick I've discovered is not to bother to write down the titles of all the books you see; instead, simply write down the Dewey Decimal or Library of Congress numbers you see most often. Armed with these numbers, you can do your selecting with the actual shelf of books in front of you. If there are many books on the topic, a quick way to decide which seem most promising is to scan the index of each book, using the subject headings that you've already found most productive or those you most desperately need material on. Then check one or two of the references to see if the book's style and approach appeal to you.

If the books that interest you aren't at the library, or you're trying to decide if the ones that are there seem worth reading, you can use book reviews to compare and contrast the books quickly. Book reviews are summarized and indexed in *Book Review Digest* and a variety of more specialized publications.

Once you have a firm assignment from a magazine, you can sometimes arrange to get free review copies of new books on your subject by contacting publishers' publicity departments and telling them which magazine you're writing for, the topic of the article, as well as the exact titles and authors of the books you want. A few publishers will automatically put you on their review list after that, ensuring a steady stream of interesting reading and potential article topics.

Go to government publications. The United States government is this country's largest publisher and information source, churning out statistics, charts, reports, maps, and other informative documents you can use to improve your articles. About half the research I needed for the "Computer Jobs" article was in one such publication, *Occupational Outlook Handbook.* If your library is designated as a United States government documents depository, Government Printing Office publications are sent to it free each month; check such directories as *Monthly Catalog of United States Government Publications, Congressional Record Index,* and *Government Reference Books.*

You can also arrange to be notified biweekly of interesting new government publications free; write to Superintendent of Documents, U.S. Government Printing Office, Washington, DC 20402, and request *Selected List of U.S. Government Publications.* Just looking over the list could trigger some good article ideas as well as provide research material for your current projects.

Quality and Quantity

Freelancers frequently wonder how much research to do on their articles. It's easy to get caught up in compulsively tracking down tiny details. In fact habitually over-researching articles can sometimes be a symptom of writer's block, a way of procrastinating and avoiding the actual writing of the article. On the other hand, there's no surer way to turn off an editor than with skimpy research, slightingly referred to as "cut and paste" work in the trade. So where do you draw the line?

While the exact quantity of research required varies according to the type of article you're writing—investigative reports require a lot more digging than self-help pieces—most writers agree that it's best to over-research slightly, especially when you're beginning. No matter how experienced you become, points out veteran magazine writer Paula Dranov, "There's always a certain unavoidable waste of effort, of going to some trouble to find out facts that prove unusable in the end."

For a typical article—Dranov specializes in women's health pieces—she starts by calling the appropriate health organization and asking for background materials and research leads. The next stop is the medical section of the library; here she tracks down nine or ten recent journal articles on her subject. To include the latest information and to gather useful quotes, she then telephones four or five leading doctors in the field and interviews them.

Dranov's method relies solely on *primary* sources, original material rather than others' reporting on the material. While *secondary* sources, reports and interpretations of primary material, can be useful for perspective, the careful writer does take that extra step and consults the original source if available since secondary sources can contain errors, create confusion by using material out of context, or fail to fully explain the original material.

To track down primary sources, carefully read your research material noting any identifiable sources mentioned in the text such as "according to the National Genetics Foundation. . . ." or "1986 census figures show. . . ." You can easily double-check all such references and obtain fresh material by telephoning the people or organizations mentioned (consult *Who's·Who* or appropriate industry directories), or if the source is written, by looking up the original journal article, book, or newspaper piece.

If you are using any books for your research, don't neglect the footnotes; often they provide excellent leads for additional information. In doing my "Computer Jobs" article I noticed that one of my reference books had a footnote crediting 1983 salary surveys from two computer magazines. Hypothesizing that they might be annual surveys, I checked the appropriate month of the current year and bingo!—up-to-date salary information I could plug into my piece; material that might have taken hours to compile through interviews if I hadn't noticed that footnote. Using your imagination can provide you with similar leads as you gradually develop research strategies that speed your search.

One questionable journalistic practice that you should avoid is the use of invented material purporting to be fact. While all magazines expect facts to *be* facts, some don't mind fictional anecdotes in softer pieces like self-help material. However, other editors, like Ruth Drizen of *Playgirl*, consider even this bit of journalistic license "an absolute last resort." To play it safe, make sure that composites are clearly identified as illustrating the "typical" case rather than some specific individual, that estimates you've made are reported as such, and that other holes in your research are handled truthfully: "While no exact figures are available on X. . . ."

Another pitfall to avoid is accidental—or deliberate—plagiarism. While facts cannot be copyrighted, words can. Extensive paraphrases have also been found to infringe on others' copyrights in some instances. (See Chapter Sixteen for a complete discussion of copyright and other legal matters.) Working from notes can lead to unconscious plagiarism as you read the notes and find catchy sentences popping into mind—just as they originally appeared in the text you made the notes from. While researching, by comparing secondary sources with the original version, I've encountered hundreds of published examples of actual or near plagiarism. To guard against unwittingly copying someone else's work this way, distinguish in your notes between your ideas and quotes and close paraphrases of published material.

A final cautionary note: since society is becoming increasingly litigious, take extra care in researching potentially controversial material. If your exposé or investigative piece is going to name names or reveal information that some might prefer to keep under cover, take extra pains to triple-check each fact through multiple sources and to check original documents, *not* secondary sources. Careful checking is your best defense against expensive lawsuits against your publisher and you.

And remember that even if there's no risk of lawsuits, mistakes can harm your reputation as a careful writer with editors, as well as provoke embarrassing reader mail. Your writing, like Caesar's wife, should be above reproach. To avoid these pitfalls and raise the level of your research, senior Playgirl *editor Ruth Drizen offers a simple suggestion: "Follow each lead to the end. You never know what's waiting for you around the next corner."*

9

"Do You Sleep In the Nude?"— Interview How-To's

T alk may be cheap to get; but when it's selectively edited and quoted in your article, it adds a valuable dimension to your writing. When the words of others are woven in with yours, an abstract story acquires the immediacy of first-hand experience: your voice assumes the authority of the experts you quote, and your style gains a richness of expression, emotion, and opinion. Interviews enhance both your writing and your research. For some articles, interviews can provide *all* your research material; for others, drawing on an expert's distilled knowledge provides a targeted research plan, letting you eliminate unproductive lines of inquiry before starting. With the right interview techniques, talk becomes more valuable still, as you glean good material in minutes and use it to sell your work.

Many inexperienced interviewers are intimidated by the prospect of locating and questioning potential sources. Often worry is equally divided between fear of refusal and fear of acceptance. While refusal is always a possibility, I've discovered that most people welcome an opportunity to talk about what they know, and enjoy seeing their names in print. Since frequently interviewed subjects like celebrities are hard for the beginner to get to, your best bet is to start with less-known figures like doctors, psychiatrists and psychologists, and other experts—all of whom are frequently used in popular articles. An advantage of this strategy is if pediatrician X is too busy, then there're always doctors Y and Z to turn to. Most experts are interchangeable with others in their field, giving you many potential subjects to approach.

Fear about actually conducting the interview can easily be countered by remembering that the interviewer is in control of the situation. While the subject may flounder for an answer, you always have the next question ready. Naturally it's easier to get some people to talk than others; one subject may drop quote after quote while another may be inclined to stick with name, rank, and serial number. While the truly difficult subject—rarely encountered, fortunately—can challenge even the craftiest interviewer, the ability to loosen lips can be learned with practice. As you grow more confident in your skills, your nervousness will disappear, and soon you'll find yourself enjoying the give and take of a good interview.

Finding Sources to Talk To

Before you can begin tracking down interviewees, you need to decide what sort of people you need for the article and where you're most likely to find them. While locating sources for an article on genetic counseling is simple—obstetricians, counselors, geneticists, and patients are most promising—other subjects can be trickier. For an article on double weddings, I decided I needed several interviews with couples who'd actually been married in tandem. But where to find them? I decided that such a complex wedding would probably require the services of a wedding consultant; by calling several I learned of five couples to interview. Categorizing your subjects will help you find them. Here are some strategies to find people within the appropriate categories:

Networking: Start with the people you know. By broadcasting my topic among friends and acquaintances, I've often learned of good sources, and heard about new books and articles on the subject. The professionals you deal with—doctor, lawyer, banker—

may also be able to provide referrals to colleagues specializing in your subject matter.

Groups: Next try trade groups, foundations, and associations specializing in your field. Many of these will have press officers who can give you names, information, and other leads. Ask for copies of publications put out by the group too; I've often received copies of previously published articles, pamphlets, and even books on the subject absolutely free this way. Frequently you can get enough material to write a good query or even the entire article. These press officers can sometimes arrange for you to interview group members too.

To find these groups, consult the *Encyclopedia of Associations* at your library. Also scrutinize articles and books you are using for lists of names and addresses to contact for further information— usually listed at the end of the text. Also note any experts cited within your research material; often you can contact these people for new interviews. If you live in a large city, try checking your telephone book under likely names: X Foundation, National X Organization, American X Association—a simple technique that has often helped me locate useful local groups.

The Yellow Pages: Want the names of some local chiropractors to interview? Letting your fingers do the walking can put you in touch with dozens of potential subjects.

Publishers and others: Since many experts are also authors, ask the publisher of their books to put you in touch with the writers. Some will give you the addresses, others will forward your letter. A fringe benefit of this strategy is that some publishers will put you on their press lists, sending you news releases and free copies of upcoming books, giving you other potential articles to write.

Checking specialized magazines in the field will also help you assemble a list of names; look for articles by experts in your area, then contact them through the magazine. Also check the ads; I found a detailed list of wedding consultants and their phone numbers by skimming through *Bride's Magazine.* Manufacturers can supply useful information for some articles; you'll find these names in the ads too.

Lecture bureaus can also help put you in touch with experts, as can newsletters and trade tip sheets.

Press agents/publicists: Some authorities are so eager to be interviewed that they're paying people to put them in the public eye. PR people will be eager to tell you about anyone in their stable who can help, and will put you on their mailing lists. Urban writers may also be able to get on publicity guest lists; as one public relations expert told me: "We'll invite anyone who has the faintest connection with the press to our parties—we need warm bodies to fill the room."

Who's Who: Not just a listing of the famous, this directory also has the addresses and phone numbers of many executives and other moderately prominent men and women, as well as biographical data. But it's only useful if you already know the person's name and simply need a way to get in touch with him or her.

The ripple effect: Once you have one expert in hand, often he or she can crack the field open for you by telling you others to contact. Always ask interview subjects for suggestions for further interviews.

Setting Up the Interview

How: Your first hurdle in arranging the interview is your lack of a magazine assignment. However, often you can't get an assignment without some interview material to give to the editor. To get around this apparent catch-22, try this approach in your initial letter or phone call:

"I'm writing an article on X and would like to ask you a few questions about it." Often you won't even be asked what publication you're working for, but if you are, a good reply is: "I'm targeting it to ABC magazine," or "I have several magazines in mind, depending on the precise direction the interviews take." The first reply is particularly good since it creates a favorable association between you and the target magazine without claiming that you are working for them.

Where: The traditional face-to-face interview can be quite time-consuming and may be geographically impractical. Reserve it for profile subjects, experts who are briefing you on confidential material and who possess extensive files or research materials or have helpful exhibits to show you, and pieces that require descriptive sections. For other interviews the telephone is your weapon of choice, allowing quick access to subjects almost anywhere on the globe.

When: While you can sometimes get on-the-spot telephone interviews, making an appointment a few days in advance frequently produces better interviews because the subject will have been mulling the topic over in the interim. When making the appointment, explain both the subject and slant of the article. If your exact subject or slant might put the subject off—it's hard to get interviews with morticians for example if you announce that you're writing an exposé of sales tactics—consider offering a sanitized version: "My article will help the reader plan an appropriate funeral, should a loved one die."

Indicate the length of time you'll need. For face-to-face interviews an hour is usually enough, except for major pieces and profiles which may require two or three hours or longer. Always meet the subject on her own turf, home or office. Not only will she be more relaxed in the familiar environment, but she'll have quick access to reference materials and personal mementos needed to illustrate points or refresh recollection. For your profile you'll find plenty of colorful details here to enhance your piece. For telephone interviews try to limit yourself to a half hour or less. Fifteen minutes is often enough to get three or four juicy quotes if you organize your questions effectively.

Once you have an appointment, be punctual in calling or arriving on time and when the agreed-upon time is up, offer to end the interview. Often you'll be invited to continue the interview; if not, finish up and leave. It's a good idea to tell the subject you may contact him or her again if any additional material is needed.

What to bring: The tape recorder versus pencil and notebook debate rages on in journalistic circles. Tape recordings are accurate and allow you to concentrate fully on the conversation, but you're at the mercy of your equipment. Horror stories abound of the interview that got away because of a malfunctioning machine. And even if all goes well, there's the somewhat daunting task of transcribing and organizing the taped material. You'd be amazed at how much a person can actually say in an hour—and how little is usable. Taking notes allows you to distill the best quotes but lets good material be lost if you get one of those rare subjects that drops terrific quotes in every phrase. Using both tape and notes gives you the best of both worlds. For tips on choosing a good tape recorder, see Chapter Eleven.

Why: To avoid shotgun interviews that yield scattered morsels of information, it's a good idea to bone up on your topic in advance. An ignorant interviewer not only annoys the expert subject but lacks the knowledge to ask probing questions. While the experts you talk to won't expect you to have their depth of knowledge, they will expect to be talking to an informed layman. If you don't know much about your topic, reading a few articles or skimming through a book on the subject should give you enough background. The expert can fill in the blanks from there.

For profile articles, better known subjects will expect you to know something about their lives. Consulting *Biography Index* and *Who's Who* will give you a capsule summary to work from; for genuine celebrities, also read previously published profiles and biographical books. For lesser luminaries, a general idea of a few of their major achievements is enough.

Having a strong angle and outline for the proposed article will also help you target your interview. Questions can then be focused to gather material you can actually use, keeping the interview short and meaty.

Getting Them to Talk

In an interview often *how* you ask is just as important as *what* you ask. These time-tested strategies set subjects at ease, helping you to get the most out of your interviewee:

Start with easy questions: build up to the tough ones. As a beginner you're likely to be interviewing inexperienced subjects. If your first question is a real zinger, the subject will immediately become anxious and clam up. The rest of the interview will be real work. Instead, you might begin with a few relaxing, basic questions that verify facts you already have about the interviewee or topic. Asking how the subject would like his or her name to appear in the article, what title or affiliation should be used, and other routine information, if appropriate, also reveals you to be accurate and painstaking. Using formal address, Mr., Ms., or Dr., until invited to be on a first-name basis is courteous and professional.

Develop a listening knowledge of your subject. Since every subculture, from computer programmers to three-card monte players, has its own jargon, taking the time to learn some of the insider talk of the profession will enhance your understanding of your interviewee's comments. Your interview will take less time too since your subject won't have to spend time explaining basic concepts.

Avoid linguistic "hot buttons." Groups that feel discriminated against, whether because of political, ethnic, racial, or sexual identity, are often highly sensitive to signs of bias in an interviewer. Update yourself on the preferred idiom, and avoid questions that convey any taint of moralistic or judgmental phrasing. You want the subject to feel you're on his or her side and sympathize with the group's concerns. This is especially important if you find yourself interviewing a member of a group you do *not* sympathize with. You can ask tough questions, but make sure the subject feels that you are trying to clear up misunderstandings about the group, not to further popular bias.

Use leading questions sparingly. Since an interviewee often aims to please, most of your questions should be phrased neutrally to avoid suggesting possible answers. Otherwise your interview may merely echo your own preconceptions, rather than being an exploration of the subject's ideas. However, leading questions are valuable in a few situations. You may wish to probe areas which might seem shocking if you didn't bring them up first. If, for example, you asked a new mother how she felt about her baby, you'd get a very different answer than if you suggested that even the most loving mother sometimes hates her baby for its constant demands, sparking an admission you'd never get with the first question. Or your article might be heavily slanted to a certain point of view—quitting a job can be a positive experience, say— and need quotes from experts who agreed. A *New York Times* reporter once told me that the best question to use to put words in someone's mouth is: "Would you say that. . . ." If the subject says yes, the question can then become the quote.

Convey approval. Whether or not the interview is going well, it's important to encourage the subject. Such remarks as "What an interesting point," "That'll make a terrific quote," and "I had no idea that so much has been done in this area," make the subject feel he or she is performing well, encouraging further revelations. Nodding and smiling also signal approval; leaning forward in your chair indicates interest. If you get a lull in the discussion, continue to scribble furiously—seeing the interviewer stop taking notes makes subjects uneasy.

Don't be afraid to show ignorance. Many people are embarrassed to reveal holes in their knowledge. However, if you don't understand something, chances are some of your audience won't either. Don't hesitate to ask for further explanations and definitions whenever necessary, and persist until you're sure you've grasped the point.

Feel free to depart from your script. A common mistake of inexperienced interviewers is to view the script as a security blanket to be clung to through thick and thin. Often you get the best material through follow-up questions like "Can you give me an example of that?" or "What's the worst experience of that type you've encountered?" Also eliminate questions that have already been answered in previous replies; rephrase and repeat questions that haven't been answered to your satisfaction. Experienced journalists may ask the same question three or four times in different ways and at different points in the interview.

Avoid overly simple or highly complex questions. Questions that can be answered with a yes or no response don't encourage elaboration and should be avoided. Also follow the rule of "one question, one answer" by asking several questions instead of a single mammoth one. If you ask, "Since gold, silver, strategic metals, and foreign currencies are your preferred investments, could you describe the outlook for each of these over the next decade?" your subject is likely to concentrate on the last item you mention and ignore the rest of the question. Instead ask, "Where do you see gold prices in ten years?" then move to each additional topic with a new question.

"Did You Happen to Kill Your Wife?"—Questions

Since the entire purpose of an interview is to get *answers*, your questions should be designed to produce the kind of material you need for your article, whether it's facts, opinions, anecdotes, or emotion. For many articles you'll want to use a mix of question types to get the most out of your subject. Most interviewers prefer to start with specific, factual questions then expand to more thoughtful, speculative questions, nailing down any remaining specifics at the end. If you're writing a profile piece or a "Q and A" (question and answer) article, you'll also need a good closing quote, so you should add a few final questions to elicit a closing statement for your piece.

Here are the most common kinds of questions:

The facts, please. Many of your questions will be aimed at eliciting the specifics of your story—especially for profiles of relative unknowns and background investigations of new topics. For profiles, constructing a chronology through an initial series of questions is often helpful: "When did you start. . . . ?" "After your first million, then what?" To get a broad overview on a field try the 5-W approach: "Where is the field going in the next ten years?" "When should a couple seek genetic counseling?" "What tests are most commonly used?" "Who is the typical patient today?" "Why is the field growing so quickly?" Expand on the basic facts by getting interesting details: "What's the most valuable item in your collection?" "What does this 'fertility pump' look like?" "How did you select those winning lottery numbers?"

Anecdotes. Since stories and examples liven up any subject, try to get as many as possible. Don't let your interviewee get away with a lot of boring generalities: "My research has impacted the lives of dozens of my patients." Follow up immediately with requests for anecdotes, examples, and case histories: "What was the strangest case you've come across?" Another approach is the non-question: "I'll bet you hear some wild excuses during a tax audit," is an opening hard to resist. Or you can tell anecdotes you already know to inspire the subject to try to top you with his or hers.

Opinions and predictions. A lot of your best quotes will result from questions asking for opinions. Oriana Fallaci, a colorful Italian journalist, used this approach masterfully on former Secretary of State Henry Kissinger: "Dr. Kissinger. . . . how do you explain the fact that you have become almost more famous and popular than a President? Have you any theories?" Kissinger's reply, after a bit of fencing, was: ". . . . The main point stems from the fact I've always acted alone. Americans admire this enormously. Americans admire the cowboy leading the caravan astride his horse. Without even a pistol, maybe, because he doesn't go in for shooting. He acts, that's all; aiming for the right spot at the right time. A Wild West tale, if you like."

Predictions and speculation are also good quotes. Ask your experts questions like "How do you think this research will improve care of premature infants in the future?" "If an investor with $10,000 followed these recommendations, how would his portfolio look in five years?" "Do you think employers of the future will discriminate against workers who have a genetic predilection to occupational diseases?"

Emotion. While the classic question to elicit an emotional response is "How did you feel when . . . ?", there're plenty of other approaches. While most people who've had a strong emotional experience seem almost compelled to describe it, if your interviewee is being coy, try the "other people" approach. "What do you think women find to be most frustrating about infertility treatments?" The subject is then apt to recount her own frustrations. Or you might gently lead the subject a bit: "It must be hard to admit to yourself that alcohol is a problem. . . ." A third approach is to ask for recommendations to help others: "How do you think lawyers *should* handle the divorce process?"

Description. To re-create events that the subject participated in and you didn't, jog memory with such questions as "What did the earthquake sound like?" "When did you realize the house was on fire?" "What was the first thing you did after you heard the alarm?" Try to conjure up sensory details: "The earthquake sounded like a freight train running through our bedroom," is a much better quote than "It was a big one, all right." Getting the interviewee to describe the event more than once is also helpful since additional details may be remembered in a second telling of the story.

Tougher Tactics

While most interviews are more like conversations than inquisitions, as John Brady writes in *The Craft of Interviewing,* "Getting tough in an interview means never having to say you're sorry you didn't get the story." However there's a big difference between being tough and being hostile. While a surprising number of people consider probing questions an intellectual battle of wits, few enjoy rudeness or cruelty. Instead you're likely to find your interview at an end. Here are some diplomatic approaches for those more difficult questions:

The aw shucks question: "I hate to ask you this, people are saying that... and I thought you might like answer them. . . ." Saying this in a low, embarrassed voice may actually make the subject feel sorry for you and answer candidly to save further embarassment on your part.

The psychoanalytic approach: Intuitions can be valuable clues for the interviewer. If you sense a certain reluctance to talk about certain topics, bring the feeling out in the open. "I get the feeling there's something about this that's bothering you . . ." can be a good question, or "Is there something you're not telling me?" Even total silence can be a good tactic in this situation; few people can let a long pause go unfilled. Many people have a secret desire to confess; if appropriate, do all you can to encourage this tendency. Another psychiatric technique is to repeat the subject's last phrase in a thoughtful tone, encouraging him or her to elaborate.

The foot in the door approach: Judiciously using information you already possess can create the impression that you already know all, so there's no point to silence: "You took some big losses after the SEC investigation, didn't you?"

Devil's advocate: A soft question can turn away wrath; preface it with "Pretending that I'm one of the opposition, what do you say to the charge that . . . ?" Or implying that you agree with the subject, pose the question as a hypothetical one: "While these design plans certainly sound meticulous, does the company actually have the capacity to deal with a major chemical leak if it did occur?"

The brass tacks question: Often your best approach is to just come right out and ask the question: "What do these three malpractice suits indicate about your ability as a plastic surgeon?" You may want to plan follow-up questions if the subject disagrees with the assertion in the first question: "Is the company headed for bankruptcy?" "If it isn't, are there business problems which account for this persistent rumor?" "Who do you think would want to create the impression that a healthy company is going under?" With a line of questioning like this, you're likely to get some hard information to sink your teeth into.

The obvious question: Confronting your interviewee with logical objections and reactions to his or her ideas is a sound, though unglamorous tactic. "Assuming the technology were developed, why would the people of the future *want* to defrost all these bodies you have in cryogenic suspension?"

Parting shots: Some journalists find they get their best material after the formal interview is over. Putting away their notebooks, they engage the interviewee in seemingly casual conversation, hoping that he'll let his guard down enough to drop a few good morsels. If you are fortunate enough to get some good ad libs this way, just memorize the remarks and scribble them down in the hall after you leave.

Putting It All Together

Depending on the nature of your interview, you'll want to use one of these three formats for the material:

Q and A: Best for informational and celebrity interviews, this type of article starts with a short introduction, then follows the format of a transcript:

Q: How safe are safe deposit boxes?

A: Quite, but it's important to remember that the bank doesn't insure their contents. However low cost coverage is available commercially.

Quotation marks are not needed in this format, but careful editing and organizing of your original transcript are.

Profile: Good for both celebrities and ordinary people, this approach combines your observations and research with direct and indirect quotes from your subject.

Here's an excerpt from a profile article I wrote for *Gallery:*

> Touring with the Globetrotters wasn't always fun and games. While testing a new shot during one of his half-time exhibitions, Reisman fell and broke his arm. "Right away the promoter rushed out and said, 'Is there a doctor in the house?' The audience laughed. They figured it was just part of the act, until the ambulance came. Two weeks later I won a championship match with my left arm in a cast. Nobody laughed that time."

As an enhancement to other articles: While the Q and A format and the profile feature interview material from a single source, for many articles you'll want to include remarks from several experts. Identify each expert in full the first time his or her name appears, by name only each subsequent time. Here's an example of how to describe and quote your expert from a piece I did for *Glamour:*

> "The medical definition of SIDS is 'infant death that occurs suddenly, unexpectedly and inexplicably,' " says Alfred Krause, M.D., associate professor of pediatrics at Cornell Medical College.

As in these examples, for quotes within quotes use double quotation marks outside, single quotation marks for interior quotes.

Selecting and Editing Quotes

For longer interviews or ones where you've made extensive notes, it's helpful to organize the interview material by subject since the answer to one question may contain material that expands some previous answer. You can do this easily by photocopying the material, and cutting and pasting it into the most logical order.

For Q and A pieces, after rearranging the material by topic, you'll want to edit out repetitions and digressions, and rearrange the entire interview into the most logical order to avoid abrupt shifts of topic or sudden regressions to earlier subject matter. A Q and A is not a literal transcript but a carefully edited and organized piece of work. If a particular answer seems interesting but not directly responsive to your original question, feel free to revise the questions to fit the answer. For profiles, arrange your notes chronologically. While most profiles begin by discussing the subject's current activities, then flashing back to the past, keeping your notes in chronological order makes it easy to find the quotes to accompany each period you discuss.

For any article using quotes selectively, your priority is to identify potentially usable material. Good quotes should leap off the page when you look over your notes. Look for vivid descriptions and pithy advice. Statements of fact and anecdotes often sound better as your own words rather than direct quotations, unless the manner in which they were stated is particularly original or vivid. " 'I was born in 1952,' says flamboyant entrepreneur Joe Smith," is a poor use of a quote. A better approach is "Born in 1952, heir to $5 million in 1953, and bankrupted in 1954, entrepreneur Joe Smith describes his origins as 'Shirtsleeves to shirtsleeves in twenty-four months.'"

Often when going over your notes or tape, you'll find that the subject has made good observations but has phrased them ineptly. While a few purists oppose any editing of quotes, the common journalistic practice is to improve weak quotes through judicious deletions and rewording. Few subjects want to be quoted as saying, "Well, er, diplomacy, I mean well, it's like an art, you know. You have to, well, kind of wear a mask and make it seem believable, if you know what I mean." Instead write "Diplomacy is the art of wearing a mask while seeming totally natural."

Normal editing of quotes doesn't ordinarily require the approval of the source, but if you take further liberties with the quotes, check with him or her. When dealing with topics you know little about, checking with your authorities is wise even when you've quoted them exactly—your expert may realize that his phrasing was unintentionally misleading, or have updated information.

Since quotes also make excellent openers and closers, look for unusually provocative, insightful, or profound remarks for possible leads or conclusions. Or see if one of your profile subject's anecdotes seems to launch or sum up his story neatly. Quotes that offer startling predictions about the future often provide natural yet dramatic last words for your piece.

10

An Article Makeover

P ulling all the threads together to weave your research, interviews, and ideas into a perfected article entails taking a hard look at your draft. Many writers fall in love with their words and find the revision process a painful stage. To illustrate the process, here is one of my articles written with co-author Susan Plummer for *Cosmopolitan,* first in draft, then in the form in which it was ultimately accepted for publication.

GENETIC COUNSELING
by Lisa Collier Cool and Susan Plummer

Problem: the reason for the first miscarriage is never explained, leaving the reader to wonder whether Joan's problem might be genetic after all.

After a miscarriage on her 30th birthday, Joan was relieved when she conceived again a month later. Despite a last-minute cesarean, she had no reason to expect anything but a normal, healthy child. After the delivery, even through the haze of anesthesia, Joan sensed that the examination of her child was taking an unusually

89

long time. Finally, she heard her doctor's voice: "It's a girl. . . . she has a cleft palate. . . . the ear is underdeveloped. . . . but she'll be fine." Later she learned that Michele had facio auriculo vertebra sequence, a cluster of birth defects affecting development of the ear, throat, upper vertebrae and face. Although Michele's case was mild—and surgically correctable—Joan sought genetic counseling to assess the risk to future children and to learn more about the syndrome itself. The news was good: the syndrome was almost certainly acquired after conception, rather than genetic, meaning that the odds of its recurrence were only slightly greater than those of the average couple.

A major problem starts to reveal itself; the article is too long and wordy. Are five case histories really needed in this paragraph? Could it be cut to three?

When our parents were young, conception was a form of genetic roulette, with each couple hoping that their combination of egg and sperm would add up to a healthy child. Today medical genetics offers high-risk couples a way to improve the odds. Couples like Sandra and Mark, who are in their late thirties and want to start a family; Nancy and Bruce, who are concerned about Bruce's occupational exposure to radiation; Linda and Ted, who have suffered three unexplained miscarriages; Sylvia and Jim, who lost a child to Tay-Sachs disease; and Miriam and Bill, who know that several of Miriam's relatives have had heart attacks before age 50; can often discover what genetic legacy they will bequeath to their children. While medical science cannot yet guarantee each couple a perfect baby, in the past twenty years geneticists have made enormous strides forward in answering every prospective parent's ultimate question: "Will my baby be normal?"

This paragraph seems okay to me.

Not surprisingly, an increasing number of couples are taking advantage of this opportunity to gaze in their own genetic crystal ball. "As technological advances are dramatically increasing the number of questions that can be answered, more and more couples are demanding those answers before making their childbearing decisions," says Lawrence R. Shapiro, M.D., director of medical genetics at Westchester County Medical Center, and professor of pediatrics and pathology at New York Medical College. The increased demand also reflects today's consumer-oriented outlook, says Ruth Berini, director of the National Genetics Foundation (NGF). "When couples are having few children, they expect a corresponding increase in the quality of those children. To many, genetics offer the hope of a 'better baby.' "

Charlotte's case history seems too long. Another problem was that the doctor I asked to review the piece for accuracy felt some of the research in this section was outmoded, and suggested changes which were incorporated into the final draft.

Who Should Get Genetic Counseling?

Though counselors are reluctant to define a "typical" patient, citing the wide range of individual concerns, Charlotte's case illustrates the range of problems counselors can encounter. Pregnant at age 36, Charlotte has three concerns. The first is genetic—she is affected by a rare bloodclotting disorder, and wonders about the risk of passing it on to her unborn child. The counselor's research indicates that, unlike hemophilia, which is inherited, Charlotte's disorder is not genetically transmitted. Though her baby will have clotting problems immediately after birth due to seepage of maternal blood, they will last only a few weeks. Her baby will be normal afterward. If you have a disorder, or suspect a family history of inherited disease, a counselor can help determine whether or not the disease is inherited, and if so, arrange testing to discover whether or not you have any risk of transmitting the disease. If a risk is found, depending on the disorder, often amniocentesis or another method of prenatal diagnosis can reveal whether or not the unborn child is affected.

Like other women over age 35, Charlotte is aware that she has a higher risk of producing a child with chromosomal problems like Down's syndrome. Her exact risk, according to her counselor, is 1 in 287. Unlike genetic disorders, which run in families, chromosomal disorders result from errors in the formation of the egg or sperm. Such errors increase with the age of the mother—and possibly the father, according to new research. With the recent trend to delayed childbearing, older women with no history of genetic problems have become the fastest growing group of counseling patients, since counseling usually accompanies amniocentesis. Recent studies show that between 75 percent and 85 percent of women who choose amniocentesis do so solely because of age. Because of Charlotte's clotting problem, and the unknown status of the fetus's blood, she is advised against amniocentesis, despite her age, because of the risk of serious complications to herself and the unborn child.

Her final concern relates to the possible effects of steroids on the developing fetus. Since steroids could improve her blood condition, decreasing the risks of amniocentesis, she asked the counselor to investigate their prenatal hazards. Used during the first trimester of pregnancy, steroids pose a 1 percent risk of cleft palate or lip, plus a slight chance of interfering with the baby's adrenal gland. Concerns over the effects of drug or toxin exposure during pregnancy are another common reason for consulting a counselor, as are illnesses or health problems during pregnancy.

In this paragraph, I felt the wording was not precise enough.

According to Nargess Ahgharian, M.D., a New York obstetrician and other authorities, counseling is especially helpful for anyone in these risk categories:

This section overlaps with the following section, causing some repetition. I decided to merge the two sections in my final draft to eliminate the problem.

Possible carriers of an ethnically linked disease, such as Tay-Sachs disease, which primarily occurs in Jews of Eastern European ancestry; sickle cell anemia, which strikes blacks; and thalessemia, occurring in those of Mediterranean ancestry. Simple, inexpensive blood tests are used to screen for carriers, who are normal men and women at no risk of getting the disease themselves, who carry the trait as a recessive gene. Both parents must be carriers themselves before a child could have the disease.

Should explain here

Parents of a previously affected child. Coun-

how genetic inheritance works. Also need to add new material Susan just dug up on new methods of treating and testing the unborn.

selors can arrange testing and provide research to evaluate whether or not the disease is inherited, and if so, the exact odds of recurrence. Frank and Marsha were devastated when their firstborn son was deaf. Genetic evaluation revealed that any future child would also be deaf. As a result, they adopted a healthy baby girl to complete their family.

Couples with a history of unexplained miscarriages or stillbirths. While there are many reasons for miscarriage, a certain percentage result from genetic or chromosomal defects in the fetus that are incompatible with life. A history of repeated miscarriage or stillbirth—two or more—may signal a genetic problem, as in the case of one patient who learned after several miscarriages that a rare genetic problem made it impossible for her to carry a male fetus to term. She was, however, eventually able to deliver a healthy daughter.

No need to identify Nargess Ahgharian again.

While certain groups of people have a significantly higher risk of transmitting inherited diseases to their children, counseling can help just about anyone, says Nargess Ahgharian, M.D., a New York obstetrician. "If you have a question or concern, counseling can help. While some people take a fatalistic attitude toward pregnancy, or worry that posing the question will be 'bad luck,' why spend nine months worrying unnecessarily? By consulting a counselor you are not committing yourself to anything, but simply getting some information that you can use—or ignore."

I decided to delete this paragraph, since it contains material better included in the section describing counseling.

A concerned couple need not look far for help: over 500 facilities, including both major centers and smaller "satellites" for rural areas, now exist, staffed by both geneticists, who are medical doctors specializing in genetic concerns, and counselors, who hold either masters or doctorate degrees. Geneticists handle diagnosis, testing, and treatment; counselors provide the latest information on the suspected problem, assess risks and explore options to counter those risks, research the patient's "pedigree" or family background, and give emotional support. Costs vary: for truly rare problems a research center might offer a free treatment, while more routine cases might entail costs between $50 and $800, depending what tests are used and whether or not amniocentesis is performed.

This is the section that will be combined with the preceding one to eliminate repetition and overlap of subject matter. The second paragraph almost completely duplicates information already presented under the heading "possible carriers of ethnically linked diseases."

What Are Your Risks?

Though it has been estimated that all of us harbor an average of four to eight potentially harmful genes among the 50,000 to 100,000 that dictate our physical and mental characteristics, genetic disorders are relatively rare. While a dominant trait of one parent would appear in 50 percent of his or her children—and 100 percent of the children of a couple who share the dominant trait—many harmful traits are *recessive: both* mother and father must carry the same harmful gene before any child could be affected. Even when both parents are carriers of a dangerous recessive gene, the odds are still 75 percent in favor of a *normal* child. Due to these favorable odds, only 1 percent of newborns in this country develop genetic disorders. Within the unlucky 1 percent, many disorders are minor, according to Dick Leavitt, science information editor at the March of Dimes: "There is a full spectrum, ranging from the almost imperceptible to the most severe. A specific trait can have a tremendous range of expression: color blindness, for example, can be a difficulty in distinguishing red from green, or it can render all colors as shades of gray."

The risk of some serious disorders is gradually being reduced by widespread genetic screening. While some genetic disorders occur randomly, others are concentrated within certain ethnic groups, which makes it possible to sift through the target group in search of carriers, who are healthy men and women with a recessive gene for the disease. Carriers have no risk of getting the disease themselves—they only risk passing it to their children. Government programs have made inexpensive blood tests widely available to potential carriers of Tay-Sachs disease, a rare and always fatal metabolic disorder, sickle cell anemia, and thalessemia, a severe anemia. Though a few potential carriers may be missed—one Tay-Sachs victim was born to a Sicilian father and Sephardic mother—such screening programs have had a dramatic impact: estimates indicate an 87 percent reduction in new cases over the past 15 years, from an average of 100 new cases each year to just *thirteen.*

Since hemophilia is such a rare disease, I decided to include less information on it, as few readers would be likely to be concerned about this particular problem.

When the disorder is both rare and randomly found in families of diverse background, like hemophilia, genetic evaluation offers those with a suspicious family history a chance to de termine if they are carriers. According to the National Hemophilia Foundation, "While a car rier test does exist, testing the entire U.S. popu lation to find the one woman in 5,000 who car ries the trait is not economically feasible. Also the current test has a relatively high rate of false positive results, which would cause needless alarm if mass testing were done." Tests are also available for a variety of other genetic diseases, through geneticists.

This subhead seemed a bit drab; and the lead could be improved with an interesting case history. I decided to pull material out of the following section, "Genetic Detective Work," to improve this one, ultimately combining the two sections.

What Counseling Is

In 1974, F. C. Fraser, the father of medical genetics, and a group of medical professionals defined genetic counseling as "a communication process which deals with the human problem associated with the risk of occurrence of a genetic disease in a family." The process begins with a complete family history, called a pedi gree, an intricate piece of detective work that covers four generations of your family history, including births, deaths, suspicious medical patterns, even miscarriages and stillbirths Sometimes counselors will ask to see family photos or medical records of other family mem bers. Your personal health is also explored, es pecially if you are pregnant, with questions about smoking, alcohol consumption and diet.

To aid doctors and individuals, the NGF, a clearing house that brings clinical genetic advances to physicians, has a questionnaire that the patient may fill out and return to the foundation for computer analysis. Patients check off answers to questions relating to 14 different categories of disease, ranging from cancer to mental illness to birth defects. For $20 the NGF will analyze the data, have it evaluated by consulting geneticists, and provide printouts of the latest information on any problems detected in the family history. If a risk is identified, a counselor discusses the options with the couple—options may include not having children, amniocentesis and perhaps subsequent abortion, artificial insemination, or adoption.

This paragraph is slightly repetitious, since the previous paragraph also describes options.

Though some fear that counselors will encourage abortion of imperfect offspring, actually, according to Dick Leavitt of the March of Dimes, the process is "an exploration of options, leading to a couple's making an informed decision in light of existing risks. The counselor explores the information available on the defect: the risk of passing it on, the seriousness of the disorder, the state of the art in treatment and prevention of the defect, and the chances of giving such a child up for adoption. Although couples often ask what the counselor would do in their situation, no ethical counselor would impose his or her own biases on the couple. The final answer is a personal decision between husband and wife."

The first case, shortened a bit, would be perfect for the earlier material on "parents of a previously affected child," since it shows that a previously affected child doesn't necessarily mean you'll have another one, but it doesn't work here with so

Genetic Detective Work

When Jeannette arrived at the geneticist's office, she was desperate. Her first child was born deaf, blind and retarded, and she and her husband had decided against future children. Now she had unexpectedly conceived again and feared further tragedy. After a detailed examination, testing and analysis of her medical history, the doctor determined that her child's defects were the result of German measles during pregnancy—a one time accident. Reas-

many case histories lumped together.

This case history should be in the opening paragraph of this section—had major news coverage, but should be rewritten for more impact.

The next case history struck me as too vague and downbeat, so I decided to delete it. Also the description overlaps with previous material on the subject.

sured, she carried the pregnancy to term, delivering a healthy baby.

Even when the diagnosis does not lead to a cure, simply finding out what is wrong can be a relief. Since 1845, over 300 descendants of a Portuguese sailor named Antone Joseph lived with a terrible secret. Over 46 of them died of a mysterious sickness, which starts with slurred speech, a staggering walk and loss of coordination, and ends twenty years later in death brought on by gradual paralysis of the breathing muscles. More than 125 of these descendants are alive today, 13 of them showing signs of the disease. Some of the clan feared that the mysterious disease was congenital syphilis, or referred to it as a "stigma," others hoped that it would die out in future generations. Finally, one of the clan broke silence and contacted the NGF. A counseling session, attended by 80 of the Josephs and several leading medical experts, was arranged, and for the first time, "the family secret" was revealed. The family's disease stems from a unique flaw in one of the genes affecting brain function, unknown outside of this particular family.

Sometimes the complexities of a case defy exact diagnosis. Since childhood, Patricia has been aware that her sister Anne was "slow." After two miscarriages, Patricia now worries that she carries "tainted blood." Her genetic evaluation begins with the construction of a detailed genetic "pedigree" for four generations of her family, listing health problems of grandparents; parents and their siblings; Patricia's siblings and cousins; and nieces and nephews. Anne proves to be the only affected family member. Since Anne herself cannot be examined, having recently been killed in a car accident, photos of Anne are checked instead for signs of Down's sydrome or other clues. Next the medical records of her mother's pregnancy and Anne's childhood are reviewed for what her doctor terms "suspicious events," such as health problems during pregnancy or labor, or childhood illnesses or injuries that might have affected Anne. Chromosome work-ups, or karotypes, are done on Patricia and her husband. Everything seems normal. Finally the couple is given information on mental retardation, showing that in the majority of cases, mild retardation is *not* genetic, but a risk does exist. Patricia opts for pregnancy and amniocentesis, and has a normal son.

While Patricia's case seems disappointingly mysterious, medical genetics, despite major breakthroughs in screening, diagnosis, prenatal testing and preventive treatment is not always an exact science. As Dr. Lawrence Shapiro puts it, "A definitive diagnosis is extremely helpful, but if one *can't* be established, genetic evaluation can still be helpful by providing information and a calculation of risks. We don't have all the answers yet, but new ones are constantly being discovered."

I realized at this point that the article should include a straightforward description of counseling, testing, and evaluation in one section, instead of having the material scattered all over the place.

This section, revised a bit, seemed like a natural for the final section of the piece, rather than coming before the material on prenatal testing as it does now. In the new plan, testing should follow the detailed description of genetic evaluation.

Genetic Prophecy

Though medical genetics, as a distinct discipline only started in the mid '60s, awareness that diseases—as well as other traits—run in families has existed for centuries. In the *Talmud*, rules for circumcision of newborns with brothers or uncles with bleeding tendencies are relaxed, while the persistent strain of hemophilia in her male descendents prompted Queen Victoria to write: "Our poor family seems persecuted by this disease, the worst I know." Experimenting with sweetpeas in the mid 1800s, an Austrian monk discovered the laws of dominant and recessive inheritance, but his theories were ignored until the 1920s. It wasn't until the '50s, however, that the secrets of human chromosomes were revealed. Since the 1959 discovery that Down's syndrome, a form of mental retardation, was caused by an extra chromosome in the 21st pair of the 23 chromosomes we all carry, over 3,000 inherited disorders have been identified. Victor A. McKusick, M.D., director of the department of medicine at Johns Hopkins Hospital and author of *Mendelian Inheritance in Man,* the bible of geneticists, suggests that even these may represent only 15 percent of genetically transmitted diseases, and Leon E. Rosenberg, M.D., chairman of the human genetics department, Yale University School of Medicine, goes even further: "There may be no such thing as an acquired disease."

The next paragraph seemed like a good bet for the ending of the piece.

The future of medical genetics is filled with exciting possibilities. By pinpointing individuals with genetically determined health "hot spots," predictive medicine might be able to forestall many potential health problems, through monitoring, early intervention, and even repair or replacement of defective genes. As the mapping of our component genes improves, we may be able to read our entire future in the genetic blueprint we are handed at birth.

This next paragraph and the following material should be in a separate section on prenatal testing. A possible subhead is "Will My Child Be Normal?"

Should add what is being tested for, and how the test is done.

Other exciting developments are found in the field of prenatal testing. The most widely used test, amniocentesis, is done between the fifteenth and seventeenth weeks of pregnancy, with the results available a month later. Such late results mean that a woman must make the emotionally wrenching decision as to whether or not to abort, in the case of adverse results, when she is already "showing" and has felt life.

Newer tests, still in the experimental stages, offer earlier results. The most widely tested, chorionic villi sampling, used at major medical centers throughout the world, entails removing a wisp of tissue from the placenta. Results from the test, done in the eighth week of pregnancy, are available in a few days. The risk of spontaneous miscarriage due to the test is 1 percent to 2 percent.

How does this risk compare with amniocentesis? Also a quote here from a doctor involved in the testing would make the material more authoritative.

An even newer development, early prenatal karotyping (EPK), has just been announced by researchers at Michigan State University. The test is done on the blood of the mother, and doesn't involve any risk to the fetus. Done in the seventh or eighth week of pregnancy, the test isolates fetal cells floating in the mother's blood and examines them. If further tests bear out the early results, the test's originators anticipate approval of the procedure within a year or two.

The ending seemed weak. Also it raises a question not addressed in the article, which might confuse readers.

These prenatal tests, plus the tremendous advances to come in the near future, offer us the chance to build a better genetic future for ourselves and our children. But the real question is, how much do we really want to know?

For further information, contact the National Genetics Foundation, 555 West 57th Street, New York, NY 10019 (212) 586-5800 or your local chapter of the March of Dimes.

Going through the article, I realized that my co-author and I had become overwhelmed by our material—we had so many case histories and facts at our disposal that the problem had become one of selectivity. Also our piece was jumping around, without following the most logical plan. To eliminate these problems and get rid of various minor quibbles, we redrafted it as follows:

GENETIC COUNSELING
by Lisa Collier Cool and Susan Smahl Plummer

Despite a last minute cesarean, Joan had no reason to expect anything but a normal, healthy child. After the delivery, even through the haze of anesthesia, Joan sensed that the examination of her baby was taking an unusually long time. Finally, she heard her doctor's voice: "It's a girl. . . . she has a cleft palate. . . . the ear is underdeveloped . . . . but she'll be fine." Later she learned that Michele had facio-auriculo-vertebral sequence, a cluster of birth defects affecting development of the ear, throat, upper vertebrae and face. Although Michele's case was mild—and surgically correctable—Joan sought genetic counseling to assess the risk to future children and to learn more about the syndrome itself. The news was good: the syndrome was almost certainly acquired after conception rather than genetic, meaning that the odds of its recurrence were only slightly greater than those of the average couple.

When our parents were young, conception was a form of genetic roulette, with each couple hoping that their combination of egg and sperm would add up to a healthy child. Today, medical genetics offers high-risk couples a way to improve the odds. Couples like Sandra and Mark, who are in their late thirties and want to start a family; Nancy and Bruce, who are concerned about Bruce's occupational exposure to radiation; and Miriam and Bill, who know that several of Miriam's relatives had heart attacks before age 50, can often discover what genetic legacy they will bequeath to their children. While medical science cannot yet guarantee each couple a perfect baby, in the past twenty years geneticists have made enormous strides forward in answering every prospective parent's ultimate question: "Will my baby be normal?"

Not surprisingly, an increasing number of couples are taking advantage of this opportunity to gaze into their own genetic crystal ball. "As technological advances are dramatically increasing the number of questions that can be answered, more and more couples are demanding these answers before making their childbearing decisions," says Lawrence R. Shapiro, M.D., director of Medical Genetics at Westchester County Medical Center and professor of pediatrics and pathology at New York Medical College. The increased demand also reflects today's consumer-oriented outlook, says Ruth Berini, director of the National Genetics Foundation (NGF): "When couples are having fewer children, they expect a corresponding increase in the quality of those children. To many, genetics offers the hope of a 'better baby.' "

Who Should Have Genetic Counseling?

Charlotte's case is typical of the spectrum of problems counselors and geneticists can encounter. Pregnant at age 36, Charlotte has three concerns. The first is genetic—she has a rare blood-clotting disorder, and wonders about the risk of passing it on to her unborn child. The counselor's research indicates that, unlike hemophilia, which is inherited, Charlotte's disorder is not genetic. Though her baby will have clotting problems immediately after birth due to seepage of maternal blood, they will last only a few weeks. Her baby's blood will be normal afterward. If you have a health problem, or suspect a family history of inherited disease, a counselor or geneticist can help determine if the disease is genetic, and arrange testing to discover your risks, if any, of transmitting that gene. Prenatal testing can often reveal if the unborn child is affected.

Like other women over age 35, Charlotte is aware that she has a higher risk of producing a child with chromosomal abnormalities like Down's syndrome. Her risk of Down's syndrome is about 1 in 400, of any chromosomal problem about 1 in 200. Unlike genetic disorders, which run in families, chromosomal disorders result from errors in formation of the egg or sperm. Such errors increase with the age of the mother. With the recent trend toward delayed childbearing, older women with no history of genetic problems have become the fastest growing group of patients. Recent studies show that between 75 percent and 85 percent of amniocentesis patients' sole concern is age. Because of Charlotte's clotting problem, and the unknown status of the fetus's blood, she is advised against amniocentesis, despite her age, because of the risk of serious complications to herself and the unborn child.

Her final concern is the possible effects of steroids on the developing fetus. Since steroids could improve her blood condition, decreasing the risks of amniocentesis, she asked the counselor to investigate their prenatal hazards. Used during the first trimester of pregnancy, steroids pose a slight risk of interfering with the baby's adrenal gland, but are generally considered relatively safe to use. Concerns over the effects of drug or toxin exposure during pregnancy are another common reason for consulting a counselor, as are illnesses or health problems during pregnancy.

In addition to those concerned by age, family history or events during pregnancy, three other groups should also consider genetic counseling, according to Nargess Ahgharian, M.D., a New York obstetrician, and other authorities:

Possible carriers of an ethnically linked disease, such as Tay

Sachs disease, which primarily occurs in Jews of Eastern European ancestry; sickle cell anemia, which strikes blacks; and thalessemia, a severe anemia sometimes occurring in those of Mediterranean ancestry. Simple, inexpensive blood tests screen for carriers—normal men and women at no risk themselves, who carry a gene for the disease. Widespread screening programs sift through target populations to alert carriers. The impact is dramatic—estimates indicate an 87 percent reduction over the past fifteen years in Tay-Sachs disease, a rare and always fatal metabolic disorder, from an average of 100 new cases a year in the U.S. to just *thirteen.*

Potential carriers of dozens of other genetic disorders can also be tested. A carrier test for hemophilia, for example, is available; but since only one woman in 5,000 is a carrier, the test is done on an individual basis, as population screening would not be cost effective for such a rare disease. If you suspect that you may be at risk for any genetic disease, a geneticist can help you decide which tests are necessary.

Parents of a previously affected child. Counselors can often provide exact odds of recurrence, ranging from 0 percent to 100 percent. Lewis and Marsha were devastated when their firstborn son was deaf. Genetic evaluation revealed that any future child would also be deaf. As a result, they adopted a healthy baby girl to complete their family. Frances, on the other hand, learned that her son's birth defects were caused by her bout of German measles during pregnancy—a one-time accident. Faced with a risk to future children, couples have a variety of options. When the risk is fairly low, many couples go ahead with another pregnancy, especially if reliable prenatal tests exist for the disorder, allowing them the option of a possible abortion. If only the father is affected, artificial insemination is another possibility. New methods of treating the unborn, such as percutaneous umbilical cord sampling, which allow fetal blood to be withdrawn for testing, and transfusions or drug therapy to be given before birth, can dramatically enhance the health and survival of a child at risk for some problems; while immediate neonatal treatment can help or even forestall others.

Though all of us harbor about four to eight harmful genes among the 50,000 to 100,000 that dictate our physical and mental characteristics, genetic disorders are relatively rare. Although 2 percent to 3 percent of the children born in the U.S. have some birth defect, only 25 percent to 40 percent of these problems are genetic, meaning that even a couple with an affected child is likely to have little or no risk of recurrence. When the problem is genetic, the odds often favor a normal child, except in rare cases where two individuals with the same harmful dominant trait have children together. If one parent has a harmful dominant trait, 50 percent of the couple's children will be unaffected. For recessive traits, both parents must have the trait before any child is affected. And, even when this is true, the odds are still 75 percent in favor of a *normal* child.

Couples with a history of unexplained miscarriages or stillbirths. While there are many reasons for miscarriage, a certain percentage result from genetic or chromosomal defects in the fetus that are incompatible with life. A history of repeated miscarriage or stillbirth—two or more—may signal a genetic problem, as in the case of one patient who learned after several miscarriages that a rare genetic problem made it impossible for her to carry a male fetus to term. She was, however, eventually able to deliver a healthy daughter.

While certain groups of people have a significantly higher risk of transmitting inherited disorders to their children, counseling can help just about anyone, says Nargess Ahgharian, M.D.: "If you have a question or concern, counseling can help. While some take a fatalistic attitude toward pregnancy, or fear that posing the question will be 'bad luck,' why spend nine months worrying unnecessarily? Consulting a counselor is not a commitment—you are free to use—or ignore—the information you receive."

Genetic Detective Work

The persistent strain of hemophilia running through her male ancestry prompted Queen Victoria to write: "Our poor family seems persecuted by this disease, the worst I know." Life under the shadow of genetic disease is just as devastating today, as over 300 descendants of a Portuguese sailor named Antone Joseph have discovered. Since 1845 this family has lived with a terrible secret. At least 48 of them have died of a mysterious illness which begins with slurred speech, a staggering walk and loss of coordination, and ends twenty years later in death from gradual paralysis of the breathing muscles. Some of the clan feared that the illness was congenital syphilis, or referred to it as a "stigma"; others hoped it would die out in future generations. Finally, one of the clan broke silence and contacted the NGF. A mass counseling session, attended by 80 of the Josephs and several leading genetic experts, was organized, and for the first time "the family secret" was revealed. The family's disease stems from a unique flaw in a gene affecting brain function, a mutation unknown outside of this particular family. Though no cure is at hand, the combination of medical information and emotional support provided by the counseling session made many of the family members feel as if they had stepped out of darkness for the first time in their lives.

Originally conceived as a "communication process which deals with the human problem associated with occurrence or risk of occurrence of a genetic disorder in a family," according to F. C. Fraser M.D., father of medical genetics, counseling now encompasses much more. According to Ruth Berini of the NGF, "Counselors can and do address just about any concern of the prospective parent or pregnant patient, whether genetic, chromosomal, environmental or emotional."

The counselor's first step is to draw up a complete family history, called a "pedigree," an intricate piece of detective work that covers four generations of your family, including grandparents, cousins, aunts and uncles, nieces and nephews, and even miscarriages and stillbirths in your family tree. As an aid to this process, the National Genetic Foundation offers, at a fee of $20, a questionnaire covering 14 categories of disease, ranging from cancer to mental illness to birth defects present in yourself or relatives. The NGF then analyzes the data by computer, followed by a more detailed evaluation by consulting geneticists. The printout includes medical information on any genetic patterns discovered. Such research may yield surprising results, as in the case of a woman who discovered for the first time that her mother had two retarded brothers, now deceased, that she had never mentioned to her children.

Since diagnosis can be complex in some cases, such as retardation which can result from either genetics, chromosomal abnormality, or events during pregnancy, birth or early childhood, the services of a geneticist, a physician specializing in genetic problems, is usually required. To aid in the diagnosis, you may be asked for medical records and even photos of family members to clarify the condition. You and your husband may also have to undergo karotyping, a chromosome analysis of your white blood cells. And in some cases, a definitive diagnosis may prove impossible, though as Dr. Shapiro points out, "While an exact diagnosis is certainly very helpful, even if one can't be established, genetic evaluation can still be worthwhile by providing information and risk calculation."

If any risks are found, the process then evolves into what Dick Leavitt of the March of Dimes describes as "an exploration of options, leading to the couple's making an informed decision in light of existing risks. The counselor will explore the information available on the defect, the risk of passing it on, the seriousness of the disorder, the state of the art in prevention and treatment of the defect, and the chances of giving such a child up for adoption. Although couples often ask what the counselor would do in their position, no ethical counselor would impose his or her own biases on the couple. The final answer is a personal decision between husband and wife."

"Will My Child Be Normal?"

After the counseling session, many patients decide to have prenatal testing, usually through amniocentesis. The procedure, done around the fifteenth to seventeenth week of pregnancy, starts with an ultrasound examination, followed by the insertion of a needle through the abdomen into the amniotic sac. Roughly an ounce of fluid is removed for study. Fetal cells in the fluid are cultured, and can be studied for more than 100 abnormalities, including neural tube defects like spina bifida, chromosomal problems like Down's syndrome and genetic problems like sickle cell anemia. Though the procedure is normally quite safe, the 1/4 percent to 1/2 percent risk of complications, including miscarriage, has made most doctors limit its use to higher risk patients and older mothers. Also, since the testing of cells takes up to a month, in the 1 1/2 to 2 percent of cases with adverse results, the expectant mother confronts the emotionally wrenching decision as to whether or not to terminate the pregnancy when she is already "showing" and has felt fetal movements.

Newer tests, still in the experimental stage, offer earlier results. The most widely tested, chorionic villi sampling, used at major medical centers throughout the world, entails removing a wisp of tissue from the placenta. Results from the test, done in the eighth week of pregnancy, are available within a few days. The risk of spontaneous miscarriage due to the test is about one to two percent. When this risk is decreased to compare with the 1/2 percent risk of amniocentesis, this new test may become the recommended procedure of the Food and Drug Administration, according to Jay Goldberg, M.D., assistant professor of obstetrics and gynecology at Mt. Sinai Medical Center in New York. "CVS will be a welcome alternative to amniocentesis, once its safety is borne out in larger studies."

An even newer development, early prenatal karotyping (EPK), has just been announced by researchers at Michigan State University. This test is done on the blood of the mother, and does not involve any risk to the fetus. Done in the seventh or eighth week of pregnancy, the new test isolates fetal cells circulating in the mother's blood and examines them. If further tests bear out the early results, the test's originators anticipate approval of the procedure within a year or two.

Genetic Prophecy

Awareness that diseases—as well as other traits—run in families has existed for centuries; but it wasn't until the 1950s that the mysteries of human chromosomes were revealed.

Since the 1959 discovery that Down's syndrome, a form of mental retardation, was caused by an extra chromosome in the 21st pair of the 23 pairs of chromosomes that we all carry, over 3,300 inherited disorders have been identified, ranging from mild disorders like frequent nosebleeds or color blindness to an increased risk for heart disease, breast cancer or diabetes. Victor A. McKusick, M.D., director of the department of medicine at Johns Hopkins Hospital and author of *Mendelian Inheritance in Man,* the bible of geneticists, suggests that even these may represent only 15 percent of genetically transmitted conditions, and Leon E. Rosenberg, M.D., dean of Yale University School of Medicine, goes even further: "There may be no such thing as acquired disease."

The future of medical genetics is filled with exciting possibilities. By pinpointing individuals with genetically determined health "hot spots," predictive medicine might be able to forestall many potential health problems, through monitoring, early intervention, and even repair or replacement of defective genes. As the mapping of our many component genes improves, each of us may be able to read our entire future in the genetic blueprint we are handed at birth, thus building a better and healthier life for ourselves—and our children.

For further information and brochures on genetic counseling, contact the National Genetics Foundation, 555 West 57th Street, New York, NY 10019 (212) 586-5800; or your local chapter of The March of Dimes.

Sounds a lot better, doesn't it? Careful editing can work wonders for your writing as well—don't neglect this vital step that turns an ordinary pebble into a sparkling gemstone.

11

Equipped for Success

While many a writer has launched a career by plopping an old Remington manual on the kitchen table and pecking out a few pieces with the two-finger typing system, the right equipment can increase productivity—and quite possibly profitability. By switching from a typewriter to a computer, for example, I found I was able to write articles between 25 percent and 50 percent faster. Adding a camera to your inventory of writing tools can be another income booster, as you sell pictures along with your text. Whether you're operating on a shoestring or have unlimited funds at your disposal, your goal is the same: to create an environment stocked with the right tools for each job, where you can focus fully on making your writing the best that it can be.

A Room of One's Own

A writer's first requirement is a place to work. You might find, as Mark Twain did, that the bed is the ideal workspot, or have the incredible concentration of Jane Austen, who wrote amid family conversations in the living room; but if you're like most writers, you'll do better to dedicate some space specifically to your creative needs. As you build up associations between a particular location and work, you'll establish an almost Pavlovian flowing of creative juices as you sit down to work, reducing or perhaps eliminating time-wasting blocks and elaborate warm-up routines, especially if you also establish a regular work schedule you religiously adhere to. In addition to generating good work habits, dedicated workspace can also create potential tax deductions to offset your writing income—an advantage that modern-day Twains and Austens would miss out on.

While most writers start out with a home office, there are pros and cons. The chief advantages are convenience and economy; the disadvantages are distractions from friends and salespeople who don't take your work seriously, potential tax audits (the IRS has targeted home offices for extra scrutiny), and isolation. Noted science-fiction writer Ray Bradbury has found the best of both worlds by having *two* offices, a home office for early morning work, and an outside office for the regular workday.

Once you've found a niche for work, start setting up your workspace for maximum efficiency. Put files, phone, and bookcases in easy reach of your desk. By doing so you'll avoid the temptation to make a trip to the file cabinet into an unscheduled coffee break.

Furnishing your office on a shoestring is easy. Visit odd lot or discontinued office furniture stores until you find a couple of metal two-drawer file cabinets that are the same height (color doesn't matter since you can always spray paint them) and a comfortable desk chair. Then buy an unfinished door at your lumberyard, lay it on top of the two file cabinets, and you have an instant desk and storage area in one. Add a bookcase, phone, and appropriate lighting for your work area and you have the bare bones of an office.

Typewriters

To find the best typewriter for your needs, consult *Consumer Reports* or similar publications for information on repair records and special features of the various models available. Before making your final selection, investigate whether service for that model is offered locally. If you live in a large city, you can sometimes buy a service contract for your typewriter which includes all annual maintenance and repair, with the work done right in your office.

There are three basic kinds of typewriters on the market today: manual, electric, and electronic. Manual typewriters are by far the cheapest, but are also the slowest and noisiest. The next step up, the electric, comes in two varieties: the first is essentially a motorized version of the manual typewriter and is sometimes afflicted by excessive noise and vibration; the second has a type ball instead of bar type on the ends of the keys, making it smoother and quieter to operate than most bar type models. An additional advantage to the type ball typewriter is that you can change your typeface by changing the ball.

The Rolls-Royce of typewriters is the electronic typewriter. The type is on a rotating "daisy wheel," which allows you to continue typing even when the wheel is returning to the left margin, as the typewriter's "memory" stores the keystrokes and prints them as soon as the wheel has returned. Other handy features in many models are: automatic return when you approach the right margin; crisp, neat typing using a film ribbon cartridge or cassette, rather than the conventional fabric ribbon; repeat spacing and backspacing; tab stops stored in memory that work both backward and forward; various automatic ways of formatting material for special typing jobs; and easy corrections—you merely hit the correction key and the erroneous character or characters are "lifted off" the page, or struck over with white-out film; the memory automatically strikes the correct keys in reverse order until the correction is complete. Further, most electronic models can be linked to a computer to serve as a letter quality printer, though a rather slow one compared to conventional computer printers.

If your budget is modest, you can often buy good typewriters at a fraction of their original cost by buying "reconditioned" typewriters from used office equipment suppliers. If the model is very old, you'll want to check on local access to service and availability of the right ribbons.

An important consideration in choosing your typewriter is the size and style of the type. Pica is by far the most popular size with editors and writers, though elite is also acceptable. Avoid other sizes of type, as well as script or other unusual typefaces. Typewriters which use "proportional spacing," like some IBM

models, result in attractive but hard-to-correct pages, since you
may have to redo a whole word to change a skinny letter to a fatter
one.

If you are just learning to type, you might want to investigate
typewriters with the new "Dvorak keyboard." The keys are arranged in a pattern said to increase typing speed by 30 percent by
eliminating the wasted motion built into the standard QWERTY
arrangement used on most typewriters. Supposedly your fingers
travel sixteen miles in a day's typing on a standard typewriter, as
opposed to just *one* on a Dvorak keyboard typewriter. However,
experienced typists may not want to invest the fifty to one hundred hours of practice required to equal, on the new keyboard,
their current speed on a standard typewriter.

Word Processors

As an aid to faster, more efficient writing, the computer can't
be beat. There's no need to retype as you redraft; at the stroke of a
finger you can insert new material anywhere in your article, delete unwanted words or paragraphs, rearrange paragraphs or
pages, substitute one word for another throughout the text—
handy if you've just finished the piece and learn that "Dr. Smith"
spells his name "Smythe"—have the computer correct your spelling errors, and finally repaginate the whole document into your
preferred format. And you can store dozens of articles and
queries in its memory and locate any of them instantly. Some programs will also suggest words to use and evaluate the readability
of your material.

With a phone hookup, your computer can communicate with
other computers all over the country. This will let you gather pre-
liminary research at home by connecting you with bibliography
and abstracting services and network with other writers and potential interviewees through various message boards and electronic conferencing services. You could even collaborate elec-
tronically with another writer anywhere in the country as your
two computers exchange files of text over phone lines, allowing
each of you instant access to the other's efforts.

But are computers complicated to use? What about the horror stories of writers obliterating their entire text by pushing the
wrong button? And what if your style of working just doesn't com-
pute? Writers who haven't tried the computer are often intimidat-

ed by such concerns, fearing that you have to be some kind of genius to become computer literate. Actually today's computers are designed to be user friendly, using commands in ordinary English, offering "help menus" to direct the novice, and even pointing out your mistakes. Most writers find, as I did, that it takes only a day or two to get into the swing of word processing, and once you do, you're likely to wonder why you ever hesitated to make the switch.

If you'd like to sample the high-tech approach before you make an investment in a computer of your own, a good trial is to borrow or rent one and experiment with it for a few weeks.

Here's how you'd use your microcomputer in your writing. To enter text, you'd type on a keyboard similar to that of a typewriter, but with a few additional keys. As you worked, a video screen would display the text you'd typed. When you'd finished writing and editing, a high-speed printer would churn out as many copies as you needed for submissions, while your original text was stored in memory or on a disk for future reference.

How does the computer do all this? You'd provide the necessary instructions by inserting programs written on plastic diskettes into a slot in the disk drive—as easy to do as putting a record on a turntable. Hundreds of such prepackaged programs are available commercially—not just for word processing, but for accounting, record keeping, games, and dozens of other purposes—making it unnecessary to learn computer programming unless you want to. The program you load is decoded by the computer's brains, the fingernail-sized silicon chip housing the Central Processing Unit, and stored in other chips holding memory.

In selecting your computer, you'll find the quality of the software (programs) is just as important as that of the hardware (the computer and its accessories). The more popular the computer model you select, the wider the selection of compatible software. While you may not want or even need a great variety of software, a lack of software support suggests that a model may he headed for extinction, creating potential problems in getting service or accessories in the future. After zeroing in on popular models in your price range, here are some desirable features to look for:

Keyboard: Many writers prefer a keyboard that is not rigidly attached to the other components so they can move it into their preferred typing position.

Screen: Having the screen separate from the keyboard also makes it possible to move the screen to your preferred viewing distance as you work. Another important factor is the size and appearance of the letters on the screen. Are they clearly defined and easy to read? Can you display a whole page at a time, or only a few lines? It's a lot more convenient to view a complete page as you edit it.

Memory: The computer you select must have sufficient memory to hold your word processing program and files of text at the same time. Most computers have room for additional memory, allowing you to add as much capacity as you need.

Printer: For the most attractive manuscripts, buy a letter quality printer. However, these are quite expensive—your printer might cost almost as much as the rest of your system. To slash costs, consider a high-quality dot matrix printer, which typically goes for half the price of a letter quality printer and is equally acceptable for manuscript typing. Make sure the characters have true descenders—that the tail of "q" or "y" does drop below the line—and check that the print-out is clear and readable: legibility can vary considerably. The printer you select must be compatible with your other hardware. Ask for a demonstration of the whole system working together before buying.

Modem: A useful accessory, a modem is a device that lets your computer communicate over phone lines. You might want to get one when you buy your computer.

Selecting Software

Your new computer will be only as useful as its software, so you'll want to select your word processing program carefully. Here are some features to look for:

Word wrap: With this feature you only hit carriage return when you reach the end of a paragraph; the computer breaks the lines for you.

Delete and insert: How easy is it to delete words and longer segments? Does the program allow you to insert anywhere from one letter to several pages by automatically moving the subsequent text over without leaving any holes?

Move: Is it easy to move blocks of text of any size within the document? Can the block start in the middle of a line?

Search and replace: Can you replace words or phrases either selectively (you approve each change) or globally (changes are made automatically)?

A Well-Stocked Office

Attractive letterhead stationery (be sure to include home and office phone numbers) lends a more professional appearance to your submissions. However, avoid identifying yourself as a "writer" on your stationery since many editors consider this the sure sign of an amateur at work. And avoid the far fetched: I've received letters at my agency from Miss X, "ecrivain," which I eventually learned was *French* for writer (pretentious, oui?) and Mr. Y, "the fastest pen in the east," both of which drew an immediate negative response. Instead, aim at something with a dash of boldness—you're a writer, not a lawyer—with an interesting type style or color choice. Computer feed stationery is also available, allowing you to print out personalized cover letters for your multiple submissions in minutes on your computer.

Typing paper need not be the expensive parchmentlike variety—any reasonable grade of bond paper will do. Editors dislike erasable paper, which tends to smudge. A generous supply of typewriter ribbons is important—editors also hate straining their eyes on faint text. If a rush project finds you without a fresh ribbon, a trick one professional writer I represent recommends is having your local photocopy shop reproduce the text on the darkest setting, then reproducing the resulting copy a second time again on the darkest setting. Repeating this process a few times will darken the text to submission quality.

To handle your mailing needs, get a supply of padded mailing envelopes (#5 size holds an article; #6, a book manuscript) or manila envelopes (9 by 12 size for articles); a postage scale and stamps in various denominations; and an inkpad and stamp with your name, address, and phone number (for return addresses and labeling manuscripts).

Other helpful items are: a Rolodex for phone numbers and addresses of editors, interview sources, and other professional contacts; plenty of file folders to organize each new project; ledgers to keep track of receipts and potential tax deductions, record books or index cards to maintain submission records; and a calculator.

Answering Machines

If you work alone, a phone answering machine or answering service will keep you from missing potentially important calls from editors while you're out mailing off submissions. Interested editors often call to offer assignments; a missed connection could cost you a rush project (as happened to me once before I got my machine).

Though the great answering machine vs. answering service debate rages on, personally I prefer the reliability and discretion of the machine—it never garbles a message or complains if you check it a dozen times a day. While any machine will do, it's nice to get one which will also play back your messages when you call from the outside—handy if you're spending the day on the road gathering interviews and research. The "toll-saver" ringing system is also desirable—the phone answers on the second ring if there are messages; the fourth if not, allowing you to hang up after the third ring when calling for your messages. This feature also allows you to leave the machine on all the time since you have four rings in which to answer when you're at home.

Getting It on Tape

While I've managed to get by without one thus far, many writers swear by the tape recorder, not just for interviews, but for taping notes for articles in the car, at the library, and wherever else inspiration strikes. Some writers also enjoy dictating their articles and having them professionally typed. Avoid microrecorders; they have the drawbacks of accepting only thirty minute tapes, tinny reproduction in some cases, and inconvenience in finding public stenographers equipped to transcribe the smaller tapes. Instead, choose a recorder that uses standard cassettes.

Good features to look for in a tape recorder are: rechargeable batteries, an audible signal when a tape is full, a tape counter to help you find relevant portions of the conversation quickly, reasonable reproduction (test the quality at the store), and an indicator that shows when the batteries are getting low.

Selling Your Pictures

While a good picture may be worth less than a thousand words—or more depending on the markets you hit—your photography skills can definitely increase your writing income, since many magazines will buy freelance pictures. Many types of articles will be enhanced by photos; travel, profile, nature, sports, human interest, and business pieces are some of the more common possibilities. You can also use your photography as a starting point, building an article around a series of photos, with an action/adventure photo essay for example. Or you can sell your photos to illustrate other writers' articles; *Photographer's Market* (published by Writer's Digest Books) can help you find promising outlets for your work.

If photography appeals to you, most professionals suggest that you equip yourself with a 35-millimeter single lens reflex camera with removable lenses. You may also want to select a camera with automatic or programmable exposure, which adjusts the aperture and shutter speed for perfect exposures—but make sure it also has manual override so you can adjust the camera for unusual lighting conditions that photograph poorly on the automatic settings. If you plan to do a lot of high-speed photography like sports/action pictures, an auto-winder might be helpful.

Depending on the type of photographs you envision yourself taking, you'll probably want some additional lenses. A wide angle lens allows you to capture a broader area than the regular lens that comes with your camera—useful if you're photographing a crowd or large group. Telephoto lenses come in various lengths; shorter ones are good for portrait photography, longer ones for sports. A zoom lens is like having several telephoto lenses, since it allows you to photograph from many different perspectives. For more information on lenses, consult *Lenses for 35mm Cameras,* Kodak Workshop Series, available at camera stores or through Eastman Kodak, 343 State Street, Rochester, NY 14650.

Other accessories you'll need for your photography are a tripod, a powerful flash unit, and a camera bag. To ensure your ability to upgrade your equipment, either select a popular brand or buy all extra lenses and accessories now.

Cameras are frequently discounted; you may be able to buy yours at 50 percent off the list price. It's well worth visiting several stores, as well as studying advertisements for specials. Some stores will undercut any advertised price you show them, or offer substantial cash discounts if you dicker a bit. Look out for "gray" market cameras—these are illegally imported, cheaper cameras, whose guarantees don't apply to the U.S. market. Economizing by buying used equipment is not generally recommended as there is no easy way to evaluate just how much abuse the camera may have suffered at the hands of its previous owner.

Generous supplies of film are vital. To ensure good photos you'll have to shoot lots of pictures of the same scene or person, being sure to bracket your exposures by shooting each picture at an f-stop higher and an f-stop lower than one you selected for the first shot. You'll also want to experiment with different angles on the scene, horizontal and vertical shots of it, and distance and close-up shots. This will use up film fast.

To submit your black and white photos, determine if the editor wants contact sheets (which have all the pictures on them in miniature) or prints. Usually publications prefer 8 by 10 glossy prints, though some accept 5 by 7 prints. Stamp your name and address on the back or write it with a thin felt tip (*not* ballpoint) pen. Color pictures are normally submitted as 35 millimeter transparencies, which can be arranged on slotted acetate pages available from your photo stores. Put the best pictures at the top of the page. Label your slides by putting your name on the slide mount.

After labeling the pictures, write some brief captions to identify and explain the picture to the editor and reader. Study the captions in the target publications for guidance as to what sort of information and style are favored in captions. If in doubt, include the five W's (who, what, where, when, and why). Type the captions and tape them to the back of your black and white prints, or number your transparencies and list all the captions by number on a separate sheet of typing paper.

To mail your pictures, protect them by placing them between heavy sheets of cardboard, and tape the sheets securely together. For added protection use a padded mailing envelope as well. Or buy special photo mailer envelopes at your camera store. Clearly label both your mailing envelope and your stamped self-addressed return envelope (a must with most publications) with PHOTOS—DO NOT BEND.

Free Photos You Can Profit From

If you lack the time or talent to take your own pictures, you can still reap the benefits of photography in marketing your work. A surprising number of manufacturers, trade associations, and public relations firms will give you *free* pictures of their products or clients, considering the resulting publicity sufficient payment. Tourist bureaus and local chambers of commerce are also good sources of free pictures—they want to attract visitors to their areas. Some large organizations have press kits available with attractive (or not so attractive) pictures you are free to use with your article. •

Many other organizations will offer to supply pictures if you merely ask. Recently I was thinking of doing an article on neonatal intensive care units, and several local hospitals volunteered to supply either color or black and white photos to illustrate my article, a selling point I was able to use effectively in my query letter.

One of the best sources for free pictures is the U.S. Government. Both the National Archives and the Library of Congress have huge collections of pictures. Most government departments and agencies also have photo libraries. Depending on your subject, you might contact public information officers at the Department of Defense, NASA, National Weather Service, National Parks Service, or dozens of others.

For further information on free or nearly free pictures, consult *Picture Sources* (Special Libraries Association) and other photographic reference books.

Taxable You

As you gear up for your writing career, you may be acquiring deductible expenses to offset against your writing income. Since tax laws are currently in a state of flux, rather than advise you on specific deductions, I suggest you save all receipts for expenses remotely connected with your writing, keep a daily log of writing related expenses and marketing activities, and retain copies of submission letters and rejections or contracts for articles—important in substantiating that your writing is a business and not just a hobby that generates the odd check, an important distinction to the IRS. If your writing is to be considered a business, you need to show a profit two years out of five according to current regulations.

Here's a partial list of items you may be able either to deduct or to depreciate. Consult your tax adviser for the latest regulations before preparing your return.

Home office: Currently you must have a room or rooms you use regularly, and solely, for your writing. You then calculate what percentage of your home your office occupies, say 15 percent, and deduct the corresponding percentage of such expenses as rent, electricity, heat, home owner's insurance, repairs, maintenance, depreciation on the dwelling. However, by current law, you'll need to show a net profit at least two out of five years to justify this and other "writer's" deductions to the IRS.

Office furniture and equipment: Rather than deduct the entire cost of your desk, typewriter, file cabinet, computer, or other furnishings that have a useful life of more than one year, such items are depreciated according to some schedule, based on the anticipated useful life of the item. Your accountant or tax preparation service will be able to advise you on the appropriate schedule of depreciation for each item. Buying a computer or other equipment may qualify you for an investment tax credit; check current regulations for specifics.

Publications and dues: Since a writer needs to keep up with the marketplace, you should be able to deduct the cost of any magazines, newspapers, and reference books you might buy. Or if you belong to any writers' organizations or other associations useful to your work, the cost of dues would be deductible.

Travel and entertainment: If you use your own car for business purposes, you can deduct mileage according to some rate the IRS supplies, currently 20.5 cents a mile. For overnight business trips, say to a writers' conference, you can also deduct for hotels, meals, tips, transportation, and other travel expenses. If you want to take an editor, interview subject, or other business associate out for one of publishing's notorious three-martini lunches, check with your tax adviser on whether such expenses are currently deductible. If so, keep a copy of the bill and a record of the business discussed.

Other deductions: Other likely deductions are phone expenses, office supplies and stationery, postage and messenger service, bank charges (if you have a separate business account), legal and accounting fees, rent on an outside office, photocopying, photography expenses, repairs and maintenance of writing equipment, courses and conferences to enhance your writing skills (only after you're established—courses that train you in a new career aren't deductible).

Getting your new office stocked and your filing and record-keeping systems organized requires a modest investment of time, money, and energy. But it pays big dividends in improved efficiency and productivity. The right surroundings also let you enjoy your work, making you eager to start each work day.

12

Irresistible Queries

While many writers write the complete article first, then try to sell it, selling first—through a query—*then* writing is a more profitable and efficient approach. A combination sales pitch and article summary, a query describes your idea in a page or two of well-written prose. Sent to the right editor, these few paragraphs can land you a profitable article assignment. This shortcut to sales really pays off: timely ideas get out quickly; you can submit more, receive faster answers, reduce research and time wasted on unsalable material. Not just for the seasoned pro, queries can work equally well for you. I've often seen my students and clients make their first sales through queries.

Most magazines prefer queries over complete manuscripts. Queries are easier and faster to read than manuscripts and allow editorial input *before* the article is written. Often an editor will hesitate to ask a writer to revise a completed piece but feels no such compunctions about suggesting a new slant for a query. My two-paragraph query proposing an article on consumer advocacy, for example, produced an assignment from *Harper's* to write on deceptive food packaging, an angle I'd never considered.

Queries can be used to propose just about any kind of article, though for humor pieces, editorials, newspaper articles, and general pieces shorter than 1,000 words (four double-spaced pages), it's best to submit a completed article. Also a few magazines insist that only completed articles be sent. To learn specific preferences, check listings in directories, such as *Writer's Market,* or ask the magazine for writer's guidelines.

Shaping Your Raw Material

According to one editor I know, the best way to get an editor's attention is to "punch him in the nose and keep fighting until you hear the bell." He means that a good query starts strong and never lets up until the editor is sold. In composing your query keep two newspaper dictums in mind. The first, the five W's (who, what, where, why, and when, used to compose the typical first paragraph of a news story) reminds you to explain the story immediately. The second, the inverted triangle (the arrangement of facts favored by newspaper writers) emphasizes the importance of putting the most interesting information *first.* Don't save the best for last or you may have lost the editor's attention by the time it appears.

Your query should include three main sections: the lead paragraph, the summary, and the author's bio. Each has a specific purpose; as articles editor Julia Kagan of *Working Woman* says, "First, tell me what the story is, then why we should buy it, and finally who is going to write it." (Figures 12-1 and 12-2, pages 129-131, illustrate the two preferred query formats.)

Hooking the Editor

Your lead paragraph should have a solid impact. This is your chance to audition before the editor, to give him or her a taste of your writing. A good lead not only helps sell the editor on your idea but can be used again in the actual article. While many writers like to open with an anecdote, other effective approaches include: provocative quotes, surprising facts or statistics, references to celebrities or news events, wittiness or exaggeration, references to dramatic events or common situations with a new twist, thought-provoking questions, commands to the reader, unusual definitions, and surprising comparisons and contrasts. Here's how I've used some of these approaches in first paragraphs of articles and queries:

Celebrity anecdote: [for an article on superstitions]

When her daughter was critically injured in an accident, *Dynasty* star Joan Collins tried to ensure the youngster's survival by becoming ill herself: "I felt that if I threw up—was sick—Katy would live. It sounds ridiculous, but some voice in my head, the old ingrained actor's voice of superstition, kept telling me to do this." As she writes in her memoirs, *Past Imperfect,* later she remembers the same voice says, "If you make the green traffic light before it turns red, she'll live. . . ."

Question: [for an editorial]

It's all very well for Melville's character to say, "Call me Ishmael," but what's Mrs. Ishmael to do if, like so many of us, she uses her married name at home, and her maiden name at work?

Play on words: [for a profile article]

Harry Browne's unorthodox economics have earned him titles like "crackpot," "charlatan" and "prophet of doom and gloom"—this last title being a favorite with the financial press, who sometimes suggest that "prophet" should be spelled "p-r-o-f-i-t." These unorthodox economics have also earned him an estimated $1 million.

Comparison: [profile article]

Though he may not be able to leap tall buildings at a single bound, sixteen-year-old Philip Marshall Hecht is considered a superman of the comic book world. In just three years of buying and selling old comic books, the teenaged tycoon has turned $60 into $60,000.

Quote:

When asked just how you get rich playing table tennis, hustler extraordinaire Marty Reisman smiles and says, "First, you need a good racquet, then you need a lot of balls." Reisman has both.

Factual lead:

Last year Americans spent over six *billion* dollars on telephone calls. For the average household, this works out to $369.16, or

$32.43 a month. Since telephone calls, like everything else, are getting more expensive, each call must pay for itself by saving you time and money. With the right techniques, you can get more from your phone—and pay less for it.

Longer Leads:

While I usually launch my queries with a single paragraph, sometimes a longer presentation works better, by creating drama or offering an imaginative presentation of a commonplace topic. Here are two longer leads I've used in published articles.

For Glamour:

Thanksgiving, 1980, was a day of celebration for Karen Segal (names have been changed) even though she spent it in a hospital room. Her son, Michael, had been born the day before, "a perfect little boy," her doctor told her. With her other son, David, two years old, her family was now complete. Karen told all of her friends that she felt as if she were "living in a fairy tale."

Her happiness lasted thirty-five days. On the morning of January first, Karen nursed Michael at her breast and put him in his crib. While she was cooking in the kitchen, Michael, without warning, died silently in his sleep.

For Cosmopolitan:

Fantasy #1: You return from lunch with an important customer. Linda, your new secretary, has transformed your office during your absence—a stack of flawlessly typed letters awaits your signature, the research you need for the sales conference is compiled, and your Rolodex has been updated and alphabetized.

Fantasy #2: You return from a boring budget meeting and stumble over your new secretary's muddy overshoes. Helga is chatting on the telephone with her boyfriend as she does her nails. Most of the work you gave her in the morning remains untouched. On your desk lie some illegible telephone messages and two unfinished letters, both pockmarked with White-Out.

Hiring your first secretary can be a trauma-charged experience. . . .

Other suggestions for your lead: While a magazine lead can—and should—be more creative than the newspaper five W's lead, it must let the reader know exactly what to expect from the article that will follow. And whatever type of lead you select, remember that it must convey the tone as well as the topic of your proposed article to the editor. You're courting rejection if your lead promises a lively anecdotal piece when you really intend to write a straightforward how-to article.

The Heart of the Matter

Once you've aroused the editor's interest with your lead, move directly to a summary of the article. This section of your query should convince the editor that you know where you want to go with the article; it should outline the points you plan to cover or provide important factual information about your topic. As Louis Tutellian of *Savvy* puts it: "Show us you've already gone halfway down the road. Give enough facts, figures and details to prove your story is real."

While some queries can be written entirely from your own knowledge, others require research. Chapters Eight and Nine showed how to get the facts you need through interviews and research. However, if you need just one or two facts, a quick call to the telephone reference number of your library (a service available in most cities) can often give you the answer immediately.

Or a call to a foundation or association can give you enough. In a recent query on genetic counseling, a call to the National Genetics Foundation (Chapter Nine tells you how to locate appropriate organizations) yielded enough information for me to write:

> Genetic disorders affect about 15 million people in the U.S., with 2-3 percent of babies born each year showing some detectable genetic disease. More than 3,000 such diseases have been identified, ranging from color blindness or a tendency to nosebleeds to such serious conditions as Tays-Sachs disease and hemophilia. Until recently, conception was a form of genetic roulette, but today medical genetics can. . . .

Your summary should be succinct and clear. Here are two methods I've used successfully. For a simple idea, the flat summary will work:

> My idea is "I Do! I Do!", a guide to double weddings: the etiquette, the logistics, from shower to ceremony, with a few interesting anecdotes thrown in (like the most *double* wedding ever, when twin sisters married twin brothers, with thirty-eight pairs of twins participating in the festivities) and quotes from ministers and other authorities.

For more complex ideas, the "bullet formation" might be preferable. In a query for an article entitled "Creative Failure," later sold to *Glamour,* I described the main idea (that failure can be good for you), then listed some key points in this format:

- *Guilt-free Failure:* The importance of understanding that failure is normal and necessary.
- *The Failure Fallacy:* How to steer clear of the debilitating belief that one failure will inevitably lead to another.
- *Creative Failure:* A program for analyzing your failures and using them as tools for future successes.
- *Running the Marathon:* Why making the effort is often more important than coming out number #1.
- *The Risk for Success Equation:* By increasing the possibility of failure, you can actually increase your potential for success.

Now mention your sources. "Tell us who you'll be talking to," says Patrice Adcroft of *Omni.* "Are your experts just the guys who've been around forever, or are they on the cutting edge of today's technology?" Add any relevant sales points: news pegs, similarity to previous articles in the publication, points of particular appeal to the magazine's readers, significant dates the article might tie into, and any other strong reasons to buy now. Then list any important nuts-and-bolts information the editor should have, such as the projected word length (rounded off to the nearest 500 words: 2,500 words, for example; each typewritten page of double-spaced prose contains about 250 words). Mention too the availability of photos or illustrations (optional) and the amount of time needed to write the piece (not more than two months for most articles).

Finally be sure to include your title somewhere in this material. If you haven't been able to come up with a good one, a working title such as "How to Hire a Secretary" will do. Avoid submitting untitled queries.

Selling Yourself

After you've sold the editor on the idea, start selling yourself as a writer. Many writers are overcome by modesty at this point, but there's no reason to be bashful. Editors expect a bit of sell in the bio—within reason. There's nothing wrong with saying "I'm highly qualified to write this article because. . . ." if a convincing reason follows.

After you acquire one or more magazine credits, use them to open your bio. With one credit say "My work has appeared in XYZ magazine." As your list of credits grows, list them all until you have about nine or ten. Then get selective by including the magazines most similar to the one you are currently submitting to, as well as any others that are particularly impressive. Also, once some of your articles are published, include photocopies of any that are similar to the new one as samples.

Until you acquire these credits, use the bio to emphasize your *other* qualifications. For example, for *American Baby* magazine having children might be your best qualification. "We often buy articles from parents," says editor Phyllis Evans. "Writing credentials are not important if you understand our readers."

Students in my writing course, most of whom enter as unpublished beginners, are often unsure what qualifications to include when writing a first query. "I don't think I have any," one complained. After reviewing her professional and personal background, I pointed out that she had on-the-job writing experience as an advertising copywriter, that she was a former teacher (her topic was choosing your child's first school), and that she had three children in school. Unqualified? Hardly.

The ideal author's bio is short but convincing. To compose it, look for relevant material from:

Your job: Does it involve any sort of writing or publishing? Or does it relate to your topic? What about former jobs? If your work experience is relevant, briefly describe it, mentioning your title (if reasonably impressive) and the name of your company.

Your hobbies: A passionate interest in your subject can be an excellent qualification. If your subject is "Profiting from Collectibles," and you've attended every stamp, coin, and miniature show in the state for the past five years while building a library of 200 back issues of various collectors' magazines, say so. If you can truthfully add that your personal collection, put together at a cost of $1,500, was recently appraised for $25,000, you've probably made the sale.

Your family: When appropriate, mention family members: "As the wife of an executive in a multinational corporation, I have moved seventeen times in the past four years, so I feel uniquely qualified to write 'Avoiding the Moving Day Blues.' "

Your personal life: If you have had any personal experience with the subject, explain the connection: "After recently ending a live-in relationship, I have many insights into 'Surviving the Break-up.' "

Your education: If you hold an advanced degree (beyond a

bachelor's) or have attended a particularly prestigious college, mention these facts in your bio. Also mention any specialized training or courses taken in the topic you propose to write about.

If you have been the subject of an article or book that deals with your query subject, either send copies of the material or name the publications you were mentioned in. Editors may also be interested in lectures or courses you've given, radio and television appearances, awards you've received, and other significant achievements.

After the bio, close with a sentence asking for the sale: "What do you think?" or "I'll be looking forward to hearing from you." Be sure your close is upbeat.

Telephone Queries

While the fastest way to get your idea before an editor is the phone, the typical editor is likely to be in a meeting, late getting in, just down the hall, out to lunch, left early, took the day off, on jury duty, on vacation, at the sales conference, out sick, or on the other line when you call. Unless the editor knows you, it's practically impossible to get through, except at very small publications.

If you do decide to call, boil your idea down to three or four catchy sentences. You won't have long to get a busy editor's attention, so practice your presentation for maximum impact before calling. Also make a list of two or three alternate ideas in case the first one doesn't appeal to the editor. But chances are that even the best phone presentation will result in a request for a written query to show to the other editors; editors know that talking a good game doesn't necessarily mean you can *write*.

Query Checklist

Is your query ready to submit? A final review will help you decide. Here's what to look for:

• *Lead:* Does your opening paragraph grab the editor's attention? Would additional facts, statistics, or quotes strengthen the lead? Is the lead appropriate for your article in tone and style? Does the lead clearly reveal the topic of the article concisely?

• *Summary:* Have you listed at least three key points that will be covered in the article? Are your facts and quotes interesting and new? Are there powerful additional points that should be added? Have you mentioned the names of any authorities to be quoted in the article? Is the message and direction of the article absolutely clear? Have you included all relevant sales points?

• *Bio:* Are all your credentials included? Is each fact about you phrased in the strongest possible way? Have you attached supporting exhibits (if any), like your *Who's Who* bio or previous articles?

• *Length:* Does your query fit on one or two double-spaced pages; or if you are using a letter query, in a one-page single-spaced letter? If not, trim the lead; sharpen the summary, retaining central points, eliminating lesser arguments; and condense the bio. It's best to err on the side of being too short, since an interested editor will often ask for more material if necessary.

• *Format:* Is your query attractively laid out and free from errors in style, punctuation, and spelling? Mistakes and sloppy presentation create as poor an impression in your query as in your resume.

• *One query or two?* If you plan to submit more than one idea to a magazine, write a separate query for each topic and add a cover letter. Different editors may want to consider the different ideas.

Once your query passes these tests, it's ready for its submission debut. In the next chapter I show you how to pitch your queries and articles to editors— and start ringing up the sales. But don't pin all your hopes on one query; now that you've mastered the basics, keep your skills sharp by immediately turning each inspiration into a polished query. The more queries you mail off, the sooner you're likely to get back another sort of query, one that says, "Could you sign and return this article contract?"

Figure 12-1
TRADITIONAL BUSINESS LETTER QUERY

Mr. William Brohaugh
Editor
Writer's Digest Magazine
1507 Dana Avenue
Cincinnati, Ohio 45207

Dear Mr. Brohaugh:

I'd like to write a piece on "How to Write a Selling Query and Author's Bio—Even If You Have No Credits at All." Here's how I'd handle it:

> How would you like to turn a few paragraphs into a profitable article assignment? A query letter, brief and to the point, can be your shortcut to sales. Not just for the experienced pro, queries can work for any writer. As a literary agent and writing teacher, I've seen queries produce writers' very first sales.
>
> Making queries work for you is a matter of mastering two skills: presentation of an idea and presentation of a writer—you. Here's how:

The article would then go on to cover, step-by-step, how to write your query and author's bio. Some main points:

- Grab the editor's attention. Tips on writing the lead paragraph, the five W's, the inverted triangle (say the most interesting thing *first*), other leads and examples.

- Give your slant. Examples of how to narrow the focus and make the idea specific.

- Outline the piece. The eye-catching "bullet formation" and other ways to make your description dramatic.

- Give a sales pitch. Ways to identify the best marketing points and use them.

- The nuts-and-bolts: include length, time needed to complete, availability of photos (optional).

- The author's bio. How you too can be an expert. Ways to toot your own horn, even if you think there's nothing to toot about.

- Formats for your query. Precise how-to's of the letter query and the cover letter plus separate query.

- How and where to submit your query.

Naturally, all this would be developed with much more detail, with examples from successful queries and author's bios, for both new and experienced writers.

As a writing teacher (I am a faculty member at Parson's School of Design, teaching "Magazine Writing") and a literary agent of more than ten years' experience, I have noticed that many people actually have significant qualifications (like the school teacher writing "When Your Child Is Having Trouble in School") and never think to mention them. I will show how professional, personal, social, romantic, academic, and other experience can be translated in the author's bio into "expertise." Also I will try to convince readers to overcome their modesty and toot their horns *loudly*—it really works.

In addition to my publishing and teaching background, I have sold my own writing to many magazines and newspapers, including *Harper's*, *Family Circle*, *Cosmopolitan*, *Glamour*, *Penthouse*, and maybe twenty others. If you wish, I could send clips of my published pieces, several of which deal with various kinds of writing.

I look forward to your reaction.

Sincerely yours,

Lisa Collier Cool

Figure 12-2
SEPARATE QUERY

One of my students, Maria Neuda, wrote this and was offered $300 for the article. I've omitted her address.

TUMBLING AWAY STRESS
by Maria Neuda

You're close to 40—or feel like you are. You have a demanding job and a mate with equally important demands. Sometimes in the middle of the day, if you're even aware enough of your own needs to notice, you feel your stomach is totally in knots. At the end of the day, your nerves feel like they're racing 100 miles per hour or you've got a migraine.

Sound familiar? It was to me until I found a sport that fit easily into a hectic schedule (one class per week), increased my sense of confidence and power, and motivated me to exercise regularly during the week.

What was it? Gymnastics: a perfect sport, I discovered, for a stress-filled life.

Benefits

- Relax in a noncompetitive environment.
- Enjoy the excitement of new sensations (try a drop seat on the trampoline).
- Develop an agile body and mind, along with an overall sense of harmony and well being.
- Feel, in the words of an expert, "light . . . powerful . . . decisive . . . free."

Who Can Do It

- You can start at any age. (I started at 39.)
- You can be any weight. (Well, almost. But Sue Ellen weighs 170 pounds and has the best balance of anyone in her class.)
- You don't have to have special talent.

Barriers

- Psychological fears in starting as an adult: how to overcome.

Requirements

- The basic equipment: floor mats for tumbling, uneven parallel bars, balance beams, horse. Also, trampoline.
- Importance of a good coach: what "spotting" means.
- Expense: class (reasonable) and clothing (minimal).
- Maintenance during week: 10 to 15 minutes of stretching, daily if possible. Why you'll *want* to do it.

[The query then added topical references and names of experts.]

My credentials: I am a professional business writer of training and promotional materials. I have first-hand knowledge of stress, having to meet deadlines, determine and meet the needs of my clients, and cope with the pressures of project delays caused by vendors. I also have first-hand knowledge of starting gymnastics as an adult. I love the sport, look forward to class. I *have* been able to cope with stress better, and I'd like to share this knowledge with your readers.

Would you agree they'd enjoy reading about it?

13

Submission Strategies That Sell

As an agent, I've frequently been hired by authors who've submitted their own work widely and unsuccessfully. Often the problem was that the author had been sending the right material to the wrong publishers: I've seen mistakes as obvious as peddling pro-choice material to Catholic publishers or sending complex, literary works to juvenile publishers. By adopting more appropriate submission strategies, I've turned such "unsalable" work into successful publications. Other times I've been able to succeed through sheer perseverance when the author has failed, as in the case when I was hired by a novelist with twenty rejections behind him. To his amazement I was able to sell the book on one submission. Why? I sent it to the *only* major publisher he had not yet approached, and luckily hit pay dirt there.

Assembling Your Submission List

There's a lot more to submitting your work than trudging over to the post office, manuscript in hand. Your first problem is deciding exactly where to submit the article or query. Let's say you've just written an article called "Meeting Men through Video-dating." Here are some strategies to use to assemble your submission list (see Figure 13-1 for sample):

1. *It often pays to be obvious.* Since this topic is clearly slanted to single women, the most logical market choices are: *Glamour, Mademoiselle, Self, Cosmopolitan, Playgirl,* and *New Woman* since these publications cater to this audience.

2. *Look for more subtle marketing factors.* Since videodating is both new and relatively high priced, magazines catering to the fashionable or successful woman might be some other good markets. Add *Vogue, Harper's Bazaar, Savvy,* and *Working Woman* to your list. Maybe there's a woman's liberation angle here—after all, videodating lets women shop for men instead of waiting for the man to make the first move. Let's put *Ms.* on our list, remembering to stress this aspect in the covering letter.

3. *Slight shifts in slant can multiply marketing possibilities.* To get more mileage out of your videodating research, why not try to sell several videodating articles instead of just the one you've already written? You could target spin-off queries to men's magazines, "Your VCR or Mine?"; regional magazines, "The New York Videodating Scene"; ethnic/minority publications, "The Black Woman's Guide to Videodating"; maybe even retirement publications, "Videodating for Seniors." Related articles could open still more markets; for business publications "Cashing In on the Singles Boom;" for humor publications "Horror Movies—My Experience With Videodating;" and for industry publications "Videodating—A Profitable Sideline for Video Store Owners."

Figure 13-1
SAMPLE SUBMISSION SHEET FOR QUERY OR ARTICLE

(title) VIDEODATING

date sent	publication	response
1/15	Cosmopolitan	2/10 rejected, competing piece in the works
2/11	Self	2/28 rejected, form letter
3/1	Glamour	4/16 not for us, send other ideas
4/20	Playgirl	5/28 sale, $750

4. *Don't limit your list to magazines.* Articles on current trends— like our videodating piece—as well as human interest stories, profiles, sports, business, new technology, and a variety of other articles may be good bets for submission to newspapers, Sunday supplements, and feature syndicates. Newspapers and feature syndicates prefer short articles, 500 to 750 words; or break a longer article into a three- or four-part series of short articles.

5. *Never stop digging for new markets until the piece is sold.* While our submission list now includes dozens of good prospects, it never hurts to learn of additional markets. Study *Writer's Market,* running your finger down the various categories listed in the table of contents. I just did and found three more potential markets for the videodating piece under the heading "Lifestyles": *Albuquerque Singles Scene Magazine, Florida Singles Magazine and Date Book* and *Modern Singles.* Also check *Writer's Digest* and *The Writer* each month for new markets that might be right for your piece.

6. *Start with the top markets and work your way down.* Why sell a piece for $50 when some other publication might pay $500? By hitting the best paying markets first, you'll avoid unwittingly cheating yourself out of potential profits. To organize your submission list, research markets until you have determined the approximate pay scale of each likely prospect. Then prepare a submission card with the best paying market on the top of the list and the worst paying one at the bottom. Taking the time to get organized before you start submitting has several advantages. You avoid missing high-paying markets through scattergun submissions. If the piece is rejected, you're ready to get it back out the same day to the next market on the list. And when you do sell the piece, you may be able to *resell* it to one or more of the markets you didn't get to the first time around.

7. *Once you have quantity, go for quality.* Once you have your basic list, upgrade it with these two steps. First, read at least one issue of each target publication to make sure your piece really is suitable. Inappropriate submissions waste your time and postage, as well as irritate editors. Second, check *Magazine Index* or *Reader's Guide* at the library to learn if any of your target publications have covered it within two years. For general interest topics like sex or money, don't worry if other articles have appeared recently as long as your exact slant hasn't been duplicated. For more specialized articles like "Adopting Foreign Children," you're unlikely to make a sale to a magazine that's done *anything* on the topic even if the other article was handled quite differently.

Manuscript Mechanics

While there are various schools of thought on such points as the use of title pages, where to put the page numbers, and other aspects of manuscript typing, here's the approach I always use:

For articles of four pages or more, make a title page. Space down to the middle of the page and center your title, typing in capital letters. Space down four spaces and center the word "by" in lower case letters. Space down four more spaces and center your name or pseudonym *exactly* as you'd like to see it in print. Type your legal name, address, and home and office numbers, with area codes, on the lower right-hand side of the page, double-spaced. See Figure 13-2 for a model title page.

If your article is three pages or less in length, or you're typing a query that will be attached to a cover letter, type your name, address, and phone numbers on the upper left-hand corner of the first page in single spacing. Space down four spaces, shift to double spacing, and type your title in capital letters, centered. Double-space and center "by" on the next line. Double-space again and center your preferred byline. Space down four lines, indent five spaces, and start the first paragraph. See Figure 13-3 for a sample first page for a short article or query.

As you type, remember that neatness does count. Put a fresh ribbon in the typewriter for nice, dark pages; and make sure your keys are clean—those smudgy "o"s and "a"s can be tough to read. Triple-check for typos—there's nothing that puts an editor off more quickly than discovering typing errors on the first page; on subsequent pages make sure there's no more than one neat correction per page; otherwise retype where necessary.

For all manuscript pages of a longer article, and all pages after the first of a shorter article, type your last name followed by two dashes and the page number on the top of each page, either at the center or on the right. Double-space all material except long book excerpts, which are single-spaced. Use one inch margins all around the page: top, bottom, and both sides. Pica type will produce twenty-six double-spaced lines on each page, resulting in about 250 words to the page.

Always photocopy your work before submitting. Most writers keep the original at home and submit the photocopy. This protects you against loss or damage in the post or at the magazine. Make sure your photocopy is from a decent shop that doesn't use that dreadful-smelling photocopying process. Also check each page to make sure it's completely legible and in the correct sequence.

After copying, attach the manuscript pages with a single staple on the upper left corner. No cover is necessary, but if you wish, you can put the article inside a plain manila file folder with a label on the front giving the title and your byline. Avoid colored folders and any form of binding; editors consider these amateurish. Attach your cover letter to the manuscript or folder with a paper clip—don't staple it.

Letters to Editors

Though a few writers don't believe in using cover letters with their submissions, I feel a manuscript without a cover letter is like encountering a stranger who doesn't bother to introduce himself. An enticing cover letter, on the other hand, can inspire a busy editor to read your piece quickly, rather than letting it languish in a pile of unread submissions. Compose your cover letter with the same careful attention you'd give to a letter accompanying your resume on a job application.

Never address your submission to "The Editor"; always address it to some specific person within the organization. Letters addressed to "The Editor" rate the lowest priority and are normally considered by junior personnel assigned to "slush," the publishing term for unsolicited material. A letter that's addressed to one of the editors, on the other hand, is usually considered by that editor's assistant or sometimes by the editor herself. Either way, it usually gets faster consideration by a more experienced person, increasing your odds of success.

But to whom should you address the submission? Start by scanning the magazine's masthead, looking for an individual designated as articles editor. If this title doesn't appear, other good prospects are one of the senior editors or the managing editor. Don't submit to the person heading the masthead, usually described as editor, because this person is usually an executive with minimal involvement in buying and assigning articles. Also avoid submitting to contributing editors. These are usually freelance writers who work regularly for the magazine, rather

Figure 13-2
MODEL TITLE PAGE

THE FASTEST GAME IN TOWN

by

Susan Struggling Scrivner

Susan S. Scrivner

19 Aspiring Lane

New Rochelle, NY 10802

(914)555-1212

Figure 13-3
FIRST PAGE OF SHORT MANUSCRIPT

Lisa Collier Cool
000 Street Address
City, State 00000
(000) 000-0000

KEEP THE CHANGE!

by

Lisa Collier Cool

I confess. I am not now, nor have I ever been, thrifty. I get no kick from cents off—I'm waiting for the day when they start passing out free samples at Tiffany's. Until then, I'm content to let others harvest the bonanzas of double coupons and warehouse sales. While I'm not adverse to finding a real bargain, the allure of taking a ten mile detour to avoid a 25 cent toll is lost on me. Frankly, I scarcely consider nickels and dimes real money. But, even though I'm somewhat mystified by the thrill some of my friends get from saving a few pennies on panty hose, I don't begrudge them their pleasure. Where I do draw the line is when they try to reform *me*.

I'll never understand why my friends—and even complete strangers—are so eager to save *my* money for me. People who'd never dream of telling you how to manage your love life or career, will, at the drop of a price tag, try to take over your financial affairs. "You buy at *retail*," they shriek as if you'd just

than acquiring editors on the magazine's staff.

If the magazine boasts a large number of senior editors, or if you're unsure which editor would be most appropriate for your submission, telephone the publication. Ask the receptionist which editor is responsible for health articles or whatever category your piece fits into. Since some secretaries treat such information as if it were defense secrets, if you have trouble getting the appropriate editor's name, call back and say you're a literary agent updating your submission records—you'll get the answer immediately. And since a literary agent is merely someone who markets an author's work, there's nothing untruthful about claiming to be your own agent.

Since publishing has a high turnover of personnel, it's often wise to call and verify that the editor you've decided to submit to is still there. A magazine you see on the stands represents the status quo of three or four months ago; your editor may have moved on to another publication or have been promoted to a different position within the magazine.

Format your cover letter like a standard business letter (see Figure 13-4, cover letter). In typing the letter, take pains to get the editor's name right and to attach the correct title to it. There's nothing more annoying, especially for the unusually named, than to see one's name written incorrectly. Address all female editors as "Ms." unless they specifically list some other honorific in the directory you're using. Also be sure to spell the publication's name correctly and put the apostrophe (if any) in the correct position— you'd be surprised how many writers slip up on these small, but important points.

In the body of your letter mention the name of the attached article or query, with a one-line description if the title doesn't make the subject crystal clear. Next, mention any special sales points: "When America's 33 million single women complain that 'a good man is hard to find,' they're speaking quite literally. With only 25 million single men available, today's single woman needs some bold new approaches to beat the odds, which is why I feel my 'Videodating' article is particularly timely right now." Also mention any other points that might help: "In June you expressed an interest in seeing any new ideas I might have. . . ." Finish with highlights of your bio: "I am highly qualified to write, 'Riches After Retirement,' since I started my nationally franchised restaurant chain at age 65, and made my first million six

Figure 13-4
SAMPLE COVERING LETTER

BRIAN FIRSTTIMER
521 Arbitrage Circle
Cincinnati, OH 15242
(513) 555-1212

October 20, 1986

Ms. Charla Lawhon
Assistant Managing Editor
Metropolitan Home
750 Third Avenue
New York, NY 10017

Dear Ms. Lawhon:

Enclosed is my article, REFINANCING YOUR HOME. With the recent drop in interest rates, many homeowners are wondering if it's time to refinance. My article explains the various considerations, and offers detailed guidance on finding the right mortgage deal.

Having spent fifteen years as a bank loan officer, I am highly familiar with the typical questions consumers ask about refinancing, as well as the technicalities of the various types of mortgages now being offered. Attached is a course listing for a seminar I taught last spring on home mortgages.

I'll look forward to your reaction with interest.

Sincerely yours,

Brian Firsttimer

months later." However, don't fall in love with the sound of your words; limit the letter to a few paragraphs at most.

In any query or cover letter, avoid any remarks that might create a negative impression. Don't say, "I'll be happy to revise it to your specifications," "I know the subject's been done before, but. . . ." "This is my first effort directed at publication," "I've rewritten this ten times," or "I'm sure you'll agree this blockbuster effort will electrify the public"—all statements I've frequently seen in submissions directed to my agency. Also avoid the humorous or cute approach; editors have heard just about every joke you can imagine; they weren't amused the first time around and won't be now.

Though a self-addressed stamped envelope—one with enough room and postage to hold your manuscript—should be attached, I think that it's best not to refer to the SASE in your cover letter at all. An SASE is for the editor's use in rejecting material, and rejection isn't a concept that should be alluded to, even obliquely, in a letter designed to sell the material. However, if you insist on including a reference to the envelope, put: "A self-addressed stamped envelope is attached for your reply."

Multiple Submissions

Let's face it. Most magazine editors are slow, slow, slow. Sending out unique submissions of each article or query isn't the most efficient way to market your work. A multiple submission gets your work before all likely markets simultaneously, ensuring quick results on each idea. The trouble is, though most publications will consider simultaneous submissions, many editors dislike them or feel the multiple submission is a tool that only top writers should employ.

Should you give up the benefits of multiple submissions because of this lingering editorial prejudice? Not at all. As one agent I know points out, there are three sets of rules in publishing: editors' rules, agents' rules, and writers' rules. Editors' rules say, "Don't send out multiple submissions because they make me work harder." Agents' rules say, "Multiple submissions are okay for me, but not for writers who are submitting to my agency." Writers let themselves get intimidated by the editors' and agents' rules, and forget that they can write their own rules, including one that says, "Use the best submission technique to sell your work quickly, efficiently, and profitably."

To counter negative editorial attitudes, the most effective way to use multiple submissions is *secretly*. Here's how: after determining which markets on your submission list will consider multiple submissions, photocopy as many copies of your query or article as you have markets. Then type a personal cover letter to each editor, avoiding any reference to other submissions. Don't photocopy the body of your cover letter—the names and addresses won't look right when you add them on your typewriter.

When assembling your letters and labels, make sure the correct letter is inside the correctly labeled envelope. Your whole secret strategy is unraveled when an editor from *Modern Bride* opens her envelope to discover a letter addressed to the editor at *Bridal Planner*.

If you're the cautious type, you can hedge your bets on a multiple submission by sending the piece only to half the potential markets at a time. If some fatal flaw is detected by the first group of editors, you can easily revise before the second round of submissions go out. (If you're even more cautious, submit only to those publishers which announce no objection to multiple submissions in their writers' guidelines or market listings.)

You're probably wondering what to do if multiple offers result from your secret multiple submissions. The answer is you should be so lucky! In my entire writing career it's never happened to me. If you do hit upon an idea that two or more editors want to buy, you have a couple of options. First, if the markets don't overlap with each other—a man's magazine and a woman's magazine for example—write *two* different articles on the subject, slanting them appropriately. If the markets do overlap, accept the highest bid and decline the other offers, informing the other publications that you received a better offer.

But won't this land you on some kind of publishing blacklist? No—actually you'll be enhancing your future prospects, though it may not seem that way at first. As an agent I've often encountered the wrath of the rejected editor. After a heated auction, I've had editors threaten never to buy from me again, to sue my agency, and once to run a large ad in my local paper denouncing me! Since editors are accustomed to giving orders and watching writers jump, they're unaccustomed to failure. But these tempests blow over in a day or two, leaving the editor with a frustrated desire to buy from that writer. Next time that editor will act swiftly to buy your work, and avoid the frustration of being rejected again. I've seen this psychology in action time and time again—and used it profitably. So can you.

Should you use multiple submissions for all your work? Three situations when a unique submission might be preferable are: for editors you know personally, for very speedy editors, and for material with a very limited audience, say two or three magazines at most.

Mailing Manuscripts

The post office can be hard on manuscripts. For finished articles, put the unfolded article plus a piece of heavy cardboard in a 9 by 12 manila envelope, or use a #5 padded mailing envelope. Type the editor's name, title, publication, and address on a letterhead or other label, being sure to add your return address if you're not using a personalized label. Queries can be folded in thirds and placed in a #10 business envelope or sent unfolded in a 9 by 12 manila envelope.

Use first-class mail—a typical article can be sent for less than a dollar at current rates. For longer manuscripts you can save a little with fourth class (manuscript rate) mail, but the pennies you save will cost you in longer mailing time. Avoid special delivery mail; I've often found it actually *delays* arrival. Unless you are on a very tight deadline, the expense of express mail or private delivery service is unnecessary.

If you'd like a record of when the manuscript arrived, ask the post office to send it "return receipt requested." Some authors like to send stamped self-addressed post cards for the editor to mail upon receipt of the material, but I've found that editors often overlook these cards; the post office's return receipt is sent automatically on arrival.

The Waiting Game

How long should you wait for a response? On their tip sheets and in *Writer's Market,* most magazines indicate how long they usually need to consider material. Typically, most magazines take between two and eight weeks to answer. If you've received no response in the specified time period, wait an extra week, then send a tactful reminder. If any new developments have occurred in the field since you sent the query, an updating note can be an effective reminder: "Perhaps you saw last week's *60 Minutes* presentation of this case, or the current *Time* magazine report on it. The subject seems to be really heating up, so I'm eager to get to work on it. How's the submission faring with you?"

Inexperienced writers often imagine that their reminders will spark rejection. Actually this *never* happens; instead your reminder might speed the inevitable, which might be a rejection or might not. A telephoned reminder—not to the editor but to his or her secretary—can also be effective.

Is no news good news? Sometimes. One writer friend of mine had an article bought *nine* months after sending the query. She'd long since written the topic off as a nonstarter and moved on to other projects by the time the contract arrived. Other times no news can just mean that your material is gathering dust or languishing in some dead end of the organization maze. Your reminder can help blast it out of whatever black hole it's fallen into.

Changing Rejection into Acceptance

Almost all writers collect a certain number of turndowns. However, keep rejection in the proper perspective. Rejection can have a bright side; I've often found that editors had gained a positive impression of my work even as they were sending back my latest query. Sounds paradoxical? Editors frequently have to return perfectly good ideas because they conflict with upcoming projects, fall into some area the publisher had labeled temporarily off limits, or just don't fit into the format. But the editor still realizes the material has merit and looks favorably on the *next* query from that writer.

Another possibility is that your taste just doesn't click with a particular editor's. Never give up after just a few turndowns; doggedly send the article to *every* possible market. Unless your writing becomes hopelessly dated—forget about that Halley's Comet piece if you haven't sold it yet—you can outwait the editors. After you've sent it everywhere, combed writer's magazines for new markets, and done everything you can think of, *don't* quit. Instead start over; editors may have left magazines you've already tried, and new, more receptive ones may have joined the publication.

Keep your eye out for new developments on the subject. I

had a query on home computers rejected by *Woman's Day* on the grounds that relatively few of their readers had home computers. Foolishly I gave up. A few years later I picked up *Woman's Day*— and, you guessed it, there was a long article on home computers. No, they hadn't stolen my idea; I was too early the first time and didn't think to go back to them when the home computer boom I'd predicted actually materialized. By keeping on top of your subject until you sell it, you can avoid my mistake by recontacting likely markets whenever events indicate that your subject is hot.

Study your rejection letters carefully. While a form rejection tells you nothing, any personal comment or criticism should be viewed as encouraging. Anyone who takes the time to criticize you is doing you a huge favor; don't let negative comments wound you. Instead see if you can correct the problem and if so, send revised material. If not, try another query on the same editor. When an editor says, "This one didn't work, send other ideas," believe it. Send three or four queries off as quickly as possible while the favorable impression is still fresh in the editor's mind.

Increase the odds of acceptance by submitting to magazines you enjoy reading. You must believe in yourself and the power of your work to sell others on it. This positive attitude about your work will register on editors and impress them.

Keep busy. Send out your queries and articles regularly. Don't languish by the mailbox waiting for answers; get back to the typewriter and keep turning those queries and articles out. Try to resubmit rejected material the day it comes back. Keep the flow going by establishing regular marketing routines—studying likely markets, creating new queries regularly, setting submission goals. Paper your walls with rejections if you must, but be persistent—*success is often waiting for you on the far side of failure.*

14
Anatomy of a Magazine

I

f I get a form rejection, has anyone actually read the submission? Do editors steal writers' ideas? Why do editors take so long to read queries? Do I have any control over the editing? When is that piece I sold last month going to be published?

The inner workings of magazine publishing are a mystery to many writers, few of whom actually met an editor personally or visited a magazine's office. Dealing with magazines by mail, as most of us do, offers very limited opportunities to study the editorial process. While an acceptance letter tells you all you need to know, you can't very well cross-examine a rejection slip to learn whether the piece was a near-miss or a total washout. Behind the closed doors of the magazine are the answers to *why* one piece sells, another misses—information you could put to use in marketing your work and increasing the odds of a sale.

To get the inside story, I traced the path of two imaginary submissions to *Penthouse* and *Cosmopolitan* by interviewing high-ranking editors and their staff.

The Envelopes, Please

Neither of your submissions would be lonely along the way—the mail carrier drops off twenty or thirty submissions a day at *Penthouse* and totes a hefty fifty more over to *Cosmopolitan*, editors estimate. At both magazines your letter is opened by an editorial assistant; three divvy up unsolicited submissions to *Penthouse* and six share *Cosmo*'s.

What prompts such a heavy volume of submissions—5,000 to 7,500 to *Penthouse* and 12,500 to *Cosmopolitan* annually? The two magazines are attractive to writers for the same reason as they are attractive to advertisers—their large circulation ensures wide exposure of ads and articles. And since advertising rates are based on circulation size, both publications share some of the wealth with their writers through high pay rates, making them doubly alluring to would-be contributors. Throughout the magazine and newspaper industry the same rule applies: the higher the circulation, the higher the pay to writers.

Both publications have enjoyed an upsurge of success in recent years. Though writers for *Penthouse*'s maiden U.S. edition in 1969 would have only reached 235,000 readers, today the publication claims to be "the Number One selling men's magazine," with a circulation of over 5,000,000 copies a month. Its article rates, which start at $2,000, are sufficiently elastic to attract such top writers as Isaac Asimov, James Baldwin, Gael Greene, Michael Korda, and Harrison Salisbury.

Cosmopolitan's success story is equally dramatic. Though the magazine was established in 1886, it experienced a complete revolution in content in 1965 when Helen Gurley Brown took over. Under her leadership, monthly circulation has risen from 740,000 to the current level of over 3,000,000, with a tenfold increase in sales of advertising pages. Currently rates start at $750, but go much higher for top contributors like Susan Jacoby, William F. Buckley, Jr., Rex Reed, Erica Jong, and John Updike.

What sort of odds does *your* submission face? In the past, *Penthouse* bought about seventy to eighty manuscripts a year, as well as book excerpts; but an increased emphasis on pictorials, both nude and action/adventure photography, has reduced the number slightly. A typical issue contains three editorial slots which are filled with articles, interviews, fiction, and book excerpts, plus a freelance-written essay and two reader-written humor sections. Nine regular columns complete the table of contents. Three of *Penthouse*'s twelve annual issues are thicker, with twice as many editorial slots.

Not only does *Cosmopolitan* run a substantially greater amount of text, but they've recently *expanded* the editorial content. A typical issue now contains twenty-five articles and features (short articles), two or three short stories or novel excerpts and one or two editorials—all written by freelancers—plus twelve regular columns. However, managing editor Guy Flatley estimates that only three or four of these articles and features start out as author's queries; the rest are staff-generated ideas which are then approved by Helen Gurley Brown and assigned to freelancers whose work the magazine likes.

The Wrong Stuff

Though editorial assistants lack the power to buy, they are free to *reject*, since their function is to screen out unsuitable material. Typically, the assistants look at both *form* and *content*. Any deviation from standard format such as a handwritten query or page after page of densely typed single spacing earns you poor marks, or even rejection. Your actual words are then scrutinized for general suitability for the magazine. According to editorial assistants Laura Berland (*Penthouse*) and Susan Benson (*Cosmopolitan*), the leading reasons for rejection at this level are:

Obvious lack of professionalism: the author has no idea of how to write a query.

Unfamiliarity with the magazine's content: *Cosmopolitan*, described by editors as being targeted to "young women interested in getting the most out of their personal and professional life," recently received a query for an article on "The History of the Spanish Civil War." Actually *Cosmopolitan*'s editorial formula is a judicious mix of seven main article topics: sex, male/female relationships, health and beauty, celebrities and gossip, careers, self-help, and profiles, plus occasional personal experience, humor, round-up, and true crime articles. Fiction usually falls into either the romance or romantic suspense category. *Penthouse*, best known for its exposé articles and equally exposed models, as well as for its lively fiction, regularly receives poetry and other equally inappropriate material.

Fuzzy writing: "If I can't figure out what the writer's trying to say by the middle of the first page, it's a pretty sure bet for rejection," Susan Benson says, adding that she always reads each query to the end.

Similarity to recently published pieces: "It's surprising how many people try to sell us something we just did a month or so ago," complains Benson. While it's impossible to know what the magazine has in the works, checking the last twelve issues will save such time- and postage-wasting submissions.

Your chances of getting past the assistant vary according to the length of time she's been at the magazine. With just two months' experience at *Penthouse,* Laura Berland estimates that she refers 40 percent of the queries she sees upward, while Susan Benson, a three-year veteran with *Cosmopolitan,* rejects four out of five queries that cross her desk. Berland uses form rejection slips to reply, while Benson personally types a polite note. Neither gives any editorial comments, though Benson refers good queries that conflict with existing projects to managing editor Guy Flatley in case he wants to encourage the author to send other ideas, or work on one of the magazine's own ideas. (To ensure the return of unsuitable material, Berland reminds authors to send a self-addressed stamped envelope with their submissions.)

Up the Organization

Your query, however, strikes an editorial assistant as professionally formatted and interesting, so it moves up a rung to an *editor. Penthouse* has five nonfiction editors, *Cosmopolitan* six. Each has an additional editor to handle fiction. In addition to considering submissions, editing assigned manuscripts, and dealing with agents and book publishers, some of these editors also edit the regular columns. None of these editors has final authority to make assignments, but can only reject the material or pass it up to his or her superior, which would be executive editor Peter Bloch of *Penthouse* or managing editor Guy Flatley of *Cosmopolitan.*

Where does the passing of the buck stop—and the assignment buck start? At *Penthouse* Peter Bloch makes the final buying decision. While no formal story conferences are held, Bloch often consults informally with other editors before giving his verdict. However, if your idea seems to have major potential for provoking controversy or lawsuits, or you demand an exceptionally large fee, Bloch might discuss it with editor-in-chief and publisher Robert Guccione before going ahead. Multimillionaire Guccione takes an active role in managing *Penthouse:* suggesting articles like the 1985 "Medical Genocide" series, meeting with the staff to talk about the future evolution of the magazine's editorial content, even photographing "Pet" pictorials on occasion. His empire also includes *Omni, NEWLOOK, Variations, Forum,* and other publishing, entertainment, and merchandising ventures.

At *Cosmopolitan,* editor-in-chief Helen Gurley Brown makes the final decision on all assignments. After one editor responds favorably to your query, he or she writes a short memo about it, passes it on to Guy Flatley for a second opinion memo, and then forwards it to Brown. (If Flatley is presenting the idea, he too must seek another editor's opinion before giving it to Brown.) While she frequently follows the editors' suggestions, Brown sometimes rejects material editors recommend to her. "Helen Gurley Brown *is Cosmopolitan,*" says Flatley. "Everything in the magazine passes through her hands for approval."

What do these top editors expect from your material? Bloch's editorial checklist for queries would include: "professional appearance, going beyond the obvious—you'd be surprised how many people simply crib recent newspaper coverage of their story—the author's background and knowledge of the subject, the inherent interest of the idea, and writing style." Of these he rates professional appearance least important—"I'd buy a handwritten query, *if* it met all my other criteria." Occasionally he will overlook an overly academic style if the author is a true expert in his or her field.

Since most of the queries Bloch reads have been pre-screened, few of his rejections are due to obvious flaws. Instead the problems tend to be more subtle; often he finds the material to be "just not quite right for us"—a catchall phrase he defines as "material that is more than adequate, but perhaps too similar to something we've already done; topics that may not be very important to our readers, or not exclusive enough; or a good subject written up in a boring way." Like most editors, Bloch's list of reasons to reject is longer than those to accept, but he looks at each idea with an open mind. "I don't start out to reject, I just want to see what it is."

At *Cosmopolitan,* Guy Flatley looks for queries that are "relevant to our readers; written in a warm, friendly style, without a lot of cliches; and seem genuine in feeling." For heavily factual topics, the author's own expertise or the caliber of experts to be interviewed is also important. As with *Penthouse,* the more expert the author is, the less important writing style becomes: "We have people who could rewrite something from, say, a psychiatrist, if the information was valuable and original enough to warrant the effort," says Flatley. Even if your query passed all these tests, it still might not be bought, cautions Bloch. "With our limited editorial space, we have to be tremendously restrained about buying. With only three editorial slots in each issue, a lot of great ideas have to be turned down simply for lack of room."

The Making of an Editor

What sort of expertise do Bloch and Flatley bring to evaluating submissions? Both started out as English majors—Bloch is a graduate of Queens College in New York City, while Flatley got his degree at St. Louis University. Both found the working world unimpressed with their diplomas; Flatley was indignant when the *New York Times* assessed his worth as a copy boy at $49.50 a week in 1959. "Even then, that wasn't a whole lot," he says. Bloch also began his editorial career at the *New York Times;* after stints in the army and as a computer programmer he planted himself in the *Times*'s personnel office and asked "for any job, however menial, that would get me started here." He was promptly hired, as a news assistant, in 1971.

Here, Bloch's and Flatley's career paths diverged: after two years at the *Times,* Bloch realized that with five people ahead of him in line for the first opening as editor, his prospects might be better elsewhere, and joined *Penthouse* as a copy editor. Working his way up through the ranks, he was promoted to interview editor, articles editor, senior editor, and ultimately executive editor, his current position. Flatley, on the other hand, flourished at the *Times,* spending the next eighteen years there: his positions include clerk on the picture desk, and a variety of positions in the *Arts and Leisure* section. He also wrote celebrity profiles and a movie column for the paper—an interest he now pursues for *Cosmopolitan* (Flatley writes the "COSMO Goes to the Movies" column and celebrity articles for the magazine, in addition to his editorial tasks). Lured away from the *Times* eight years ago, Flatley started at *Cosmo* in his current position, managing editor.

Sold!

Once Peter Bloch or Helen Gurley Brown approved your query, one of the editors would offer you an assignment to write the piece. *Penthouse* uses a printed contract and normally buys world rights or world periodical rights; *Cosmopolitan* types an assignment letter, usually for world publishing rights, but other arrangements are possible. While inexperienced authors often assume that the contract they are offered is "standard," actually both publications are somewhat flexible about terms—*if the author raises the point.* (It's hardly in an editor's interest to instruct writers on the art of negotiation.) Often you can arrange to retain dramatic and book-publishing rights to your article or fiction, but since both magazines have foreign editions which reprint articles from the American edition as well as originate their own material, foreign rights are important to both publications and are seldom, if ever, relinquished to the writer. If one or more of the foreign editions did pick up your piece, you would probably receive additional checks.

Penthouse would pay you $2,000 or more for a feature of 2,500 words; $3,000 and up for articles of 5,000 words. A feature of 2,500 to 3,000 words would earn you at least $750 at *Cosmo,* an article of 4,500 words, $1,500 or more. Both magazines give periodic raises to writers who work for them frequently. Your kill fee in case of rejection of an assigned article would be 25 percent of the acceptance price at *Penthouse,* 15 percent at *Cosmopolitan. Cosmo*'s typical deadline is two months; *Penthouse* allows you anywhere from one month to one year, depending on the complexity of the subject and the urgency of publication. How important are these deadlines? Very, says Claudia Valentino, managing editor of *Penthouse:* "Writers have no idea of the production problems that can result from a week's delay in delivery." At *Cosmopolitan* the exact date of delivery is less important for most articles, but editors suggest that writers ask for an extension *before* the deadline passes.

You and Your Editor

While many writers have no further contact with their editor until the piece is complete, Bloch finds some writers like to report in when the research is completed to discuss their findings. Flatley usually reviews the project with the author over the phone when offering an assignment, explaining his editorial preferences and any pitfalls to avoid. After you begin work, consulting your editor about any questions or problems you encounter is a wise move—a quick phone call may prevent time-consuming rewrites. If you plan any dramatic shift in direction from the approach described in your original query, it's essential to get editorial approval; your new angle might not appeal to the magazine or conflict with other projects, causing possible rejection.

When your completed piece is delivered, your editor reads it first, then passes it up through the chain of command. Peter Bloch and Helen Gurley Brown render the final verdicts for their respective publications. If your piece has major problems, both publications offer you a chance to revise before putting through a kill fee. Guy Flatley tries to indicate the odds of acceptance after revising, providing detailed editorial comments to guide the author. To increase the likelihood of approval after revision, editors suggest that you study the exact comments given you very carefully, and avoid the temptation to revise material that was *not* criticized, lest you create new problems. For minor problems, you might be asked to revise, or the editors might accept the piece and edit it themselves. Requests for revisions are relatively rare at *Penthouse,* fairly frequent at *Cosmopolitan.*

Approval takes one to three weeks. Flatley tries to read assigned pieces the day they arrive, but needs an additional week to gather a second opinion and Brown's verdict. Bloch estimates that three weeks are required to get the OK from *Penthouse.* Vacations and holidays may delay the process, but there's no harm in sending off a tactful reminder if you're kept waiting more than four or five weeks. Such notes never *cause* rejection, as some authors fear, but merely accelerate the verdict, whether positive or negative. *Cosmo* pays you ten days after acceptance; *Penthouse* takes about three weeks. If you don't receive your check after a few weeks, telephone the editor's assistant, who will trace it through the organizational maze.

The Editor's Craft

When your work is complete, the work of *Penthouse* and *Cosmopolitan* is just beginning. While writers are often baffled by the long delay between acceptance and publication, bringing out a monthly magazine is a complex process. The first step is to select a publication date for your piece. While *Cosmopolitan* only schedules articles after acceptance, *Penthouse*, like many other magazines, sometimes schedules articles by reliable authors as soon as the assignment is given, allowing for speedier publication. Late delivery by the author creates inconvenience, possible extra expense, or can even prevent publication of the piece, as well as damaging your odds of repeat sales to the magazine.

How quickly your piece is scheduled for publication varies. Extraordinarily timely articles might appear in *Penthouse* just four months after acceptance, but typically it takes eight months to see your work in print. Twenty percent of *Penthouse*'s accepted articles are never published at all, usually for one of three reasons: a turn in events that makes your piece out of date before publication; a hotter topic preempting your space; or a subsequent purchase of superior material on your topic or a related one (like an excerpt from a best-seller on the subject). If this happens to you, you can usually get the rights back eventually.

At *Cosmopolitan*, speed of publication depends on the category your article falls into. If there's a heavy inventory of emotional/self help pieces, a year or more could pass before publication; but if there's a shortage of sex articles, the piece could be in print in five or six months after approval. Accepted pieces are filed according to originating editor and assigned a color-coded marker on a large bulletin board listing all pieces currently in house. To plan an issue, Flatley first selects the nine "major" or long articles to fit the seven categories, using the colors to remind himself which pieces are available, then selects a mix of fourteen or fifteen features. (Fiction is scheduled by fiction editor Betty Kelly.) This breakdown is then reviewed by Helen Gurley Brown, who might change some of the selections. The selected pieces are then distributed to one of the six editors for editing. (Flatley does no editing himself.) Since *Cosmopolitan*'s articles are less topical than *Penthouse*'s, virtually every accepted piece eventually is published, says editor Susan Korones, though some writers may have to wait as long as three years to see their work in print.

At *Penthouse* the editor who bought your piece would also edit it. If Peter Bloch were your editor, he'd work on your piece at home, since his time at the office is consumed by interdepartmental meetings, phone calls, and lunches with agents, authors, and book publishers. Bloch's philosophy of editing can be summed up as "less is more," since preserving the author's voice is a priority with him. "The less editing I do, the happier I am," he says. "*Any-*

thing could be reworded, but where's the advantage in that?"

At *Cosmopolitan,* editing may be light to vigorous, reports features text editor Susan Korones. "I start by looking at length—most articles can benefit from some trimming and tightening." Trimming is also beneficial to the magazine; by squeezing in a few additional ads here and there each issue becomes more profitable. Style is then modified, if necessary, to fit *Cosmopolitan's* customary friendly, enthusiastic tone; and finally subheads may be added to break up long chunks of text. A word count is also taken to aid in calculating how many lines of text the article will occupy in the magazine.

After editing, *Cosmopolitan* retypes your article and sends it to you for review. To make sure your changes can be included, a deadline for your corrections will be attached to the edited copy. Reading and returning your edited piece with any necessary corrections promptly will prevent annoying mistakes or careless editing from making their way into print. However, confine your changes to corrections—rewriting is no longer possible at this stage.

What if you don't care for the editing? While Flatley finds that most authors like the way their piece is edited, if you don't, "a compromise can usually be negotiated with the copy department." At *Penthouse* your edited article is sent off to the typesetters before you see it, then sent to you if you've requested to see edited copy or if heavy changes have been made. *Cosmo* sends your piece off for typesetting after you've reviewed it.

After typesetting, your piece is returned to the magazine in galleys—long strips of paper containing the printed text in columns of the correct width, minus its headline and blurb, which are usually set separately along with other display type. After proofreading, the copy department checks spelling of names and places, confirms quotes, and may ask for documentation of some of your facts. Retaining a list of telephone numbers and addresses of the people you interview and your research bibliography until publication lets you respond quickly and easily to such queries, preventing repeat trips to the library to confirm facts you already compiled. But don't expect the magazine to ferret out *every* error you've made—it's not practical for either publication to double-check everything you've written. Instead, fact checkers concentrate on easily verified material and statements that appear questionable in some way. "After a certain point you just have to trust the author to be reliable." Bloch says.

Next comes a legal review; *Penthouse* reserves it for more controversial investigative reports. "Anyone can threaten to sue," Bloch notes ruefully, "and a magazine like *Penthouse* is a natural target. People say to themselves, 'Bob Guccione has a lot of money, maybe he'll settle for $50 thousand.' But we never settle, and so far we've never lost a case—which shows just how careful we are." *Cosmopolitan* runs less controversial material, but takes an even more cautious approach—every single article in the magazine is reviewed. The legal department may request additional documentation from authors, especially of profile, gossip, or exposé articles. Good research is your best defense against potential lawsuits; be sure to use multiple sources for potentially libelous statements.

The Art of the Matter

Meanwhile the art department has not been idle. *Penthouse* sometimes commissions artwork as soon as the assignment is given, *Cosmopolitan* after the piece is accepted and scheduled. The art department, working with editors, decides on what sort of art treatment would best suit your text, and how much space to devote to it. Although magazines rarely consult authors on artwork, if you have suggestions, include them in your cover letter when you submit the piece. If you can provide artwork of professional quality, mention this in your original query—you might pick up an extra fee for your photos or sketches. If not, the magazine can draw on a network of photographers and illustrators. For a profile *Penthouse* might hire an artist to do a portrait or caricature of your profile subject; or *Cosmopolitan* might commission sketches for your emotional piece. Both magazines also use freelance photography and stock shots from photo services, as well as art.

Once the artwork is in house, it is sent off to an engraver to be photographed. Color artwork is shot by special cameras that separate it into the three primary colors, plus a fourth separation for black to enhance outlines, shadings, and contrast. Each of these separations consists of minute dots of red, yellow, blue, or black which the eye will merge into the full spectrum of colors as it looks at the printed page. (Black and white photos, rarely used by *Penthouse*, are also color separated by a special process for optimum reproduction; at *Cosmopolitan*'s engravers, the offset process is used: the black and white picture is photographed through a screen with 130 to 150 intersecting lines per inch, rendering the picture into tiny black dots.) The color illustrations are then color-corrected at the magazine.

Assembling the Jigsaw

As artwork and text are being shuttled back and forth between the magazine and the typesetter, the magazine's production department is creating a layout for the issue, or "book" as it is often called in the trade, a process *Cosmopolitan*'s production chief Tom Sedita compares to "putting a jigsaw puzzle together," since editorial material—text, artwork, pictorials, cartoons, and ads—must be arranged to fit harmoniously together in some multiple of 32 pages. Both magazines are printed in "signatures," or units of 32 pages—a typical issue of *Penthouse* might have 160 pages, while *Cosmopolitan* might have 352, depending on the number of ads sold for that issue. A last-minute ad sale, which might be worth as much as $85,000 to these magazines, can force the editors to cut text out of your article to make room for the ad's insertion. On the other hand, if additional material is needed to fill a signature, filler features, artwork, or even ads like public service announcements are inserted to create the correct page count.

Both magazines use a similar format: columns and *Cosmopolitan*'s features go in the front of the book; a central section called "the well" contains major articles and pictorials; and the back of the book has "jump pages" or leftover bits of articles or features, *Cosmo*'s fiction section, and additional *Penthouse* columns and cartoons. *Cosmopolitan*'s well consists of 64 to 68 ad-free pages of editorial material; *Penthouse*'s, is longer, but includes ads.

Whether you're working with *Cosmo, Penthouse,* or another magazine, it pays to study article placement. Since most magazines use the same format, a glance at the well will let you quickly identify the most important articles in the publication. Concentrating on the slant and style used in these "major" pieces, and promising in your queries to use the same approach in your finished article, could be the key to turning a small sale into a big one. At *Cosmopolitan* major articles pay double the fee of minor ones; at *Penthouse* a major piece is worth an extra $1,000.

Once the pages are theoretically full, based on word counts for articles, the next problem is to make sure reality matches estimate by comparing the printed text with the space available for it. *Cosmopolitan* uses a wall of corkboard to represent the magazine, pinning pieces of galleys and accompanying artwork into the positions they would occupy on the page. As the materials arrive, the entire magazine takes shape along the wall in the sequence the reader would see it. Each time a section of 32 pages has been organized and approved by Helen Gurley Brown, it is closed and no further changes, except corrections, are made. *Penthouse* has the typesetter lay out each page of text, using templates, or standard page layouts the magazine provides. The result is a "representational" galley which returns from the typesetter with the text printed exactly as it would appear on the magazine page, with holes for color artwork.

Often the text doesn't fit perfectly into the space available. If it's too long, it is sent back to the editors for cutting. By eliminating "widows" (one word lines) or subheads, or by rewording small portions, Susan Korones of *Cosmo* finds that "I can usually cut ten lines without the author's even noticing the difference." If the text is too short, artwork is expanded or fillers like "helpful hints" or jokes are inserted at the end of the text.

After the text fits, the typesetter or printer creates page proofs, which are corrected and then photographed. The film of the text and the art separations are sent off to the printer, where they will be merged into printer's proofs, showing the magazine pages with text and color artwork in final form. These are also checked and corrected, if necessary, before printing begins.

Cosmopolitan is printed in photo offset, the most common printing process, while *Penthouse* uses two printing methods, offset for front and back matter, and photogravure, a high quality art printing process, for the well—another good way to spot *Penthouse*'s major articles. Since *Penthouse* is a relatively short magazine, it is "saddle-bound," consisting of folded double pages attached by staples through the centerfold. *Cosmopolitan* is too long for this procedure, so is "perfect bound," with each page cut out separately and glued to the inside of the cover like a paperback book.

After *Cosmopolitan* and *Penthouse* are printed—the process takes about two weeks—the magazines are loaded into railroad cars and sent off to distribution points all over the country. A few days later, you and millions of others can enjoy reading your words in their favorite magazine.

15

The Rights Stuff

an I resell the article I sold last month? Is it all right if I use a quote in my current article that I used in a piece I sold last month? Can I use that article as a chapter in the book that I'm writing?

I'm often asked such questions by clients of my agency and students in my courses. While the answer is often yes to these questions, sometimes I have to tell a surprised caller that he or she no longer owns the article. Recently the best answer I could give to one caller was a qualified maybe. The author couldn't remember whether or not there was a written agreement, let alone what the agreement might have said.

You can easily avoid such confusion by reading and understanding any magazine contract offered to you *before* putting your name on the dotted line.

Knowledge is the key to making the best deal for yourself. Whenever you sign a contract without reading or understanding it—and some very successful writers are guilty of this—you may be cheating yourself out of potential profits. If legal documents intimidate you, take heart. The typical magazine contract is both short (usually one or two pages) and relatively simple. By mastering a few basic concepts, you'll be able to decipher just about any article agreement you're ever likely to be offered.

If you're selling an unwritten article through a query letter, an interested magazine will propose one of two arrangements. If you are an inexperienced writer or have not worked for that magazine before, you may be asked to write the piece *on speculation* or *on spec*. This means that you will be paid only if the article is found acceptable. If not, you will get nothing. Writing on speculation is risky, but it's frequently the only way for the novice to break in. If you are asked to work on spec, ask the editor what fee will be paid if the piece is accepted and what rights the magazine will acquire, and agree upon the length and deadline for the piece. If the discussion is oral, send a confirming letter mentioning the agreed-upon terms.

If you are a more established writer or the magazine is familiar with your work, a magazine will often give you an *assignment*. This assignment may take a variety of forms. An editor may telephone with an offer, send an informal note with the price and terms, or ask you to sign a formal agreement. All oral arrangements should be confirmed in writing, either by the editor or by you.

If you are selling a completed article, a written agreement is still important. When there is no written agreement, the new (1978) copyright law usually considers the writer to have given the magazine nonexclusive rights to publish the article in one or more issues of the same publication. This could present a problem to the author if he or she wishes to include it in a book at a later date, because the magazine could republish the article at any time, making it difficult for the author or book publisher to license either first (before book publication) or second (after book publication) serial rights to the book.

As a literary agent, I have long since discovered that it doesn't always pay to jump at the first offer you receive. Many writers treat a contract as if it were engraved in stone, hesitating to suggest even the slightest change. Others assume that certain terms are "standard" and therefore nonnegotiable. Frequently I have gotten more money and better terms for my articles than those originally offered by the magazine. The secret? It's simple: I just ask. You'd be surprised how often an editor will agree to pay an extra $50 to $100, cover expenses, or let you keep more of the rights simply because you politely suggest it. This is especially true if you have already written an article or two for the magazine. And if the editor does refuse to sweeten the deal, you still have the original offer to console you. If this is your first magazine sale, however, leave the negotiating until your *next* sale—you need the credit to build up your bargaining position.

Dollars and Sense

The bottom line, the fee to be paid, is likely to be a free-lancer's first concern. A typical arrangement for a previously published author specifies two possible fees. The first is the price to be paid for an acceptable article. The exact amount of this fee varies widely from magazine to magazine, depending on circulation, fee policies, your writing background, whether you have previously written for that magazine, and other factors.

But what happens when a magazine hires you to write an article, but rejects it? This is where the second fee, the rejection price or "kill fee," comes in. Since you will be spending time and possibly money on the article, the kill fee assures you of some compensation for your work. The kill fee is usually expressed as a percentage of the acceptance price: 10 percent to 35 percent is typical. For a $500 article, the kill fee might be anywhere from $50 to $165. Some magazines do not pay kill fees.

Once you know *how much* you will be paid, determine *when* you will get the money. Many magazines pay *on acceptance,* which means that you will get a check soon after the editor approves the article. Others pay *on publication,* which can be months or even years after acceptance. One of my articles was published two and a half years after acceptance—that's when you really appreciate payment on acceptance. Worse still, many articles are accepted but never published for one reason or another. Then you don't get paid at all (but can get the rights back and resell the article). However there are two solutions to this problem. The first and best is to try to persuade the editor to change the terms to pay ment on acceptance. Failing this, suggest *payment on publication, or twelve months after acceptance, whichever is the sooner.* With this clause you know you'll be paid for your work.

Some magazines are also willing to reimburse you for some or all of the expenses connected with the article, such as long distance calls, travel, and other costs. While most magazines expect you to absorb minor expenses, if the article entails more substantial expenses, ask about reimbursement. Some magazines will pay for all documented expenses; others specify a budget.

Knowing Your Rights

In exchange for the fee, the magazine will ask for certain rights to your article. An article is not just a one-shot deal; if circumstances are right, it could appear in other magazines, in English and foreign languages, be part of a book, or even serve as the basis for a teleplay, motion picture, or theatrical performance. A client of mine more than doubled his book's earnings by selling its chapters as magazine articles as he wrote the book. Even if your piece on hat design doesn't seem likely to set Hollywood on fire, why sign away something that you *might* be able to sell later?

There are three basic categories of rights that pertain to magazine articles:

Serial rights: Also known as *periodical* rights, serial rights refer to publication in a magazine or newspaper. The term *serial* as used in a magazine contract has nothing to do with being published in installments, but refers to the magazine itself, a "serial" or continuing publication.

Book publication: Prolific writers often gather collections of their articles or groups of related pieces into a book. Also many books get their start as a single article, which the writer then develops. Some magazines also publish "best of" collections of articles in book form, or license others to do so.

Dramatic rights: Television producers sometimes option articles, particularly those dealing with personal experiences, human interest stories, or slice-of-life pieces as a basis for made-for-television movies. Articles may also be optioned for motion picture, theatrical, or radio use. It is also possible, but unlikely, that an article could be used for cassette or videotape recordings.

While other rights exist, such as *commercial rights* (T-shirts, toys, games, and other tie-in products) and *information retrieval rights* (electronic reproduction), these are seldom mentioned in magazine contracts and rarely prove valuable to either the magazine or the writer. If the magazine does ask for these rights, you may wish to try to reserve them for yourself, or work out some split of income from these rights between yourself and the magazine, but generally the point is moot.

Where Will the Rights be Used?

After you determine *what* rights you are selling, you'll want to determine *where* the rights can be used. Your contract will spell out which *territory* and which *languages* the magazine is buying. Since many languages are spoken in more than one country—an article might be sold for English language publications in either the United States, Canada, Australia, Ireland, the United Kingdom, South Africa, Hong Kong, or Japan, for example—both definitions are essential to understanding exactly what you've sold. Any rights you haven't sold are yours to exploit for extra profit (Chapter Seventeen will tell you how to hit the resale jackpot), so you'll want to take a careful look at these provisions. Here's how it works:

Language: Some articles, particularly profiles of celebrities, have a very broad appeal and can be sold for publication in other languages. Most magazines will offer to buy either *English language rights* or *English and translation rights,* though a few may specify certain languages and exclude others. If the magazine buys translation rights, propose a 50/50 split on earnings. Otherwise the magazine can sell your article dozens of times and pay you nothing more than the original price.

Territory: When your contract is for English language rights only, your contract will spell out which territory the magazine controls. Almost all magazines will insist on buying both American and Canadian rights *(North American rights),* since many U.S. magazines are also sold in Canada. Some will also ask for rights in the United Kingdom and Australia, and others will demand English language rights throughout the world. If you sell only North American English language rights, you can resell the article in the United Kingdom, as well as other countries.

Frequency of Use

After determining what rights and where you've sold the piece, the third question is *when* the piece may be used. An article's initial publication may be just the beginning of a series of profitable sales of the material. The wording of your contract will tell you who collects these profits, you or the magazine. If you sell *first serial rights, one-time use only,* you are free to resell the article to other magazines and newspapers after the first magazine publishes it. You can also resell to the original magazine if it decides it would like to publish the piece again. Such sales are called *second serial rights* or "reprint rights."

A number of magazines will ask to buy both *first and second serial rights* to your article. Accepting such an offer prevents you from reselling your article to other magazines. A good compromise in this case is to try for a 50/50 split on income from second serial sales. Otherwise the magazine can keep any reprint income. Also, unless your agreement states otherwise, the magazine can republish the article without further payment to you.

An alternative approach is to sell *simultaneous rights.* This method, suitable for either published or unpublished articles and newspaper features, is often referred to as "self-syndication." Self-syndication entails selling your piece to several publications at the same time. To find out how, check Chapter Seventeen.

Telling Rights from Wrong

In its contract the magazine will offer to acquire some or all of these rights. The most common packages of rights are:

All rights: Sometimes written as *world rights* or *all rights throughout the world,* this means exactly what it says. You have sold everything except your copyright. This is about the worst possible agreement for the author since it prevents you from making *any* further use of the material. A similar, but slightly worse, arrangement is the *work for hire* agreement, which not only transfers all rights, but also the copyright to the magazine. Selling all rights doesn't transfer the copyright unless the agreement contains the specific phrase *work made for hire* or a nearly identical wording.

If you do sell *all rights,* sometimes you can get the magazine to reassign the rights to you after publication. While the magazine has no legal obligation to do this, many magazines have no real use for these rights and opt to return them. Under the 1978 copyright law, you can get your rights back without the magazine's consent after thirty-five years, small comfort as this may be. A more immediate solution if you are unsuccessful in getting a reversion of rights is to write *new* articles on the same subject. All you've sold is a particular collection of words, *not* your basic idea or research. In doing a new article, avoid duplicating the previous piece by adding new ingredients, a slightly different slant, new quotes, updated facts, fresh examples.

All publishing rights: Occasionally written as *all print media rights,* these terms allow the publisher to use both periodical and book rights, but let you keep all dramatic and other rights. These terms apply to both English and translations of the printed material.

All periodical rights: Sometimes written as *world periodical rights,* this represents a considerable improvement over all rights or all publishing rights because it lets you keep both book and dramatic rights. However you cannot resell the article to other magazines.

English language periodical rights: You keep all nonperiodical rights, as well as the right to make first and second serial sales of translations of the article.

North American English language periodical rights: You can sell nonperiodical rights, foreign translations, and first and second English language serial rights outside of the United States and Canada.

First North American English language rights, one-time use only: The best possible deal for the writer, this leaves you free to sell any of the rights, except for North American first serial rights, which can be sold only once.

One-time rights: This refers to any sale, first or second serial, in which the magazine or newspaper acquires the right to publish the piece once, and places no restrictions on future sales.

How Long, How Long?

Most magazines will give you two to four months to write the article, unless the topic is especially timely. Occasionally timeliness is irrelevant. I once received a contract saying "Write the piece whenever you have a spare year—we have a huge inventory of articles right now." If a deadline is mentioned, immediately determine whether or not you can write the piece by the agreed-upon date. If some event must occur before you can write the article, make sure the editor knows this and revises the date, if necessary. While one of my clients once delivered an article a *year* late and still had it accepted, few writers can expect to share his good fortune. If, after signing the agreement, you find the deadline cannot be met, inform the editor *before* the deadline to see if an extension is possible.

A final point which should be included in the contract is the exact length of the article, usually expressed in words (1,000 words, for example) or in a range of words (2,500 to 3,000 words, say). While no one expects you to sit down and count the exact number of words, as one naive client of mine did and spent days anguishing over an "extra" 47 words he couldn't eliminate, try to avoid being more than 10 percent over or under specifications. If photos or illustrations are to be included, the contract should also list the exact number and kind (black and white, color transparency) desired and the amount of extra payment, if any.

Writing Your Own Contract

If the magazine doesn't send a written contract, the following confirming letter, adapted to your needs, is one I've often used. Format it like any business letter, using either your own letterhead or typing your name, address, and phone number at the top of the page. Make one carbon or photocopy to attach for the editor's signature. Make sure the letter is dated, sign both the original and photocopy, and provide space for the editor's signature. Include SASE with contracts for return of your copy.

> Dear (name of editor):
> I'm delighted that you want to (assign me to write/buy/assign on speculation) my article (give title) for $ (give exact price and kill fee, if applicable). This is for first North American serial rights, one-time use only (or other terms, if specified in previous discussions). The length will be (number of words), and I will deliver it on (date).
> Please sign and return the attached copy of this letter to indicate your agreement.

Many writers are surprised to learn that even if they have a signed agreement with a magazine, they cannot be forced to write the article. If your profile subject skips the country one jump ahead of the feds before you get the interview, a mud slide destroys your notes (as happened to one writer I know), or some other problem arises, just send the editor a brief explanation as far ahead of the deadline as possible. The magazine cannot sue you for not delivering an article.

The Check's in the Mail—Or Is It?

The contract *does* obligate the magazine to pay you on approval or publication, depending on the agreement. While many magazines notify you of the publication date, some don't, so check the newsstand each month. If payment is called for on publication, send the editor an invoice for the article. I've found that sending an actual bill, which may be phrased in a short, friendly note, greatly accelerates payment.

If your agreement calls for payment on acceptance, send in the article with a request for payment of the acceptance price if the piece is found satisfactory. Allow the editor four to six weeks to decide. Then send a tactful reminder or call. Once the editor has read the piece, expect one of three responses. If the piece is rejected, send a bill or note requesting the kill fee, if any. If revisions are requested, get back to work promptly. Some writers are discouraged by editorial suggestions, but revision is to be expected, especially at better-paying markets. If the piece is accepted, allow two to six weeks for the magazine to draw up a check, then call or send a tactful reminder. (If collection seems difficult, Chapter Sixteen will offer tips on getting the tardy to pay up.)

Once your piece is accepted, keep those assignments rolling in by sending the editor a fresh batch of ideas. It won't be long until the next contract—and check.

16

Keeping on the Right Side of the Law

A few years ago two of my clients found themselves facing a lawsuit for copyright infringement. In compiling a resource book, they hired researchers to compile lists of various types. One of these researchers copied a short list from another book and presented it to my clients as original research. Result? A whopping suit against my clients, their publisher and its distributor, costing well over $100,000 in legal fees alone. And after years of court hearings, the clients lost the case—and most of the profits from their best-selling book.

Lawsuits are becoming increasingly common—and expensive. When someone decides to sue, typically the complainant names both the publication *and* the author—which could be *you*. Although anyone can initiate a suit—no matter how misguided and unjust it might be—most courtroom battles can be avoided by taking simple, common-sense precautions *before* you submit your work. Many magazines have lawyers on staff to review your material, but an ounce of prevention on your part is the best defense.

This chapter is not intended to substitute for the expert guidance of an experienced publishing lawyer. Instead, my purpose is to familiarize you with common legal pitfalls and offer ideas on how you can make the law work *for* you, not against you. If you anticipate any legal controversy about your writing, consulting a lawyer is a sensible (and possibly tax deductible) move.

Copyrights and Wrongs

Although the 1978 copyright law doesn't make for light reading, if you'd like to look over its text and receive materials on copyright, write to Copyright Office, Library of Congress, Washington, D.C. 20559.

Here are answers to some commonly asked questions about copyright:

What does copyright protect? Essentially, it prevents others from copying the material in your published or unpublished literary, dramatic, musical, pictorial, or recorded works. The exact words in your article are protected; your basic idea, title, facts and research, opinions and theories, or plan of organization are *not*. You are equally free to use the ideas, opinions, research, and organizational plans of other writers, without referring to them in your piece, as long as you do it *in your own words*.

Titles are occasionally trademarked; don't reuse titles that have the small "tm" symbol next to them. Also, copying a very well-known title like *A Farewell to Arms* could open you to claims of "unfair competition" if you used it in a way that might confuse the public, such as using it on another novel. On an article, however, the title "A Farewell to Arms" would not be confusing, so you'd be free to use it.

Paraphrasing—writing something similar but not identical to passages of a copyrighted work—is a tricky area. Successful suits have been brought against some writers who've paraphrased long sections of text from another work; line by line comparisons ruled out the possibility of coincidence. On the other hand, similarity between small sections of your work and portions of another might not be actionable, since plagiarism suits are normally based on economic loss: the idea that the copying of the work damaged the original author by diminishing sales or reducing the value of the work. In the plagiarism case mentioned at the beginning of

the chapter, however, the dispute centered on a very short section—three pages—of a book; the copyright holders maintained
that this particular list was a key ingredient of their book, and the
court agreed. To fully protect yourself, avoid *any* copying or
paraphasing from copyrighted works.

Where does research end and plagiarism begin? An old ad-
age is that research is stealing from several sources; plagiarism is
stealing from one. These definitions oversimplify the issues, but
reading several different pieces on your subject and taking ideas
or even a choice phrase or two from each wouldn't normally be
considered plagiarism. Courts have taken the view that most nonfiction writing simply builds and expands on the accumulated
thought of the past, rather than breaking entirely new ground.

Paraphrasing a sentence or two from some other source is
unlikely to land you in court; neither is copying such sentences as,
"John F. Kennedy was born in 1917." This sentence construction
is so common and widely used that it cannot be considered original in the first author's work.

To avoid accidental plagiarism, clearly distinguish between
quoted material and your comments or summaries in any notes
you take while researching, and review all reference materials after you've completed the article to spot duplications or close paraphrases you may have made of the original text. Alex Haley, author of *Roots*, was sued by another writer who claimed that substantial portions of her earlier work *Jubilee* were paraphrased in
Roots. Haley settled with her, explaining that the similarity to the
previous work was the result of confusion between his own words
and research notes on other works. Backtracking to your research
materials—and revising any offending sections of your article—
keeps you from succumbing to Haley's pitfall.

What's the best way to include copyrighted material in my article?
Your freedom to use material from copyrighted works varies according to the length of the quotation and that of the work containing it. If you plan to use a short excerpt from a long work, like
a paragraph or two from a book, this is considered "fair use."
Since magazine and newspaper articles are much shorter than
books, limit fair use quotations to a sentence or two at most. The
length of *your* article is a factor as well: it would be excessive to include 100 words from a book in a 250-word article without written
permission. If the quote you have in mind seems to fall under fair
use, all you need to do is include the name of the book or maga-

zine and author along with the quote: "As Margaret Mead, author of *Coming of Age in Samoa,* writes: '. . . .' "

If you'd like to include remarks some authority or celebrity made in another article, your best move is to contact that individual and interview him or her again. If this is impossible, you could include the material by writing, "Robert Redford was recently quoted in the *New York Times* as saying, '. . . .' "

If the work you'd like to quote from is quite short, like a song, you'll usually need permission to quote even one line. The American Society of Composers, Authors and Publishers (ASCAP) handles permissions for many songs. However, it's okay to mention the *titles* of songs without formal permission. For quotes from other short works like poems, or longer quotes from long works, you need written permission from the copyright holder. Contact the magazine you are working for; different publications use different permission forms.

Bear in mind that some copyright holders charge for these permissions—usually modest fees like $25, but possibly much more—so agree in advance who'll pay, you or the magazine. No permission is needed for quoting from material in the public domain, whether from older works whose copyright has expired (in most cases, 56 years after publication would be a safe estimate) or works published without copyright.

Do I need to copyright my work? Usually not. Although you can copyright unpublished articles (contact Copyright Office, Library of Congress, Washington, D.C. 20559 for the forms; the fee is $10), few writers bother. You can also give unpublished works a "common law copyright" without filling out forms or paying a fee by placing a copyright symbol (the letter "c" inside a circle) plus your name and the year in which you wrote the work somewhere on the manuscript. However, common law copyrights don't fully protect your work: registering the copyright with the Library of Congress is a prerequisite to filing any lawsuit to protect your work.

Since nearly all magazines in the U.S. carry copyright notices, usually a single notice covering the entire contents of the publication, your work is automatically protected as soon as it is published. Some magazines will agree to have your article copyrighted individually in your name and to run a separate copyright notice covering your particular article.

Even if you don't have the article copyrighted in your name, you may still own the copyright. The only way you can give up your ownership is by transferring it *in writing* to the magazine. Otherwise, the copyright is still considered to belong to you, with the magazine having only acquired the right to reproduce and distribute the article in one or more issues. If your article is published with a single copyright for the entire contents—and you haven't transferred the copyright to the magazine—you can register the article with the Copyright Office in your own name after publication by filling out a form and paying $10.

Why bother registering your articles in your own name? If someone plagiarized from your article, you'd want to avoid having your suit against that individual dismissed on the grounds that the copyright notice was defective—i.e., that it listed the magazine as copyright holder, when you actually owned it—a possibility if you'd failed to have your article registered in your name. Also you want to be sure that you—not your publisher—collect any monetary damages awarded as a result of the infringement.

If the magazine mistakenly omits its copyright notice or runs a defective notice, you have five years after the initial publication to register your claim with the Copyright Office. However, if you agree to have your work published in a magazine that is not copyrighted and don't ask to have a copyright notice applying to your work included, your article could fall into the public domain through your negligence.

How long does my copyright last? If your copyright became effective on January 1, 1978, or later, it lasts your lifetime plus fifty years, unless the work was written anonymously or pseudonymously, in which case copyright protection lasts 75 years after initial publication. The same 75-year protection applies to the employer/copyright holder who commissions writing on a "work made for hire" basis. Anonymous and pseudonymous authors can extend their copyrights to lifetime plus fifty years by disclosing their identities to the Copyright Office before the 75 years are up. If you write the article with one or more collaborators, the copyright lasts the lifetime of the longest lived author, plus fifty years.

Lies, Mistakes, and $2 Million Misunderstandings

Two words practically guaranteed to strike terror in publishers' hearts are "libel suit." Though libel suits are relatively rare—

neither I nor any writer I represent has ever been the target of one—they are costly. One survey of libel awards showed that the average damage judgment exceeded $2 million—three times as high as the average malpractice award of about $600,000. However, only 10 percent of libel cases actually come before a jury; and of those that do, surveys show that 75 percent to 80 percent of the awards rendered by juries are later reversed by higher courts: a former Miss Wyoming recently won a $26.6 million dollar libel verdict against *Penthouse* magazine in one court only to have a higher court find that the short story in question did *not* libel her. She didn't collect a cent.

Even in the 20 percent to 25 percent of cases when the jury's findings are sustained in higher courts, the megaverdicts are usually reduced drastically. Though a jury valued actress Carol Burnett's loss of reputation at $1.6 million when a *National Enquirer* story suggested that she was seen drunk at a restaurant, a higher court cut the award to $200,000. The largest jury award sustained on appeal and actually paid to the plaintiff is said to be about $500,000, paid to Elmer Gertz, a lawyer accused by a John Birch Society publication of being "a Leninist," with a police file that required "a big Irish cop to lift."

Defendants win the overwhelming majority of libel cases, but the cost of defense alone can be in the millions. Though most publishers now have libel insurance and lawyers on staff or retainer, naturally, they are more interested in preventing libel suits than successfully defending them—a point a writer would do well to keep in mind.

But where does freedom of speech end and libel begin? Is it libelous to characterize best-selling author A. E. Hotchner as "a toady," "a hypocrite" and "an exploiter" of Ernest Hemingway's fame, as the author of *Hemingway in Spain* did? Yes and no, according to the courts. A lower court said it was and awarded Hotchner $125,000; the upper court said it wasn't and gave Hotchner nothing. Confused? It gets worse—each state has its own libel laws, and new court rulings constantly change the exact definitions of libel.

So how do you avoid libel when even the experts can't agree on what it is? There is a generally accepted definition of libel: the offending remarks must be published and defame an identifiable entity, such as a person, corporation or organization, causing provable injury, such as out-of-pocket losses, injury of reputation, humiliation, mental anguish or related suffering. They must also be untrue, or stated in a manner that creates a false impression. In some cases the plaintiff must also demonstrate fault on the part of the writer as well.

Publication, the first element of libel, is pretty straightforward. Just about any combination of writing the comments down and distributing them could be considered publication: in a recent case three families wrote a letter to the local police chief, complaining that a policeman had kicked pet animals, threatened children, and used offensive language. The policeman named in this letter was awarded $52,300 in libel damages by a jury. It is not necessary that anyone actually read the remarks; the fact of their distribution determines that "publication" has occurred.

Identification, the second element of libel, could occur in several ways. First, if you mentioned a specific politician's name in your article and stated that he or she took bribes, this statement could be potentially libelous (unless you had strong proof to support it). Not using the name doesn't always protect you; a description like "the red-haired principal of a Fernwood public school" could be just as recognizable as a name. Using fictitious names could be equally hazardous—even if you successfully disguise the identity of the real person you're talking about, you might unwittingly open yourself to suits from individuals bearing the name you've selected to substitute for the real name. Check your telephone book to make sure your fictitious name isn't that of a real person in the area; or use identifiers like "Laura P. (not her real name)."

Even if you bury the individual in a group, you may not be protected: when a book called *U.S.A Confidential* asserted that "some Neiman models are call girls—the top babes in town," the court found that the phrase did identify the nine Neiman models in a libelous manner. However, a similar statement in the book about Neiman-Marcus saleswomen, of whom there were 385, was held to refer to such a large group that no particular saleswoman could consider herself identified. The precise size of a group in which individual members can be identified for the purpose of a libel action has not been established, but the larger the group, the safer you are from libel suits.

Damage, the third element of libel, means that the statement or statements must cause a provable injury, by exposing a person, organization, group of people, business or corporation to hatred, ridicule, or contempt; causing economic losses; or causing people to shun that individual or group socially or professionally. Examples of statements that are considered libelous per se include claiming that someone is immoral or practices sexual perversions; has a loathsome disease; is dishonest or has committed illegal acts; or manufactures or distributes defective, hazardous, or inferior merchandise; as well as many other remarks. Naturally, these statements must be untrue to be libelous.

Fault: Although truth is your best defense against libel, errors in your writing may enjoy a certain constitutional protection, according to the Supreme Court. In the landmark case of *New York Times v. Sullivan* (1964), the Supreme Court ruled that public officials cannot recover damages for "defamatory falsehoods" unless they can prove that the remark was made with " 'actual malice'—that is, with knowledge that it was false or with reckless disregard of whether it was false or not." This tolerance for mistakes—even ones that might damage a public official's reputation—was intended by the Court to keep debate on public issues "uninhibited, robust and wide open."

Your Constitutional Right to Be Wrong— Sometimes

In deciding the question of fault, courts have identified several categories of plaintiffs, with regulations applying to libel based on the status of the person or group identified. Here are the applicable guidelines.

Public officials: The *"New York Times* rule," as this decision came to be called, doesn't mean that it's open season on public officials. In order to enjoy Constitutional protection, the defamatory statements must pertain to the official's fitness to hold office or "official conduct," not his or her personal life. Accusations of criminal conduct, either now or in the past, would be protected if they weren't made with reckless disregard for truth; as would be other statements pertaining to the official's qualifications or lack of them, honesty and ethics, and general competence. Touching on the official's private life could be protected if it related to fitness to hold office: falsely reporting that the head of the school board was once investigated for child abuse in his home might arguably reflect on his fitness to hold office.

Who are public officials? Not every government employee

down to the town file clerk qualifies; an official must hold a job important enough that there is public interest in his or her qualifications: examples are elected officials and those running for office, commissioners and cabinet members, the police, government contractors, government attorneys and doctors, school teachers and officials, building inspectors, and military personnel. However, a low-ranking functionary could elevate him or herself to public official status by speaking out on an issue: the town file clerk would subject himself to public scrutiny if he claimed the mayor was rigging blind bids to favor certain contractors. The public would then have an interest in evaluating his official conduct; thus an erroneous report that the clerk was a regular at the local saloon might be considered to fall under the *New York Times* rule.

The shadowy "public figure": The "actual malice" standard was then extended by the Court to apply to "public figures." In deciding the case of *Curtis Publishing v. Butts* (1967), in which a football coach sued the *Saturday Evening Post* for falsely reporting that he had thrown a game, the court observed that "many who do not hold public office. . . . are nevertheless intimately involved in the resolution of important public questions, or, by reason of their fame, shape events in areas of concern to society at large." Despite deciding that the coach was a public figure, the Court still found in his favor since such mistakes as an inaccurate date, unattributable quotes, and other flaws in the article demonstrated "reckless disregard of truth" in the Court's opinion.

Unfortunately for the journalist, no exact definition of a public figure has been established; as one judge put it, defining a public figure is "like trying to nail a jellyfish to a wall," especially when deciding whether the "actual malice" criterion or some lesser standard will be used to define libel. At one point the Supreme Court suggested that anyone—no matter how obscure—involved in a matter of public concern would have to prove actual malice to collect for libel. Subsequently however, the Court retreated from that position, and two types of public figures emerged. Here's how to identify them.

The first is the *celebrity or household name,* who because of "general fame or notoriety" and involvement in "the affairs of society" becomes "a public personality for all aspects of his life." In lawsuits, such individuals as Johnny Carson, Jacqueline Onassis, and Linus Pauling have been placed in this category.

The second kind of public figure enjoys a higher degree of protection under the law, since only certain aspects of his or her life are of public concern. To determine whether a particular individual, group, or business falls into this category, courts have considered such questions as whether the person is involved in a "matter of public interest" (divorce proceedings don't qualify, the Supreme Court ruled), whether he or she has thrust him or herself into the forefront of that controversy, and whether the individual has taken steps to attract public attention, like appearing on TV talk shows to talk about the issue.

Private individuals: The private individual involved in a matter of private concern enjoys the greatest protection, according to a recent Supreme Court decision, since lesser standards than actual malice can be used to determine damages from defamatory statements. Private individuals also have a right of privacy, which may prevent you from writing true statements about that person without his or her permission (granting you an interview would be an example of approving publication).

Avoiding Libel

The best way to avoid libel is through meticulous, painstaking research that will demonstrate your regard for truth should anyone dispute it through a libel suit. Careless mistakes and sloppy reporting in other sections of your article would help demonstrate a reckless disregard for truth if a particular section aroused legal controversy. Another point to consider is that repeating libels that others have put into their work—even accidentally—could open you up to libel actions. Going back to the original source—the courtroom transcription, land deed, marriage license, or whatever—will avoid secondhand libel.

One exception to the secondhand libel problem is *privilege*, which applies to certain kinds of reporting that might contain libelous material. You may accurately report on the happenings inside legislative, judicial, or other official proceedings without worrying that some statements made by one of the participants and repeated by you will turn out to be libelous, if your report deals with some matter of public interest, like the disposition of child custody cases.

Another good way to deal with potentially libelous material is to contact the person or group identified and include the other point of view in your article, along with the controversial material: "Dr. X feels that the five malpractice suits result from 'a systematic plot to destroy my reputation.' "

After determining the truth—facts that you could prove in a court of law—you may want to consult with your publisher's lawyers or your editor about the handling of certain material. After you've written the piece, you may also want to show it to your own lawyer—sometimes a simple change in wording can reduce the risks considerably. One of my clients was once advised not to refer to one of his eccentric friends as "a madman" in print, while the same lawyer felt that "a wildman" would not be actionable in describing this particular individual. The friend didn't sue.

If your material seems too risky, removing the names and identifiers of specific individuals and groups can help a lot. In an article in *Law and the Writer* (edited by Kirk Polking), Michael S. Lasky describes an instance where a magazine decided at the last minute to remove the names of specific doctors from a piece on dubious practices of some area physicians. According to the editor Lasky interviewed, "Our lawyer said that while it was defensible, the doctors would feel obligated to sue just for the record—so they would have something to tell their patients and the medical association."

Here is a three-pronged approach Lasky recommends in evaluating your manuscript for potential legal hazards:

Is the material defamatory to an identifiable individual or group?

If it *is,* then is the information privileged?

If it is *not,* then is it fundamentally true?

If the answer is then yes, the final decision rests with you and your publisher.

Lust, Prurience, and Community Standards

Do you have a Constitutional right to be obscene? The Supreme Court views the First Amendment as protecting your right to create material "which arouses only normal, healthy interest in sex," but obscenity enjoys no such protection.

In a recent Supreme Court decision on obscenity (*Brockett v. Spokane Arcades* (1985), the Court indicated that material lacking "serious literary, artistic, political, or scientific value, material which, while arousing normal, healthy sexual responses overall, yet contains an isolated example of obscene material—described as '. . . its predominant appeal is to prurient interest, i.e., a shameful or morbid interest in nudity, sex, or excrement, and if it goes substantially beyond customary limits of candor in description or representation of such matters'—that a publication of this nature [still has] constitutional protection."

When the Check Isn't in the Mail

Tired of getting excuses instead of checks from your publisher? Here's a program that will accelerate payment from just about any publisher. After you present your initial bill and wait a reasonable period of time, your next strategy should be to telephone the accounts payable department—*not* your editor—and determine if your editor has filled out the proper payment voucher. If not, contact the editor's assistant to get the paperwork moving—and continue checking with the accounting department until they acknowledge receipt of the payment voucher. Many payment delays can be traced to editorial inefficiency in completing paperwork—unfortunately filling out forms rates a low priority with some busy editors.

Once the payment voucher is with the accounting department, learn the name of the individual responsible for sending your check to you and concentrate all subsequent dunning efforts on that person, keeping a log of your inquiries and the responses.

If your reminders simply produce excuses and unfulfilled promises, getting tough has proved 100 percent effective in my experience. Here's a plan of escalating collection tactics that should produce results:

1. Trace the check through the maze. Make sure paperwork has been filed with the proper person in the accounting department. Obtain the name of the person actually responsible for paying you. Ask when payment should be expected.

2. If the promised date passes, call or write the same person inquiring as to the reason for delay and when payment should be expected. Send a confirming letter as to the new payment date.

3. When the second date passes, send a duplicate invoice and a letter asking firmly for payment: "I'll hope for this tardy check by return mail."

4. (optional) If the excuses you get seem fairly reasonable, you may want to repeat steps 2 and 3.

5. Proceed to mild threats: "I'm amazed by the long delay in payment. Despite several reminders from me and promises from you, payment has not been made on this account. If the check is not received by the first of next month [or some other deadline], I'll have no choice but to explore other collection options." For added impact, find an attorney willing to receive a duplicate—he could be your brother-in-law—and mark the letter "c.c. Joseph Smith, esq." or whatever the attorney's name is.

6. Proceed to stronger threats. "Since several months have passed without payment from you, despite repeated requests, I am contacting my attorney with a view toward initiating proceedings against your firm. You can forestall such proceedings with immediate payment."

7. (optional) If you live near the publication, consider paying a nuisance call to the accounting department. For maximum impact, arrange to have several friends telephone you while you're there, ask for a few back issues to look over, and generally play the part of the squeaking wheel that's said to get greased quickly. For best results, stop by a half hour before lunch time or quitting time, which makes it harder for the accounting department to avoid you. Or if the sum involved justifies it, you may be able to hire a local college student to do your dunning for you.

8. Label this letter "final notice" and bring out the big guns—figuratively speaking, of course—with your ultimate threat, "As my several previous letters have failed to elicit your seriously overdue payment, I have decided to initiate legal proceedings against your organization thirty days from the date of this letter." This was the letter that extracted payment from two out of three seriously delinquent publishers.

9. Sue. There's nothing like getting a subpoena to wake up even the most sluggish payer. With this move I finally collected from the toughest case I encountered—the check was sent over by messenger the day before the scheduled court hearing. You can have your day in court, at very modest expense, without a lawyer, by suing in small claims court in your state. The two times I've sued in small claims courts, the process was simplicity itself and the results outstanding.

If you do decide to sue, keep two points in mind before proceeding against a magazine located in another state. It is not always possible to sue a nonresident business in small claims court. Many, but not all, states have "long arm" laws, originally designed to protect those involved in automobile accidents with nonresident motorists but extended, in some cases, to apply to nonresidents doing business in a state. If the magazine is distributed in your state, this would be an example of "doing business," even if the publisher's offices were in another state. Check with small claims court to see if "long arm" statutes apply in your state.

Secondly, even if "long arm" statutes apply, the publisher may fail to respond to your suit, causing you to win a "no show" victory. You would then theoretically be entitled to collect on your judgment, but if the publisher had no assets to attach in your state, collection could be a drawn-out and expensive process. As lawyer Mark A. Norman puts it, "Collection litigation is not for the faint of heart, nor for those who think a pot of gold awaits them at the end of the litigation rainbow." Actually, unless the sum in question is substantial, collecting from the out of state deadbeats may prove too expensive to be practical; however, it's certainly worth sending a few dunning letters before giving up.

Another practical consideration: although all fifty states have small claims courts—though they are known by different names in different states—all limit the amount you can sue for: the ceiling may be anywhere from $200 to $5,000. To decide whether it's worth suing, consider whether the amount involved is worth your time (one survey found that the total time consumed by a small claims suit averages between eleven and twenty-seven hours—though I only spent three hours on my case); and how convincing your evidence is—correspondence with the publication, receipts for expenses arising from writing the piece, and your contract or confirming letter are all helpful.

Once you decide to sue, many states require that you first write a demand letter to the offending party, recounting the facts of the matter and the remedy you expect, i.e., the amount of payment due to you. Even if this isn't legally necessary, it's still a good idea for two reasons. First, this final demand might shake loose payment at last; and second, it is a handy summary of your case to give the judge.

Next, all you need to do is find out where small claims suits are handled in your area and fill out a short form. Be sure to use the exact business name of the publication—copy it from the letterhead of any correspondence you've received or a recent copy of the magazine. Also prepare a short statement of your grievance to include on the form.

When your case comes to trial, avoid the temptation to turn into a Perry Mason on the witness stand. Instead, stand up when you address the judge, stick to the facts, support them with documentation, and when your turn is over, avoid interrupting your opponent's presentation. Using these simple strategies, experts say, could soon have the long arm of the law reaching for your overdue check—and grasping it.

Although the preceding paragraphs may give the impression that it's a struggle to collect from magazines, actually it's rare to encounter serious payment problems. In my experience, magazine payment departments fall into a bell curve, with a small number of very fast payers (two weeks or less), many average players (four to eight weeks), some slow payers (two to four months), and a few real delinquents (four months to eternity).

Some 98 percent of the publishers I've dealt with will pay in two months or less. Most of the longer delays resulted more from simple inefficiency than deliberate dishonesty: secretaries leaving payment vouchers lying on their desks while they vacationed, checks being sent to the wrong address, computer breakdowns, and other woes typical of the large bureaucracy. And when the typical magazine tells you that "The check is in the mail"—the odds are good that it is!

17

Sell It Again, Sam!

How would you like to make $7,500 from just one article? Recently I read about a writer who did; not by cracking some super high-paying market, but by reselling one of his articles 256 times! Another writer I used to work with made between $10,000 and $20,000 on each of his articles through overseas sales of his work. Reselling your published articles can be as easy as mailing a letter; a few weeks ago I spent less than a dollar photocopying and mailing one of my old articles and realized a $200 return on the investment with a new sale of the material.

Reselling articles can be just as easy and profitable for you as it's been for me. Since multiple sales of the same piece multiply income with little extra work, you'll want to explore the various ways to fully exploit your published and unpublished articles. Unsold articles present no potential problems in making multiple sales; but for previously sold articles, your first move is to review your magazine contract (see Chapter Fifteen) to determine which rights you control. Depending on the contract, you may be able to sell second serial rights, British and translation rights, book rights, or dramatic rights to the piece—or all of these rights.

Here's how.

Multiple Articles Sales

There are four basic ways to make multiple sales of the same article.

Syndicates: The easiest, but least profitable way to make multiple sales of one of your published or unpublished pieces is through a newspaper feature syndicate which will either pay you a flat fee or a percentage of sums collected from syndication of your piece to newspapers all over the country. Syndicates are interested in articles of 500 to 750 words or three-, four-, or five-part series of articles of that length. To make longer pieces suitable you may want either to condense them to a single short article or revise the piece into a series—usually the best bet.

Syndicates also handle columns for newspapers—consider if you'd like to write a regular newspaper column on the basic topic covered by your piece, and if so, submit a brief description of the proposed column, your qualifications for writing it, and the article as a sample column. If your proposed column is to appear more than once a week, you'll also need to write enough additional samples to provide a week's worth of the column. A list of newspaper syndicates can be found in *Literary Market Place*, available at the library or through the publisher, R. R. Bowker.

Self-syndication: Equally suitable for published or unpublished articles, self-syndication is a multiple sales technique that entails selling *simultaneous rights* to your article to several noncompeting markets. You can sell either simultaneous first or second serial rights, depending on whether the article has already been sold. To find simultaneous markets look for several publications that serve similar readers but would be unlikely to overlap in circulation.

Since the readers of the *Miami Herald* don't overlap significantly with those of the *Boston Globe*, for example, you could easily sell the same piece to both papers for simultaneous publication. Similarly, bicycle store owners don't read the same trade magazines as pet store owners, though both groups of readers might be interested in a piece on "Selecting Business Partners." Two other possibilities are religious magazines (imagine the possibilities for a good Christmas piece!) and company, college, club, and other organizational publications. Many of these publications are looking for good general-interest pieces on topics like gardening, home improvement, food, travel, hobbies, as well as more weighty topics.

To locate potential simultaneous markets, consult *Gebbie House Magazine Directory* (contains listings of house organs of various companies and associations), *Association Publications in Print* (lists magazines and books published by 13,000 associations, with 400 subject categories), *Ayer Directory of Publications* (lists newspapers, magazines, and trade publications), *Writer's Market, Standard Rate and Data* (lists magazines and other publications containing ads), *Editor and Publisher International Year Book* (contains American and foreign daily and weekly newspapers, syndicates, and news services), and other directories (see Appendix for complete list).

In preparing your submission list, select one publication within each category for your first round submissions—you don't want to have two Philadelphia publications clamoring for the same piece. Mark each photocopy "exclusive, your territory, one-time use only" or "exclusive, your circulation, one-time use only,"

Since pricing your piece can be tricky—each newspaper or magazine may have its own rate schedule—it's best not to include a price until you become more familiar with the customary rates of these markets. Include SASE and a deadline for reply—thirty days after the anticipated date of receipt is good, unless the material is super timely. Start the second round of submissions one week after the deadline established for the first round, and continue until you've made a sale in each territory or have exhausted the possibilities of this submission approach.

Second serial sales: Since there is no limit to how many second serial sales you can make of the same piece, whenever you sell something and retain second serial rights, you should always be on the alert for resale opportunities. As soon as the piece appears, study magazine and newspaper directories for markets that are noncompetitive with the original publication. You can submit the same piece in several different fields at once, so be imaginative in looking for additional possibilities.

Consider also whether minor rewrites might increase market prospects. By promising to add regional information, you might be able to sell versions of the article to regional magazines all over the country. Or the piece might be adapted for ethnic publications, hobbyist, entrepreneurial, or other special interest publications. To sell revised versions, send a covering letter detailing the proposed changes, and the piece as it originally appeared, to all likely prospects.

A year or two after publication consider also submitting to magazines within the original field. Chances are that many of the readers of *Glamour* missed the original publication two years ago in *Playgirl*, or have forgotten the piece if they did see it. Always indicate in your submission letter the date and place of original publication, as well as the specifics of any subsequent appearances of the piece. Also make sure the markets you're submitting to accept second serial submissions.

If you have several articles to resell, another approach is to prepare an alluring description of each, prepare fifty or so copies and send these descriptions to every remotely likely market with a suitable cover letter and checklist "order form" to examine the actual articles. The great advantage of this approach is super low cost—most copy shops only charge a few cents a page for multiple copies of the same document, and you'd save on postage by not having to mail the actual articles and SASE unless the publication was really interested.

Keep a sharp lookout for any new magazines that might have cropped up since you first sold the article. Since new magazines often have a tight budget, they tend to be highly receptive to second serial submissions. Keeping up-to-date on market conditions by reading *Writer's Digest* or other freelancer-oriented publications can also alert you to shifts in editorial direction at existing magazines that might create a more favorable climate for your piece than that which existed when you first submitted it.

Updates, round-ups, and spin-offs: After your original article has ripened on the vine for a few years, consider whether it's time to offer an updated version. Since most magazines have a three-year turnaround time on repeating the same subject, take advantage of this cyclical pattern by offering updates to anyone who's ever run the article. Submit the original piece plus a letter detailing your update plans two and a half years after the first publication in that magazine to allow the right lead time.

Other update prospects are any publications that expressed the faintest interest in either the original query or earlier second serial submissions. Changes in personnel and inventory could well tip the balance in your favor at this point. Resubmitting to *any* magazine that has previously considered the piece is perfectly appropriate if you're offering something new, i.e. the update, or you've learned that some editorial purge will let you approach a new person.

Enhance the prospects of update sales by making a point of clipping all newspaper and magazine articles you see on subjects you've written about in the past. Recent news events could make an old subject even more marketable the second time around: a sensational hijacking case could spark interest in a terrorist piece you'd already written; or your profile subject might step out of obscurity and win a Nobel prize, creating worldwide demand for that piece you did on him way back when. This kind of conscientious effort could also lead to your being considered an "expert" on certain subjects, increasing your fees for those articles.

Check for significant anniversaries or dates that might increase the marketability of an update. If the city you wrote about in your travel piece is about to have its centennial, or the President designates the following year "The Year of X" and you have an old piece on X in your files, dust the old articles off and get them out with a covering letter describing the reason for their new timeliness.

After you've recycled your article to every market you're aware of—and there are always more if you really look—consider whether you could cannibalize portions of your article, or the research or interviews you did for it, into *spin-offs*. For example, your research and interviews on "Breaking Into Modeling" could be spun off into "Getting Your Child into Modeling" and "The Teen's Guide to Modeling Careers" without too much additional effort.

To consider whether there's a good spin-off to your article—there may be several—consider if any portion of it could be expanded into a new article for the same market. If your last piece was on "Minor Head Injuries," you may already have research and quotes that could be turned into a query on "Memory Disorders" which you could send off to the same editor that bought the original piece. This approach is particularly good because you have already established credibility with this particular editor on medical pieces, so have created a favorable climate for the spin-off piece.

Experts and profile subjects you've already used could be recycled into new pieces, especially if you plan ahead. In an interview with a surgeon for a piece on "Avoiding Unnecessary Operations," for example, you could easily gather enough material to write spin-off articles on *each* of the unnecessary operations: "What Every Parent Should Know about Tonsillectomies," "Do You Really Need a Hysterectomy?" and "New Surgical Options for Breast Cancer."

Aspects of the piece could also lend themselves to related articles for a variety of other magazines which would not be interested in second serial rights to your original piece. Your travel piece might contain information that could be developed into a piece on "Fishing the Mountain Streams" and sold to angling magazines. Whenever you're investigating a new subject, keep your antennae up for spin-off ideas and gather the spin-off information along with the material for your original article.

To recycle your material into *a round-up article,* wait until you have several completed pieces that parallel each other in some way. If, for example, you'd written articles on "Modeling," "TV Jobs," "Careers in Advertising," "Breaking Into Publishing," and "The Fast-Paced Political Job," you could offer editors a piece called "The Five Most Glamorous Careers—And How to Break into Them" which would pull material from your five previous pieces for the "new" article. Your travel pieces could be rounded up into "Romantic Honeymoon Spots," or you could organize your profiles into "Millionaires Before Age 30—Five Success Stories."

Increase the odds of selling an easy to do round-up by concentrating on a few basic topics in your writing rather than selecting dramatically different subjects for each one.

Money from Abroad

How would you like to start getting checks in Swiss francs, pounds, deutsche marks and lira? While not every article you write will "travel," writers often neglect the thousands of markets that wait across the border. Some of the articles you write might be good bets for second serial sales in Canada, or first or second serial sales in other countries. Best bets for foreign sales are celebrity profiles, life-style pieces, material on current American trends and fashions, popular medical or scientific pieces, and some general-interest pieces if they aren't too American in outlook.

There are two ways to sell foreign and translation rights to your work. For the major European countries and Japan, you may be able to hire foreign agents. *International Literary Marketplace* lists them by country. You can expect to pay 10 percent to 25 percent as a commission on agented sales. Or you can submit to foreign publications directly. *Ulrich's International Periodicals Directory*, available at your library, lists more than 70,000 publications throughout the world. Some of the bigger foreign publications also have New York offices, making for faster submission results.

Don't worry about the language barrier when making submissions to foreign editors; any reasonably large publication will have English readers on staff. But instead of a stamped self-addressed reply envelope, enclose International Reply Coupons, available at your post office. Foreign submissions can be quite slow; don't worry if a few months pass without a reply.

Making Book on Your Articles

Many of the books I've sold got their start in life as articles. If you find yourself drawn to a particular subject in your article writing, consider whether the pieces might be gathered into a book, possibly with the addition of a few extra chapters. Or use a single article as a sample chapter to complement your book proposal.

Writing a book will help your magazine career in several ways. First, editors are quite impressed by book credits and will often increase your fees. Second, a combination of book and article projects will ensure that all your writing time is spent profitably, as you sandwich freelance assignments into your book-writing schedule. Third, your book will establish your credentials as an expert on whatever topic you write on. And fourth, you can sell the chapters of the book to magazines as you work (if you've retained first serial rights in your book contract), boosting your income still further.

Before writing your book proposal, consult *Subject Guide to*

Books in Print, available at libraries and book stores to see how much competition there is in your subject area. The more competitors there are, the stronger your slant must be to sell yet another work on the subject and to attract a readership once your book is out. Also read the competition so you'll be prepared when an editor asks how your book will differ from the works already out on the subject.

Selling a nonfiction book is much like selling an article. Instead of writing a query, you write a proposal containing the same three vital ingredients, but give each one more space. Start with a compelling lead, followed by a detailed description of your book's basic subject, being sure to mention enough highlights to whet the editor's appetite. Include sales points. Next provide a chapter-by-chapter outline, giving each chapter a catchy title and a few sentences of description. Finish with your author's bio.

The best length for your proposal is between ten and twenty pages, not including the sample article or articles. You may also want to write additional samples such as the introduction or one of the really exciting chapters. For more information on book proposals, consult *How to Write a Book Proposal* by Michael Larsen (Writer's Digest Books)—a valuable guide though its advice differs slightly from mine on some points.

To locate likely publishers, consult *Literary Market Place* and *Writer's Market.* Check your bookstore too, noting the names of publishers of books likely to appeal to a similar audience as the work you have in mind. Avoid publishers with something very similar on their list unless the other work is over five years old and therefore might be likely to go out of print soon. Use *Literary Market Place* to identify editors at the house you're thinking of submitting your book to. You may want to telephone to find out which editor would be the best bet for your book.

Once you've assembled your submission list, compose a one- or two-page query letter briefly describing your book, being sure to mention that a detailed proposal and samples are available, and, as with all communications with publishers, enclose SASE. Interested editors will then request the material. Using multiple submissions will speed results considerably.

If you'd like some professional help in marketing your book, a literary agent usually charges 10 percent to 15 percent commission. In dealing with major publishers—except for genre fiction—an agent is becoming increasingly essential as some publishers no longer consider unagented material. You can obtain a list of reliable agents by sending a stamped self-addressed envelope to the Society of Authors' Representatives, P. O. Box 650, Old Chelsea Station, NY 10013. You can also contact the Independent Literary Agents Association, Box 5257, FDR Station, New York, NY 10150, or consult *Literary Agents of North America* in the reference section of a library.

In recent years the number of literary agents has greatly increased. Since there are no special requirements to start an agency, I believe writers do best to select a literary agent who is a member of one of these organizations as both have established criteria for membership which ensure that the agent you select will be reasonably well established and successful. I also think you should avoid agents who charge a criticism fee, unless it is very small, say $15 or less. Some agents really earn most of their money through these fees rather than through sales of their clients' work.

What about an agent for your articles? Very few agents are willing to handle someone who only writes articles since the amount of work involved relative to the anticipated commissions makes such representation impractical for most agents. Once you have a book project, however, you may also be able to entice an agent into representing your articles as well as your books. However I find it hard to imagine an agent putting the same dogged marketing effort into peddling an article that its author would and think that most writers do better to sell their own articles and save the 10 percent or 15 percent.

Should you or your agent place the book, the typical publishing contract normally provides for a guaranteed advance plus royalties on each copy sold. Some smaller publishers don't pay advances, just royalties. Typical advances for first nonfiction books range from $2,000 to $12,000, depending on the size of the potential market and the degree of editorial enthusiasm for the book. Some first books sell for much higher sums. Typical hardcover royalties start at 10 percent of the jacket price of the book and escalate to 15 percent as the book reaches higher sales levels. Earnings from paperback reprint sales are normally shared between the author and publisher. You can also sell your book directly to a paperback publisher without going through hardcover first. Typical paperback royalties are 6 percent of the cover price and escalate to 8 percent.

Your Article Ought to Be in Pictures!

Your article could be the start of something big—a movie or TV contract. While relatively few articles make it to either the big or small screen, *Saturday Night Fever, Hardbodies,* and *The Best Little Whorehouse in Texas* are some notable exceptions. Your article could be another.

To have a shot at Hollywood, your article should have some kind of story line that could be developed in the dramatic version. The most likely prospects are "slice of life," human interest, personal experience, true life drama, and true crime material.

If you can envision dramatic use of your article, a dramatic agent is all but essential to selling your article to producers, many of whom will not consider unagented submissions or will expect you to sign long, complex legal releases before they will even look at the material. The agent lists provided by the SAR or ILAA include dramatic agents, or consult *Literary Market Place* or *Writer's Market* for additional listings.

If your article interests a movie or TV producer, typically you'd be offered an option agreement which provides for a payment for a six-month or one-year option, a second payment if the option is renewed, and a substantially larger payment if the option is exercised. A small movie sale might provide for $2,500 as an option payment, against a purchase price of $25,000; larger ones are sometimes possible. Your contract would also provide for additional payments for TV series or mini-series use, theatrical release (as opposed to TV release), and other dramatic uses. In addition you might be able to persuade the producer to pay you a consulting fee to help with the script—or even to hire you to write it.

If your article were made into a movie, chances are that you could make a profitable sale of book rights to the tie-in book (if you didn't give them to the producer), then possibly resell some of its chapters to magazines. A good article, you see, can be a gold mine that can be worked many times before the mother lode is exhausted. And even then your persistence could lead you to discover new sales veins to exploit in the future.

18

Seven Keys to Success— and Two Pitfalls to Avoid

I f you can sell one of your articles, you can sell a hundred of them—or a thousand. Why not? You've already made the toughest sale you'll ever have to make—convincing an editor to buy from a novice. You've proved that you've got what it takes to succeed as a writer: talent, initiative, and marketing ability. Now that you've gotten your foot in the door, how can you capitalize on this promising beginning?

Your best strategy is to immediately follow up on each sale with new submissions to that publication, other publications in the same field, and bigger publications that serve a related audience—as well as continuing to submit any other queries or articles you've previously developed, updating the author's bio to include the sale. By doing your best to duplicate the conditions of your first success, you'll be following the winning formula that keeps authors like John D. MacDonald, Stephen King, and Shana Alexander appearing on the best-seller lists regularly.

Sounds easy, right? Following the logical submission path will produce new sales, but to realize your full potential as a writer you need to know how to push *yourself* as well as your work. I'm talking about a success attitude that keeps you at the typewriter during those dark periods when it takes days to write a few simple paragraphs, the mailman leaves nothing but bills, and your outstanding submissions appear to have dropped into some black hole at the publishers' offices. It's an attitude that sends you trudging over to the post office with more submissions the very day that editor A rejects that article you labored long and hard over, and editors B and C return your two best queries with form rejection slips. Thinking like a winner even when the black dog of failure is nipping at your heels is crucial to success in any career, and freelance writing is no exception.

To cultivate this vital self-confidence, you first need to identify and eliminate negative attitudes that may be sabotaging your efforts, then replace them with habits and an outlook that promotes success. In talking to hundreds of successful and not-so-successful writers about their work styles and attitudes, I've noticed several common threads to these discussions in problems that hold some writers back and lead others on to success.

Stumbling Blocks

In typing out 1099 forms listing the taxable income of my clients, I've noticed that some writers seem to make practically the exact same income each year—it could be $10,000 or $100,000. In analyzing this plateau phenomenon I've concluded that some of us work until we reach a level of psychological comfort, then lose that sense of hunger that drives others on to reach greater and greater heights. Executive recruiter John Wareham, author of *Secrets of a Corporate Headhunter*, theorizes that what he terms "family destiny" influences the level of success reached in a career: "The typical executive pays back his father by adopting his values, walking in his footsteps, and marginally improving upon the father's status as it was perceived in childhood at about age five."

Such psychological barriers may also stop you from trying to crack better markets. Some writers feel comfortable enough working in the minor leagues and may carve out a niche in which they can sell regularly to low-paying markets. By streamlining their operation, such writers can earn a respectable salary by turning out their work in volume. But when it comes to the major markets, somehow they can't seem to find the time or the energy to submit. Subconsciously they feel that they're not good enough for *Redbook* or *Esquire* and would rather not test the assumption.

Powerful as such psychological constraints may be, breaking them is often as much a matter of being willing to *try*, repeatedly if necessary, as sheer talent; Wareham's research on family destiny turned up a spectacular exception to his rule: a million-dollar-a-year executive who was the son of a *crane operator*. And what about that fellow who went from the log cabin of his childhood all the way to the White House?

If you've written yourself into a limiting life script, why not apply your literary talents to revising it? Each time you achieve some success, you should be asking yourself, "Where do I go from here?" The answer might be asking your current publisher for a raise—you'd be surprised how few magazine writers do this—aiming queries at bigger markets until you hit some, or launching a book project. What you have now is not all there is. The best *is* yet to come, if you're willing to work for it.

While psychological anxieties hobble your steps as you travel the road to success, writer's block can stop you in your tracks if you let it. Many writers have the misconception that writer's block is something like the common cold, an incurable affliction that eventually runs its course, impervious to any known treatment. But unlike the sniffles, a case of writer's block can be arrested with prompt action.

Let's look at a typical untreated case. Ginger, one of my students, was severely afflicted. When I first encountered her in my class she hadn't written a word for several months, and no longer made any real effort to write. Occasionally she'd open her notebook and stare at a blank page for a half hour or so. Taking my course was her final attempt to snap out of it. For the first assignment, to write down six article ideas, she was able to produce four ideas. The next assignment, to write lead paragraphs for two articles, brought on a new attack. Ginger wrote nothing. Her record was equally spotty on the next few assignments. Encouraged to discuss her problem, she confided that she'd "lost her inspiration"; that she couldn't "get in the mood to write."

Not in the mood? Underlying her remark was the erroneous assumption some writer have: *that writing is a spontaneous process that naturally occurs when you "get in the mood."* What nonsense! This attitude may be okay for someone who's keeping a diary for personal pleasure, but it's a damaging assumption for anyone who hopes to write professionally. Can you imagine an insurance salesman telling his boss that he wasn't in the mood to peddle policies this week? Though salespeople have their own dry spells, like tribal shamans of old they keep doing the rain dance until the clouds start cooperating again.

But what about the creative process, you may say. You can't just turn it on by command, can you? I say you can—because I do, every weekday from 9 to 3 (when my children come home from school). Some days my fingers fly across the keyboard for six straight hours, writing up to fifteen finished pages; other days I struggle to finish a couple of paragraphs. But I don't consider these bad days wasted effort; often I find that the next day is uncommonly productive, as if my subconscious had been writing the difficult pages as I slept.

Another writer I know found herself completely cured of writer's block after having a baby. While in her childless days she'd lounged around waiting for the mood to strike or a deadline to loom, now her workday was telescoped into just three hours, the baby's naptime. Amazingly, she reported, inspiration would regularly strike during the appointed three hours, and her output rose far above the levels she'd formerly reached with "full-time" freelancing on her old haphazard schedule.

I attribute her cure not to the baby but to improved work habits. A regular writing schedule, unswervingly followed, will train "inspiration" to come on cue. Writer's block frequently becomes a vicious cycle because writers have conditioned themselves to work when in a certain mood. No mood, no work. How likely is it after such a setback that the proper mood will return the next day? The "mood" is basically a reflection of the writer's own confidence in his or her work; and that is why a bad day is so devastating to the mood writer. The regular schedule approach, on the other hand, only demands that you punch in at the typewriter on time and do your best to write until quitting time.

If you're suffering from an old writing block that has turned mountainous, there are ways to blast past it. The best is to reinfect yourself with the writing fever through exposure to other writers. Take writing courses, join writers' groups, travel to a writing conference in another city. Find a few fresh ideas to work on, research them carefully, and set up a schedule to work once you've restored your enthusiasm. Start your workday by reading some of the good work you've done in the past to boost your confidence.

My blocked student, Ginger, was encouraged enough by the class's interest and my suggestions to get back to work. While she had a few lapses into her blocked state, for the final class of the semester she proudly read a long, delightfully written piece she'd written the day before. Soon after the course ended I got a note from her—she now had a regular job with a small newspaper, writing most of the articles that appeared each week.

Secrets of Success

Avoiding negative attitudes which may inhibit your writing or selling efforts is only half the battle. To realize your full writing potential, you'll also need positive strategies. Here are seven steps to start you on the way to your first one hundred sales.

1. Read omnivorously. Every successful writer I know is a compulsive reader. "I'll read absolutely anything," one writer told me. Not only will your reading help you find good article ideas and increase the knowledge you bring to your work, but it will keep you in touch with today's top writers. As you read you'll be absorbing their successful techniques along with their ideas.

What should you read? Read it all: the classics, the popular best-sellers, literary works, and of course, all the magazines you can get your hands on. Educating yourself through reading improves your writing by expanding the sense of possibility you bring to your work. As John Gardner writes in *On Becoming a Novelist:* "The uneducated writer is, for one thing, locked into his own time and place. Not knowing. . . . about Homer or Racine or the contemporary fiction of South America, not knowing the many different ways in which a story can be told, from the rough hemp tale-spinning of the saga poets to the dandified French allegorical tricks of the Middle Ages to the strange ways of India and China or avant-garde contemporary Africans, Poles, or Americans, he is like a carpenter with only a few crude tools: a hammer, a knife, a drill, a pair of pliers."

Your reading can also help you catch rising trends in time to sell them to editors. Ever wonder who dictates that bulimia, anorexia nervosa, and hypoglycemia are out as article topics, but that stress is hot; that bodybuilding is passé, while stretching is in vogue? Where do these magazine trends start? While it might seem that word comes down from Mount Olympus just in time for the June issue, magazine editors actually learn about trends from two main sources, both accessible to the writer. The first is newspapers, particularly the *Wall Street Journal* and the *New York Times,* as well as news and people magazines. (If you live outside New York City, your local paper may also tip you off to human interest and human drama stories you can sell to New York editors.)

The second and less well known source of information on trends is the book publishing scene. Most magazines receive advance proofs of forthcoming books for first serial (before publication) excerpting and for book reviews. When a magazine editor learns that a book publisher will be spending big bucks to promote books on the F Plan diet or the G Spot, articles on these trends on dieting and sex are sure to follow. You can mine this lode too. Three times a year, in February, May, and August, *Publishers Weekly,* the publishing industry's trade journal, comes out with the thick announcement issues for important spring, summer, and fall books (winter doesn't really exist in book publishing). *Publishers Weekly* is available at your library or by subscription (205 East 42nd Street, New York, NY 10017). By skimming through the ads and announcements, you'll be gazing into the same crystal ball the publishers use.

2. Strike while the brain is hot.   One of my clients once told me that he'd talked away five good books at a neighborhood tavern. Loose lips, he found, sink writing. After talking about those five books night after night he found that he had no desire to actually put them on paper. The freshness of the original inspiration was gone; in his mind he'd already written the books and was tired of them. By spending his evenings at the typewriter, instead of the tavern however, he went on to write a dozen books with combined sales of well over one million copies.

Talking when you should be writing is an easy pitfall to succumb to, but avoid test-marketing your ideas into tedium. Describe your ideas to editors, not friends, with a pithy query sent out promptly after you get the idea. Not only don't friends have the power to make assignments, but they have an annoying habit of pouring cold water on your enthusiasm with such comments as "I think I saw something on that recently," or "But everybody already knows about that"—both common reactions that say absolutely nothing about your ability to market the article, as I've explained in Chapter One. Even positive comments, gratifying as they are, can take the edge off your enthusiasm. Confide in your typewriter, and let your friends read your articles when they appear in print.

3. Create winning formulas to follow.   Since time is money in freelance writing, the more ways you find to streamline your writing, the more profitable your time at the typewriter will be. Students in my writing class are often surprised that I can give them an instant outline to follow in writing an article on any topic they happen to name. The secret is standardization. Having read literally thousands of magazine articles over the years. I've absorbed dozens of organizing techniques that work, and can conjure up an appropriate one for a new topic with little conscious effort. You can easily devise effective formulas for your articles and queries too.

Here's a frequently used formula for articles. Start with an anecdote touching on the basic problem or situation to be described in the article, followed by a second paragraph clarifying your topic and theme or slant. In the middle section, provide the latest information on your topic, with anecdotes. For further background, provide a historical section. Next describe any solutions, new techniques, recommendations from experts and other helpful advice. End with thoughts on the future through exciting quotes, speculation on the benefits to be realized by overcoming the problem, uplifting advice, or interesting sequels to your story.

While this precise formula won't fit every article you have in mind or may not appeal to you, the point is that by making a conscious effort to analyze other writers' organizing principles and to develop winning formulas for your own articles and queries, you'll shorten both writing and research time. And using pre-fab organizing plans doesn't mean you have to sacrifice originality. The words and ideas you choose to flesh out your organizational skeletons will give each article its unique "fingerprint," something another writer with the same plan and topic could never duplicate.

Standardizing covering letters speeds submissions. As an agent I normally devise a prototype covering letter for each project and reuse it on each submission, adding any special marketing points peculiar to that particular market. My covering letters borrow freely from any previous submission letters that have proved effective for other projects.

4. Keep the production lines rolling. Can you imagine a manufacturer producing the goods to fill one order, then letting the assembly line sit idle while the sales personnel then looked for additional orders? Inefficient submission techniques are just as wasteful and costly—a surprising number of writers all but guarantee themselves periodic unemployment by failing to submit new queries and articles while they wait for results of previous submissions. As a freelancer your ultimate goal is 100 percent employment, and to get it you must keep a constant stream of submissions pouring out of your typewriter at all times.

Here's a program that should get the production lines in motion. Start by writing a minimum of one new query each week, or as many more as you can cram into your writing schedule. Send each new query out on a broad multiple submission to all likely markets, then *forget* about it and move on to the next topic that interests you. Resubmit all rejected queries immediately until potential markets are temporarily exhausted. When you land an assignment, continue marketing just as aggressively until you've lined up three or four months' worth of work. As you write your assigned pieces, continue to submit new ideas periodically to keep yourself steadily employed. As your writing skills and confidence grow, consider marketing book projects as well—you can sandwich your article assignments in between writing the book chapters.

Keep careful records of your submissions to avoid missing potential markets. Schedule periodic follow-ups to outstanding submissions, every four to six weeks, say. Also maintain a file of rejection letters to remind you of any encouraging comments or requests for additional queries you might receive, as well as to demonstrate to the IRS the businesslike nature of your professional efforts.

Learning to interrupt one project to market another requires some ability to compartmentalize your work, but the skill is easily acquired with practice. While you're working on assignment, your confidence and creative skill are likely to be high, making this an excellent time to conceive and market new projects. Don't worry about overkill in marketing—there could be worse fates than scrambling to finish a dozen assigned pieces! With practice you'll learn to regulate submission and writing flow to maintain a comfortable pace of work.

5. Beg, borrow, or steal more writing time. Too busy to do much writing? Studies show that the average person spends six hours a day watching TV. Undoubtedly you too have more free time than you realize. I've heard about ingenious writers who dictated articles to a tape recorder as they waited in lines, carried projects with them to edit on the beach, reviewed research material on the train to work, composed queries during their lunch hour, and wrote for an hour or two before leaving for the office. Before you decide that you lack time to work, consider this: an agent I know tells his clients that they can write a book in just three months by composing three pages a day. By writing just *one* page a day, you can finish an article every two weeks, twenty-six a year. Creating a respectable body of work is more a matter of *how often* you work than *how long* you spend in each writing session. Working just three hours a day will give you plenty of time to turn out queries and articles in volume.

6. Raise your marketing IQ. If you don't know that a particular market exists, you can't sell to it. Make a point of adding market study to your writing schedule. In addition to studying *Writer's Digest* and *The Writer* for market updates, try to read at least one new magazine every week. Study *Writer's Market* for additional ideas about new markets for your work. Ask your friends which magazines they read regularly and investigate these magazines as promising outlets for your work. From time to time go to the library and read the last twelve issues of a magazine that you'd like to submit to, making notes of the types of subjects and approaches which seem to be favored by that publication.

7. Keep the faith. I've saved the best secret of success for last. The greatest asset you can bring to your work is a firm belief in the power of your writing. The air of confidence attracts editors, creates sales. Convince yourself that your work is good enough to sell. Write affirmations, notes saying, "Editors want to buy my writing," and "I'm a good writer," or whatever message you think would build your confidence, and tape them around your office. Do everything in your power to make your work good: searching for salable ideas, taking time to research and plan carefully, rewriting and rewriting again as necessary, meticulous proofreading and typing, and dogged, never-say-die marketing.

Recently I heard a story about a writing teacher who told a promising student that one day her work would appear in the *New Yorker*. "Sure," said the student, "I'll believe that when I see it." "No," said the teacher, "you'll see it when you believe it."

And you will. You'll see those first hundred sales—and more—when you believe in yourself and your work.

A Letter to the Reader

Do you have any comments about this book? Though I cannot offer to represent magazine writers or provide editorial services of any kind, I'd be interested in hearing about the results you've achieved with my methods and any successes you've had after reading the book.

If you'd like an answer to your letter, please send SASE.

Sincerely yours,

Lisa Collier Cool
% Writer's Digest Books
1507 Dana Avenue
Cincinnati, Ohio 45207

Appendix

The Writer's Bookshelf

FINDING MARKETS

Since many of these directories are both expensive and specialized, if you decide to buy one for home use, I recommend either *Writer's Market* or *Writer's Handbook* for magazine markets and *Literary Market Place* for book publishing information.

Association Publications in Print. R. R. Bowker. Annual. Lists magazines and books issued by 13,000 associations, with 400 subject categories.

Ayer Directory of Publications. Ayer Press. Annual. Geographically organized directory of magazines and newspapers.

Dobler World Directory of Youth Publications. Citation Press. Comprehensive listings of juvenile and teen publications.

Editor and Publisher International Year Book. Editor and Publisher. Annual. Covers American and foreign daily and weekly newspapers.

Editor and Publisher Syndicate Directory. Editor and Publisher. Updated periodically. Contains detailed listings of newspaper syndicates.

Gebbie House Magazine Directory. National Research Bureau. Periodic updates. Gives market information on company, organization, and group publications.

International Literary Marketplace. R. R. Bowker. Annual. Contains listings of foreign publishers and agents.

Literary Market Place. R. R. Bowker. Annual. Lists U.S. book publishers and their personnel, agents, syndicates, and other publishing related information. The standard directory of book publishing.

Magazine Industry Marketplace. R. R. Bowker. Annual. Detailed listing of magazines and personnel, limited market information.

Standard Rate and Data. Standard Rate and Data Service. Organized by subject, this directory lists magazines, newspapers, newsletters, and government publications.

Ulrich's International Periodicals Directory. R. R. Bowker. Biennial. Helpful in locating overseas markets.

Writer's Handook. The Writer, Inc. Annual. Contains dozens of helpful articles on writing, plus about 2,000 market listings.

Writer's Market. Writer's Digest Books. Annual. The favorite market tool of the freelance writer, this directory lists about 5,000 paying markets for freelance work.

Magazines about Writing and Publishing

Publishers Weekly, 205 East 42nd Street, New York, NY 10017. Weekly. Oriented toward book publishers, this magazine contains personnel changes at book publishers, publishing news, and reviews of new books. Available at most libraries.

The Writer, 120 Boylston St., Boston, MA 02116. Monthly. Contains articles about writing and market information.

Writer's Digest, 1507 Dana Avenue, Cincinnati, OH 45207. Monthly. Contains articles about writing and market information.

Writer's Yearbook, 1507 Dana Avenue, Cincinnati, OH 45207. Annual. Contains how-to, current trends, interviews, and analysis of 500 freelance markets.

Tricks of the Trade

Appelbaum, Judith and Evans, Nancy. *How to Get Happily Published.* Plume/New American Library. Revised edition, 1982. A general guide to writing and publishing articles and books.

Author Aid/Research Associates, editors. *Literary Agents of North America.* Author Aid/ Research Associates (340 East 52nd Street, New York, NY 10022). Annual. Detailed compilation of agents for articles, books, and screenplays.

Bernstein, Theodore M. *Watch Your Language.* Atheneum. First paperback edition, 1976. An amusing guide to style based on the author's experiences in the news room of the *New York Times.*

Brady, John. *The Craft of Interviewing.* Vintage Books. First Vintage edition, 1977. *The* definitive guide for interviewers, this zesty book is filled with lively anecdotes and practical tips.

Emerson, Connie. *Write on Target.* Writer's Digest Books, 1981. Explains how to profile a magazine's interests and readers by studying its contents.

Engh, Rohn. *Sell and Resell Your Photos.* Writer's Digest Books. First edition, 1981. An excellent guide to breaking into professional photography.

Larsen, Michael. *How to Write a Book Proposal.* Writer's Digest Books. 1985. Although the author recommends using longer book proposals than I believe necessary, this worthwhile guide covers all the basics of writing and marketing book proposals in a concise and detailed manner.

Newcomb, Duane. *A Complete Guide to Marketing Magazine Articles.* Writer's Digest Books. Reprinted 1980. Filled with valuable tips for the magazine writer; emphasis is on selling to smaller magazines.

Polking, Kirk and Meranus, Leonard S., editors. *Law and the Writer.* Writer's Digest Books. Revised edition, 1981. A highly readable legal guide for authors, with many distinguished contributors.

Provost, Gary. *Make Every Word Count.* Writer's Digest Books. 1980. Written in a lively and entertaining style, this book discusses effective fiction and nonfiction writing techniques.

Provost, Gary. *The Freelance Writer's Handbook.* Mentor/New American Library. 1982. All aspects of professional writing are covered: magazines, books, newspapers, scripts, reviews, speechwriting, public relations, and advertising; the emphasis is on articles and books.

Strunk, William, Jr. and White, E. B. *The Elements of Style.* Macmillan. Second edition, 1972. A classic of its kind.

Tarshis, Barry. *How to Write Like a Pro.* Plume/New American Library. 1982. Techniques of nonfiction writing.

Weisbord, Marvin, editor. *A Treasury of Tips for Writers.* Writer's Digest Books. First paperback edition, 1981. Helpful hints from members of the American Society of Journalists and Authors.

Zinsser, William. *On Writing Well.* Harper & Row. Second edition, 1980. A delightful guide to nonfiction writing.

FINDING FACTS

An * indicates library reference material. The other books on this list may also be available at the library, or you may want to buy them for home use.

Bartlett, John. *Bartlett's Familiar Quotations.* Little, Brown and Company. Revised periodically. An easy way to find good quotes on just about any subject, as well as verify the exact wording of quotations you already know.

Biography Index. H. W. Wilson. Annual, with quarterly updates. Indexes biographical information from books and magazines.

Business Periodical Index. H. W. Wilson Company. Accumulated annually, with monthly updates. Use it to find business news from 150 magazines.

Chase's Calendar of Annual Events. Contemporary Books. Annual. Helpful in finding marketing tie-ins for your articles.

Cottam, Keith M. and Pelton, Robert W. *Writer's Research Handbook.* Barnes and Noble. First Barnes and Noble edition, 1978. A short, concise guide to the most common reference books, with helpful research tips.

Encyclopedia of Associations. Gale Research Company. New editions periodically, supplemented with quarterly updates. Detailed data on thousands of groups in the U.S.

Horowitz, Lois. *Knowing Where to Look.* Writer's Digest Books, 1984.

Horowitz, Lois. *A Writer's Guide to Research.* Writer's Digest Books, 1986. Horowitz, a professional researcher, explains how to find the facts you need, either for an overview or an in-depth study.

Magazine Index. Information Access Co. Updated monthly. Available on microfilm readers at the library, this is the periodical index of choice for general reference.

McWhirter, Norris and McWhirter, Ross, editors. *The Guinness Book of World Records.* Sterling Publishing Co. Revised periodically. Filled with terrific tidbits.

National Geographic Atlas of the World. The National Geographic Society. Updated periodically. A pleasure to behold, and useful besides.

The New Columbia Encyclopedia. Columbia University Press. Revised periodically. "The best 10½ pound [encyclopedia] available," say the authors of *Writer's Research Handbook.*

Newlin, Barbara. *Answers Online: Your Guide to Informational Data Bases.* McGraw-Hill. 1985. A concise, detailed guide to getting research information via computer.

Newspaper Index. Information Access Co. Updated monthly.

Photographer's Market. Writer's Digest Books. Annual. Where to sell your pictures.

The Random House Dictionary of the English Language, Unabridged Edition. Random House. Contains the entire English language, an atlas, and much, much more.

*Readers' Guide to Periodic Literature. H. W. Wilson Company. Annual, quarterly, and monthly compilations. Indexes almost 160 popular publications.

Roget's International Thesaurus. Harper & Row. Revised periodically. Here's where to find that elusive word.

*Subject Guide to Books in Print. R. R. Bowker. Annual.

U.S. Bureau of the Census. *Statistical Abstract of the United States.* Annual. Best statistics source.

*Who's Who in America. Marquis Who's Who. Annual. A companion volume is *Who Was Who in America,* covering prominent people who are now deceased.

The World Almanac and Book of Facts. Newspaper Enterprise Association. Annual. Great source of facts.

Index

Other Books of Interest

Annual Market Books

Artist's Market, edited by Susan Conner $19.95
Children's Writer's & Illustrator's Market, edited by Connie Eidenier (paper) $14.95
Novel & Short Story Writer's Market, edited by Laurie Henry (paper) $17.95
Photographer's Market, edited by Sam Marshall $19.95
Poet's Market, by Judson Jerome $18.95
Songwriter's Market, edited by Mark Garvey $18.95
Writer's Market, edited by Glenda Neff $23.95

General Writing Books

Annable's Treasury of Literary Teasers, by H.D. Annable (paper) $10.95
Beginning Writer's Answer Book, edited by Kirk Polking (paper) $12.95
Beyond Style: Mastering the Finer Points of Writing, by Gary Provost $15.95
Discovering the Writer Within, by Bruce Ballenger & Barry Lane $16.95
Getting the Words Right: How to Revise, Edit and Rewrite, by Theodore A. Rees Cheney $15.95
A Handbook of Problem Words & Phrases, by Morton S. Freeman $16.95
How to Increase Your Word Power, by the editors of Reader's Digest $19.95
How to Write a Book Proposal, by Michael Larsen $10.95
Just Open a Vein, edited by William Brohaugh $15.95
Knowing Where to Look: The Ultimate Guide to Research, by Lois Horowitz (paper) $15.95
Make Every Word Count, by Gary Provost (paper) $9.95
On Being a Writer, edited by Bill Strickland $19.95
Pinckert's Practical Grammar, by Robert C. Pinckert $14.95
The Story Behind the Word, by Morton S. Freeman (paper) $9.95
12 Keys to Writing Books that Sell, by Kathleen Krull (paper) $12.95
The 29 Most Common Writing Mistakes & How to Avoid Them, by Judy Delton $9.95
Word Processing Secrets for Writers, by Michael A. Banks & Ansen Dibell (paper) $14.95
Writer's Block & How to Use It, by Victoria Nelson $14.95
The Writer's Digest Guide to Manuscript Formats, by Buchman & Groves $16.95
Writer's Encyclopedia, edited by Kirk Polking (paper) $16.95

Nonfiction Writing

Basic Magazine Writing, by Barbara Kevles $16.95
How to Sell Every Magazine Article You Write, by Lisa Collier Cool (paper) $11.95
The Writer's Digest Handbook of Magazine Article Writing, edited by Jean M. Fredette $15.95
Writing Creative Nonfiction, by Theodore A. Rees Cheney $15.95
Writing Nonfiction that Sells, by Samm Sinclair Baker $14.95

Fiction Writing

The Art & Craft of Novel Writing, by Oakley Hall $16.95
Best Stories from New Writers, edited by Linda Sanders $16.95
Characters & Viewpoint, by Orson Scott Card $13.95
Creating Short Fiction, by Damon Knight (paper) $9.95
Dare to Be a Great Writer: 329 Keys to Powerful Fiction, by Leonard Bishop $15.95
Dialogue, by Lewis Turco $12.95
Fiction is Folks: How to Create Unforgettable Characters, by Robert Newton Peck (paper) $8.95
Handbook of Short Story Writing: Vol. I, by Dickson and Smythe (paper) $9.95
Handbook of Short Story Writing: Vol. II, edited by Jean M. Fredette $15.95
One Great Way to Write Short Stories, by Ben Nyberg $14.95
Plot, by Ansen Dibell $13.95
Revision, by Kit Reed $13.95
Spider Spin Me a Web: Lawrence Block on Writing Fiction, by Lawrence Block $16.95

Storycrafting, by Paul Darcy Boles (paper) $10.95
Writing the Novel: From Plot to Print, by Lawrence Block (paper) $9.95
Special Interest Writing Books
The Children's Picture Book: How to Write It, How to Sell It, by Ellen E.M. Roberts (paper) $16.95
Comedy Writing Secrets, by Melvin Helitzer $18.95
The Complete Book of Scriptwriting, by J. Michael Straczynski (paper) $11.95
The Craft of Lyric Writing, by Sheila Davis $18.95
Editing Your Newsletter, by Mark Beach (paper) $18.50
Families Writing, by Peter Stillman $15.95
Guide to Greeting Card Writing, edited by Larry Sandman (paper) $9.95
How to Write a Play, by Raymond Hull (paper) $12.95
How to Write Action/Adventure Novels, by Michael Newton $13.95
How to Write & Sell A Column, by Raskin & Males $10.95
How to Write and Sell Your Personal Experiences, by Lois Duncan (paper) $10.95
How to Write Mysteries, by Shannon OCork $13.95
How to Write Romances, by Phyllis Taylor Pianka $13.95
How to Write Tales of Horror, Fantasy & Science Fiction, edited by J.N. Williamson $15.95
How to Write the Story of Your Life, by Frank P. Thomas (paper) $11.95
How to Write Western Novels, by Matt Braun $13.95
Mystery Writer's Handbook, by The Mystery Writers of America (paper) $10.95
The Poet's Handbook, by Judson Jerome (paper) $10.95
Successful Lyric Writing (workbook), by Sheila Davis (paper) $16.95
Successful Scriptwriting, by Jurgen Wolff & Kerry Cox $18.95
Travel Writer's Handbook, by Louise Zobel (paper) $11.95
TV Scriptwriter's Handbook, by Alfred Brenner (paper) $10.95
Writing for Children & Teenagers, 3rd Edition, by Lee Wyndham & Arnold Madison (paper) $12.95
Writing Short Stories for Young People, by George Edward Stanley $15.95
Writing the Modern Mystery, by Barbara Norville $15.95
Writing to Inspire, edited by William Gentz (paper) $14.95
The Writing Business
A Beginner's Guide to Getting Published, edited by Kirk Polking $11.95
The Complete Guide to Self-Publishing, by Tom & Marilyn Ross (paper) $16.95
How to Sell & Re-Sell Your Writing, by Duane Newcomb $11.95
How to Write with a Collaborator, by Hal Bennett with Michael Larsen $11.95
Is There a Speech Inside You?, by Don Aslett (paper) $9.95
Literary Agents: How to Get & Work with the Right One for You, by Michael Larsen $9.95
Professional Etiquette for Writers, by William Brohaugh $9.95
Time Management for Writers, by Ted Schwarz $10.95
The Writer's Friendly Legal Guide, edited by Kirk Polking $16.95
A Writer's Guide to Contract Negotiations, by Richard Balkin (paper) $11.95

To order directly from the publisher, include $3.00 postage and handling for 1 book and 50¢ for each additional book. Allow 30 days for delivery.

Writer's Digest Books
1507 Dana Avenue, Cincinnati, Ohio 45207
Credit card orders call TOLL-FREE
1-800-543-4644 (Outside Ohio)
1-800-551-0884 (Ohio only)
Prices subject to change without notice.

Write to this same address for information on *Writer's Digest* magazine, Writer's Digest Book Club, Writer's Digest School, and Writer's Digest Criticism Service.